DISCARDED

D1130791

DISCARDED

Keynesianism, Social Conflict and Political Economy

Keynesianism, Social Conflict and Political Economy

Massimo De Angelis
Lecturer in Political Economy
University of East London

First published in Great Britain 2000 by
MACMILLAN PRESS LTD
Houndmills, Basingstoke, Hampshire RG21 6XS and London
Companies and representatives throughout the world

A catalogue record for this book is available from the British Library.

ISBN 0–333–75137–X

First published in the United States of America 2000 by
ST. MARTIN'S PRESS, LLC,
Scholarly and Reference Division,
175 Fifth Avenue, New York, N.Y. 10010

ISBN 0–312–23146–6

Library of Congress Cataloging-in-Publication Data
De Angelis, M. (Massimo)
Keyesianism, social conflict, and political economy / Massimo De Angelis.
p. cm.
Includes bibliographical references and index.
ISBN 0–312–23146–6 (cloth)
1. Keynesian economics—History. 2. Social conflict—United States—History–
–20th century. 3. Economics—United States—History—20th century. I. Title.

HB99.7 .D4   2000
330.15'6—dc21

99–055733

© Massimo De Angelis 2000

All rights reserved. No reproduction, copy or transmission of this publication may be made without written permission.

No paragraph of this publication may be reproduced, copied or transmitted save with written permission or in accordance with the provisions of the Copyright, Designs and Patents Act 1988, or under the terms of any licence permitting limited copying issued by the Copyright Licensing Agency, 90 Tottenham Court Road, London W1P 0LP.

Any person who does any unauthorised act in relation to this publication may be liable to criminal prosecution and civil claims for damages.

The author has asserted his right to be identified as the author of this work in accordance with the Copyright, Designs and Patents Act 1988.

This book is printed on paper suitable for recycling and made from fully managed and sustained forest sources.

10	9	8	7	6	5	4	3	2	1
09	08	07	06	05	04	03	02	01	00

Printed and bound in Great Britain by
Antony Rowe Ltd, Chippenham, Wiltshire

Contents

List of Figures and Tables

Preface and Acknowledgments

This book has been a long enterprise. Some parts of its material have been published in various forms. The substance of Chapter 2, 3, and 10 has seen the light in the American journal *Research in Political Economy* (De Angelis 1997); some sections of Chapter 9 are forthcoming in the *Review of Radical Political Economy*; while a large part of the section on capital movements in Chapter 11 has been published in the *Journal of Post Keynesian Economics* (De Angelis 1999). Grateful thanks are extended to the publisher of all journals for permission to reproduce this material here. The main ideas of most chapters have been the result of my work for a Ph.D. at the Department of Economics, University of Utah, finished in 1995, under the supervision of Rajani Kanth and Norman Waitzman. To both go my thanks. More poignantly, this work would not have seen the light if it had not been for the decisive and apparently indefatigable work of Harry Cleaver at the University of Texas at Austin, who was my external supervisor. To him goes my most comradely affection. Ferruccio Gambino and Bruno Cartosio must be thanked for the invaluable insights they gave me in various conversations on the history of the American labor movement, and Ed Emery for his vividly colored stories of struggles that evoked the spirit of an epoch. Since the completion of my thesis, several people have contributed to the development of this work with their encouragement, comments and useful criticisms. Silvia Federici and Mariarosa Dalla Costa have enlightened me on the conditions of the women's movement in the 1970s. Philip Arestis, Chris Fuller, Peter Howells, Andrew Kliman, Gary Mongiovi, Bruce Pietrykowski, Angelo Reati, and Ernesto Screpanti have enabled me to sharpen various aspects of my argument, while George Caffentzis has provided encouragement for the overall project and insights on the condition of the global economy today. To all of them goes my gratitude, bearing in mind that the usual caveats apply. This book is dedicated to the memory of John Merrington, historian and translator with a passion for people not roles.

MASSIMO DE ANGELIS

Abbreviations

AFL	American Federation of Labor
ASEED	Action for Solidarity, Equality, Environment and Development
CIO	Congress of Industrial Organizations
EZLN	Zapatista National Liberation Army
FDD	five-dollar day
FDI	foreign direct investment
G7	Group of Seven
GATT	General Agreement on Tariffs and Trade
GDP	Gross Domestic Product
GM	General Motors
GNP	Gross National Product
IMCU	International Money Clearing Unit
IMF	International Monetary Fund
IWW	Industrial Workers of the World
MAI	Multilateral Agreement on Investments
NAFTA	North American Free Trade Agreement
NAIRU	non-accelerating inflation rate of unemployment
NRU	natural rate of unemployment
NWLB	National War Labor Board
OECD	Organization for Economic Cooperation and Development
UAW	United Automobile Workers
WLB	War Labor Board
WPB	War Production Board
WTO	World Trade Organization

1

Introduction: The Social Meaning of Economics

1.1 Conventional wisdom

The conventional wisdom that has informed the economic policies of governments around the world over the last two decades is rooted in neoliberal ideology. This is the old laissez-faire idea that markets operate for the better when left on their own, now set in the context of increasingly integrated global markets (the result of the deregulation of financial markets and trade liberalization), and combined with modern political discourses that recognize a government role in promoting competition and facilitating standards of market deregulation. Basic old-style Keynesianism – the idea that government should intervene through manipulation of aggregate demand in order to reach "full employment" – seems a closed chapter in the history of economics.[1]

Yet the legitimacy of the neoliberal conventional wisdom is being undermined by the specter of an epoch of global economic and social turmoil. The current economic and social crisis has certainly contributed to increase the scope of debate on alternatives to neoliberalism. This is a healthy sign. The last twenty years have been dominated by a claustrophobic theoretical and ideological closure around the neoliberal priority of the market over everything else. After the late 1970s' collapse of Keynesianism, the late 1980s' collapse of the Soviet bloc was celebrated as the end of history, the end of ideologies. However, the current crisis has revealed that this consensus coincided with an apology for only one admissible historical path, and only one admissible ideology, that of the market.

As the specter of global economic turmoil threatens the living conditions of workers, pensioners, farmers, women, children, and the unemployed around the world, the ghosts of old prophets are making their appearance. One of these prophets is of course Keynes, whose analysis was inspired by a global recession and whose policies were adopted by a new generation of post-war economists who hoped to avoid any repeat of the financial and economic turmoil of the 1930s. Can this be done again in the context of the present crisis?

An indicative answer will be provided in the Conclusion (Chapter 11). Here suffice to say that current debates would *prima facie* indicate that we are witnessing a shift away from pure neoliberal policies and towards more traditional growth promotion with a Keynesian flavor. Economists such as Stanley Fischer (IMF first deputy director), Jeffrey Sachs, Joseph Stiglitz (World Bank chief economist), and Paul Krugman have all, with different nuances, espoused some form of Keynesian antidote for deflation, be this lower interest rates, lower taxes, or stimulating global demand to counter the depressionary tendencies of the global economy. They have even expressed openness to the idea that some sort of regulation of capital controls may be required. They also recognize the necessity for lower unemployment, echoing what in this book will be an important theme of old Keynesianism – that is, the maintenance of political stability, and not merely price stability, in the global economy.

Yet, if we could define Keynesianism in terms of fiscal stimulus alone, then, the massive increase in military-led public spending during the Reagan's presidency would certainly qualify as ultra-Keynesian. One of the purposes of this book is to draw from the important lessons of the post-war experience to argue that Keynesianism is defined in terms of an expansionary strategy of growth, embedded within a *social* and institutional framework that enables the different interests in society to remain in a dynamic balance within a regime of capitalist accumulation. In political terms, maintaining this dynamic balance means being able to control, at the social level, the fundamental parameters of capitalist accumulation. Following Marx's broad theoretical framework, in this book I will refer to these fundamental parameters of accumulation as the social rate of exploitation or the balance between necessary and surplus labor – that is, the spread, in society at large, between labor productivity and wage rate. Not only is this basic requirement a condition for the viability of Keynesian policy, but it is also reflected in the formulation and basic structure of Keynesian theory which informs that policy.

A basic point of this book therefore is that Keynesianism was never just an economic theory, it was also a form of social practice – it needed institutions that allowed the theory to work, and it implied a vision of power relations among classes in society. This almost trivial point acquires sharpness if we add the more substantive argument that this social practice has never been "class-neutral," but has had the function of the co-optation, or what I will call the "recuperation," of widespread social antagonism from below and its transformation into an engine of growth and capitalist accumulation.

1.2 The social meaning of Keynesianism

The post-war state intervention in the economy did not come about because of Keynes' book *The General Theory*. Rather, Keynes' book became relevant for informing those practices of economic and social management required for sustaining capital accumulation in a world that had manifestly become socially unmanageable under the classical liberal doctrine. As the philosopher of science Thomas Kuhn reminds us, scientific revolutions happen only to the extent they are able to shift a paradigm and induce a large majority of the scientific community to accept the tenets of the new paradigm. With this come new "problems available for scientific scrutiny," and new standards by which the profession determines "what should count as an admissible problem or as a legitimate-problem-solution" (Kuhn 1970: 6). A shift in a paradigm within a social science such as economics implies the existence of social forces that define the boundaries of what is considered to be an "admissible" problem and set of solutions.

To the extent that a Keynesian revolution occurred and became institutionalized practice in the world's universities and think-tanks in the post-war era, it had to define a new problem around which a new economics could unfold – unemployment. It also had to define a means for the solution of the problem – growth – and a set of instruments through which growth could be managed and achieved – monetary and, especially, fiscal policies. It is this triad – problem, means, and instruments – that define the Keynesian revolution *as the world experienced it*, independently of any idiosyncrasies that distinguish it from Keynes' original message. It may be true that there are idiosyncrasies in terms of the modeling of time and the use of the concept of equilibrium. It may also be true that, for the sake of the correct analytical classification of doctrines, we should add the adjective "bastard" in front of the noun "Keynesian" to characterize post-war economic orthodoxy (Robinson 1962). Yet, I believe that the shift in the central *problem* of economic theory and policy and the active engagement of the government and the state apparatus in the managing of the economy legitimately entitle the new economic strategies to a revolutionary status. The triad defined above, and especially the nature of the problem, constitutes my working definition of *Keynesianism*, understood as the orthodoxy, the "conventional wisdom," of the mainstream paradigm of the post-war economic community, which influenced teaching, research and the policies of Western governments.

However, there is a fourth element in the post-war Keynesian revolution that – although it constituted a cornerstone upon which the entire post-war Keynesian edifice was built – has not been given much attention in standard textbooks. It is the relation between wages and productivity, a relation that not only defines profit margins and therefore, ultimately, the entire *raison d'être* and motivation of capitalist production, but also uncovers the political and social dimension behind the veil of pure economics. Kalecki (1943), in his seminal paper "Political Aspects of Full Employment," points out this relation when discussing the question of the *maintenance* of full employment:

> Indeed, under a regime of permanent full employment, the "sack" would cease to play its role as a disciplinary measure. The social position of the boss would be undermined, and the self-assurance and class consciousness of the working class would grow. Strikes for wage increases and improvements in conditions of work would create political tensions. It is true that profits would be higher under a regime of full employment than they are on average under laissez-faire; and even the rise in wages rates resulting from the stronger bargaining power of the workers is less likely to reduce profits than to increase prices, and thus affect only the rentier interest. But "discipline in the factories" and "political stability" are more appreciated than profits by business leaders. Their class instinct tells them that lasting full employment is unsound from their point of view, and that unemployment is an integral part of the "normal" capitalist system. (Kalecki 1943: 351)

It is arguable whether full employment is the only condition for political instability in a capitalist system. Indeed, as I will discuss in this book, the post-war government "pledge" for full employment originated out of the social turmoil following the First World War, the Russian Revolution, and the strike waves of the 1930s and 1940s. Yet, Kalecki addresses a crucial issue. He shifts the focus from the mere distributional effect of full employment to the effect on the dynamic of *social relations.* "Discipline in the factory" and "political stability" are closely related, and they are both "more appreciated than profits by business leaders," because they define the framework not merely for a certain quantity of profit-making, but for the *activity* of profit-making itself, and therefore the social existence of profit-makers.

Kalecki moves from full employment to the question of productivity – that is, "discipline in the factory" (Glyn 1995) – and wages. To shed light on the institutionalization of Keynesianism, I wish to reverse the chain of causation. The ability of a social system to offer a stable relation between productivity and wages, a stable relation between work as human activity *measured* by productivity, and the income stream that goes to the performers of this activity, defines *a priori* the central pivot around which, in principle, anything is possible, even full employment policies. An institutional arrangement that is able to keep in check this relation not only against the ebbs and tides of the business cycle but, more importantly, against the political instability provoked by the lack of discipline in the factories, is a *precondition* to any promise of full employment. Expansionary Keynesian policies of the post-Second World War period presupposed necessarily such a stable relation, or at least the appearance of such stability, in order to appease the "business leaders' class instinct."

There is some indication that Keynes, who considered Kalecki's article "exceedingly good" and "very acute" (Osiatynski 1990: 573), looked at such a stable relation with a hopeful eye. As early as 1926, in his polemic with the cotton industrialists of Lancashire, Keynes pointed to the disastrous effect of cuts in money-wages in a situation of pressing international competition and technical inefficiency (Keynes 1926a). Instead of attacking the money-wages "directly," the reduction in the cost of production should have been pursued "indirectly" through the restructuring of the productive processes, through a social restructuring of the working day, which implied capital concentration, greater technological efficiency in the industry, and better and more rational use of the labor power (Gobbini 1972: 56). But the rationalization of production and restructuring of the working day cannot be implemented without raising discipline problems in the factories. Keynes thus seems to find an answer to this issue by looking back to the experience of "war socialism", the "social pact" between capital and unions during the First World War:

> War experience in the organization of socialized production has left some near observers optimistically anxious to repeat it in peace con-

ditions. War socialism unquestionably achieved a production of wealth on a scale far greater than we ever knew in peace, for though the goods and services delivered were destined for immediate and fruitless extinction, none the less they were wealth. (Keynes 1926b: 286)

Almost twenty years later, in 1943, Keynes maintained that the task of keeping "efficiency wages" (wages per unit of output) stable is a political rather than an economic problem, and in 1944 he acknowledged the problem of restraining real wages in the presence of full employment and collective bargaining (Winch 1989: 107; Glyn 1995: 37).

Yet, in the *General Theory*, Keynes explicitly accepts the second postulate of classical theory, that wages are equal to the marginal product of labor, thus linking any increase in employment to a reduction in real wages. Later, in *"How to Pay for the War,"* Keynes states again his caution in handling the issue of wages: "I have not attempted to deal directly with the problem of wages. It is wiser, I expect, to deal with it indirectly" (Keynes 1940: 55). Here again Keynes prefers to appeal to the indirect economic mechanism of money illusion to keep wages in check, rather than explicitly dealing with the overt political issue of bargaining. As Dillard notes (1984: 320), "Keynes always dealt with the wage problem indirectly and never developed anything that could properly be called a theory of wages. He strenuously objected to reductions in money-wages rates during depression periods, but on the other hand he did not advocate higher wage rates."

I have defined *Keynesianism* as the triad problem–means–tools (unemployment–growth–monetary/fiscal policies), and I have termed the institutional arrangement that is a precondition of full employment policies, as discussed above, the *social microfoundations of Keynesianism*. How did the problem of unemployment, and full employment policies, which are central to the definition of Keynesianism, and the social microfoundations which made it operational without upsetting class balances, came about? I offer two interrelated hypotheses.

First, the recognition of unemployment as a problem by economic theory (namely Keynesianism) originated out of the failure of the downward movements of the business cycle to provide the traditional economic disciplinary device for both the employed and unemployed labor force. The reason for this resides of course in a variety of historical factors. The central one, however, seems to be the organizational and confrontational maturity of what was, following the Soviet revolution, Fordism and the Great Depression, a new kind of working class. Second, the social microfoundations of Keynesianism – that is, the basic institutional arrangement to keep control of the spread between productivity and wages, and thus maintain "discipline in the factory" – originated out of a process of the institutionalization, especially during the Second World War, of workers' organizations: the trade unions.

In this book I thus provide a retrospective look at the rise and fall of Keynesian economic orthodoxy in relation to social conflict. In a seminal paper, Antonio Negri (1968) first interpreted the meaning of Keynes' theory within the context of the class struggle in the post-Soviet Revolution period. "The October Revolution had once and for all introduced a political quality of subversion into the material needs and struggles of the working class, a specter that could not be exorcised" (Negri 1968: 11). The working class became a "political entity" despite the Taylorist reorganization of work and the application of scientific management. The ruling class and state power had to *recognize* the unavoidable antagonism embodied in the working class: "Once the antagonism was recognized, the problem was to make it function in such a way as to prevent one pole of the antagonism breaking free into independent destructive action" (Negri 1968: 13).

In other words, the aspirations of the working class had to be integrated within the process of accumulation. And this integration had to be a conscious act of government policy, since economic liberalism had been defeated by people's refusal to act as non-human commodities. Keynes' theory thus represents the scientific attempt to *acknowledge* and *recuperate* (co-opt and subsume) this power of the working class. Clearly this acknowledgement is spelled out in a language compatible with this recuperation, the language of economics. The political demands of the working class were thus translated into the problematic of effective demand and its role within capitalist accumulation. Thus "for Keynes the problem is how to establish a balance of effective demand, in a context where the various balances of power making up effective demand are conceived as unchanging" (Negri 1968: 28). The approach to effective demand, then, can be summed up by saying "that it assumes class struggle, and sets out to resolve it, on a day-to-day basis, in ways that are favourable to capitalist development" (Negri 1968: 30).

Negri's contribution is however limited to Keynes and does not tackle the relation between Keynes' "Keynesianism" and that of the economic orthodoxy of the post-war era. Indeed, this is an important distinction, as Keynes and the post-war Keynesians confronted two different social contexts. Keynes lived in a period in which social turmoil, from the Soviet Revolution through the Great Depression, revealed the fragility of the capitalist social system in its entirety, a period that lacked the presence of a clear institutional pattern of management of class relations. The post-war Keynesians, especially those in the United States, lived in a period in which the institutionalization of the trade unions and of productivity deals allowed some light at the end of the tunnel as far as the management of factory conflict was concerned. As I will show, these two social contexts were reflected in the analytical categories used by economists.

Since Keynes' approach gained acceptance within the post-war economic profession in the United States (Salant 1988) and was successfully diffused abroad (Hirshman 1989) as a pillar of the Pax Americana, the central chapters of this book will focus on the analysis of the class struggle and the institutional setting developed for its containment in the United States. After 1945 every country in the Western bloc was informed by Keynesian policies, although with different forms and nuances. The aim of this book is not to compare and contrast these national Keynesianisms but to focus on the social basis of this economic strategy as it developed in the most powerful country.

1.3   The structure of the book

It is not an easy task to illustrate the intertwining of the social with the theoretical dimension and to show that the social is embedded in analytical categories, categories which therefore are *political*. First, it requires juxtaposition of discourses and methodologies that are traditionally left separated and, second, it necessitates a reader willing to admit, against a strong positivist tradition in economics, that at least *in principle* the *same* categories may mean different things to different schools of thought and theoretical perspectives. The structure of this book thus reflects the necessarily tortuous journey of discovery of the social meaning of an economic theory, a journey that must take us into fields as diverse as labor, social and economic history, economic theory, political philosophy, and political theory.

In Chapter 2, I survey what has been called "Keynes' early political intuition" (Negri 1968). I show here how Keynes' criticism of laissez-faire economics originated and how Keynes' categories developed under the pressures of growing social turmoil. In Chapter 3, I discuss two key elements of Keynes' main work, *The General Theory*, which was published in 1936 and which played a crucial role in the establishment of post-war Keynesian orthodoxy. Here I attempt to deconstruct Keynes' use of the concepts of aggregation and time. Because these concepts, in somewhat modified form, will become the pillars of post-war macroeconomics, I interpret them in political terms – that is, I show how they allow the acknowledgment of social conflict and help provide the theoretical framework to handle it. Chapter 4 briefly examines Henry Ford's strategies of labor organization and the recuperation of class conflict in the first two decades of the twentieth century. This case study gives us some insights into strategies that, although in different form, will be attempted at the social level in the post-war period and which constituted the basis for the operationalism of Keynesian policies: the attempt to implement a "social deal" in the context of mass production. In Chapters 5 and 6, I outline various developments during the Second World War that led to the realization of this "social deal." These chapters include discussions of the pattern of class unrest, despite the trade unions' no-strike pledge; the legitimization and institutionalization of trade unions; the growing influence of economists and social scientists on state planning, part of the attempt to bypass the pressures coming from grassroots activities; and the formation of an economic orthodoxy calling for the active state promotion of economic growth and full employment to avoid a political "danger laying ahead." After having analyzed the general features of the post-war consensus in economics, in Chapter 7 I examine the institutional features of post-war Keynesianism. Here emphasis is put on those key elements such as union contracts and state laws against rank-and-file militancy that served the realization of productivity deals in the United States. In Chapter 8 I deconstruct the theory of post-war Keynesianism, also called the Neoclassical synthesis. Following up on the themes already discussed in Chapter 3 in regard to Keynes, I here enquire into the political meaning of the concepts of aggregate and time in the Keynesian orthodoxy. In Chapters 9 and 10 I dissect two main "tools" of post-war Keynesianism, namely the fiscal multiplier and the Phillips curve. I show how both these analytical devices implicitly presuppose the stability of class relations, which are thus assumed to be under the sway of productivity deals, the evolution and institutional forms of which were analyzed in Chapters 5, 6 and 7. Here economic theory meets the flesh-and-blood history of social conflict and the efforts to recuperate it institutionally. The growth of the social movements in the 1960s and 1970s disrupts these productivity deals, thus destroying the social basis of Keynesianism. A new orthodoxy is on the horizon, with monetarists, supply-siders and neoliberals of all kinds replacing the Keynesians in positions of power. In Chapter 11, I summarize the lessons we can draw for today from this historical/theoretical account of the parabola of Keynesianism and postulate the general conditions and social costs that a new form of Keynesianism will have to meet if it is to become a viable capitalist strategy.

2
The Making of the Keynesianism of Keynes

2.1   Introduction: economic liberalism before the Keynesian revolution

The basic tenets of economic liberalism is that free enterprise and the free wheeling of the market are the solutions to all the economic problems of society. Laissez-faire, since its establishment as economic doctrine of the state starting from the beginning of the nineteenth century, took many forms, with different degrees of state involvement to provide a buffer for those social problems that the operation of free markets were originating. In Great Britain, for example, during the course of the nineteenth and early twentieth century, the state intervened to set a limit to the working day, regulate the work of children and women, to provide or regulate a minimum social security that, although miserly in comparison with the one established after 1945, was generous in comparison to the social provisions of earlier phases of industrialization (Checkland 1983). Also, as Karl Polanyi (1944) noted, markets did not grow out of a spontaneous process, but were the result of conscious policies and institutions set in place by states. Still, in the conventional wisdom of the time, state interventions represented detours from the main highway leading to prosperity, detours that even the father of economic liberalism, Adam Smith, was willing to acknowledge as an occasional necessity.[1] The hard core of the doctrine of economic liberalism preached that in the main highway towards prosperity there ought to be no speed limits, no government regulation, the market had to be sovereign.

Markets can regulate economic activity to the extent that demand and supply are free to set their price. Alfred Marshall, the mentor of modern neoclassical economics, insisted in his *Principles* (1890) that

11

demand and supply act as the two blades of a scissors, meeting at a point and cutting a piece of paper. That cutting point is where the price is set. The price therefore is the result of two opposite forces: one, that of the suppliers, who wish to get the most out of the good supplied; the other, that of the consumer, who wishes to pay the least for the good purchased. The price, as the meeting point of these two forces, represent the synthesis of opposite self-interests, enabling for their reconciliation the maximization of consumer's utility and of the producer's profit, and representing the starting point for the next round of market negotiations, and so on, indefinitely. The theory of General Equilibrium proposed by Lausanne's economist Leon Walras enabled economists to project to the level of society as a whole the mechanism of one market. Society was represented by the set of markets and, if market forces were left to operate on their own, all demands and all supplies will meet, will determine a set of "clearing prices" in which no good will be overproduced and no worker will be left unemployed. It was a mathematical refinement of what the French economist John Baptist Say has already announced back in 1809 with his law: supply creates its own demand.

In pre-Keynesian economics, therefore, commodity prices represent the strategic variables enabling social harmony and well being. However – and here is the big *if* – only if market forces are set free to operate. No rigidities of any kind are tolerated by this vision of social organization.

Rigidities to the free market are always there and often they have nothing to do with government policies. One among the many commodities commercialized in the bazaars of capitalist society is a strange commodity, it not only speaks, but also has needs, desires and aspirations. The commodity "labor," as economists call it, or more correctly, "labor-power," as the critics of economics prefer to name it (Marx 1867: 270), faces the mechanisms of the market with human eyes, with human feelings, and with human determination. The very existence of a price set by the market for this commodity is, on its own, already a negation of this humanity, as the non-laboring pre-capitalist intelligentsia always has reminded us.[2] But even granting that we must live under the rule of money, when it is time to evaluate the quantitative aspect of this price, those who demand and those who supply "labor" are in sharp disagreement. How much the wage is for a given time spent working is a question that has different meanings for those who supply labor (the workers) and those who demand it (the capitalists). For the former, wages are means to satisfy needs. For the latter, wages represent a cost to subtract from revenue and which defines profit. What basic economic theory does not tell us is that the meeting point between labor demand and labor supply which leads to the formation of a market wage, is one in which human needs clash with the needs of capital accumulation.

Not only the "price of labor" as such, not only its quantitative aspect, but also, more importantly, the use of this human commodity in the process of production is looked upon by the workers with human eyes. How long is the working day? How intense is the working activity? How is the relation with other workers? How many breaks can the worker take? How many opportunities to socialize with fellow workers, to turn a production activity into playful time? These are questions which answers define the lived experience of those human beings working. But in the eyes of those who demand labor, the capitalists, each one of these questions is replaced by a simple one: How much profit to get out of labor activity? This is all that counts. The welfare of the workforce assumes a central character in the administration of a competitive business, only instrumentally, only to the extent that such welfare allows the business to operate more efficiently and competitively on the market.

Thus, the market sets a price for labor power, and both the quantitative dimension of this price, and the activity required from those who sell this commodity, are realms of conflict. Here is where our market rigidities come from. When workers get together, set up trade unions, organize strikes, factory occupations, demonstrations, lobbying campaigns to shape public opinion, when they do this, they infringe the free working of the market, they build their power and erect market rigidities. Of course, by acting as human agents in defense of their needs, desires, and aspirations, or even by initiating a process in which these needs and aspirations are collectively beginning to be defined, workers, unemployed, and citizens of yesterday as today, although in different forms, find themselves against the police and the army, government's anti-union laws, and the dogmas of economic liberalism. At times these are able to set the market again on its course, by abolishing workers's organizations, crushing unemployed demonstrations, etc., and calling for responsible behavior in front of the constraint of the global economy. But other times, the entity of these struggles is so spread and co-ordinated that its impact makes laissez-faire in all its form an almost impossible way to organize society.

Keynes' revolution in economics can be understood as a reaction to working-class struggles in Europe and general insurgency in other parts of the world. It is the product of the change in the balance of forces between classes during the struggles of the 1920s and 1930s and during the Second World War. The next section aims at showing how Keynes' distancing from traditional economic liberalism took shape in relation to the social conflict of the period.

2.2 Social conflict and Keynes' early political intuition

Introduction

In 1919, an editor of *The Nation* wrote an article entitled "The Revolt of the Rank and File" that summarizes one crucial dimension of these social forces:

> [t]he most extraordinary phenomenon of the present time, the most incalculable in its after effects, the most menacing in its threat of immediate consequences, and the most alluring in its possibilities of ultimate good, is the unprecedented revolt of the rank and file.

This was a "world-wide movement" in which the "common man" has forgotten "the old sanctions," lost faith "in the old leadership [and] has experienced a new access of self-confidence, or at least a new recklessness, a readiness to take chances on his own account. In consequence, as is by this time clear to discerning men, authority cannot any longer be imposed from above; *it comes automatically from below*" (in Brecher 1972: 101, my emphasis). I find no better description of the sense of fear and uncertainty raised by this "common man" who is ready "to take chances on his account." These words speak for an epochal change which for the first time raised the specter of a post-capitalist society as a real *international* challenge.

There is evidence of Keynes' concern about the growing militancy of the working class and the change in the condition of capitalist accumulation and regulation of the class relation, as well as the influence of this concern in shaping the evolution of his thinking up to the formulation of his most famous book *The General Theory* (1936). On the occasion of the Treaty of Versailles he stressed the need to consolidate central Europe as a strategic pole for the containment of the circulation of struggles emanating from the Soviet Revolution and against the shortsighted policy of revenge of the victorious nations. The imposition of heavy war reparations on the defeated Germany would have the "disastrous" effect of setting the historical course toward civil war:

> If we aim deliberately at the impoverishment of Central Europe, vengeance, I dare predict, will not limp. Nothing can then delay for very long the final civil war between the forces of reaction and the despairing convulsions of revolution, before which the horrors of the late German war will fade into nothing, and which will destroy, whoever is victor, the civilization and the progress of our generation. (Keynes 1919: 170)

This "gloomy" prediction was reinforced by the acknowledgment of the foe's understanding of the economic mechanisms for the subversion of the status quo:

> Lenin is said to have declared that the best way to destroy the capitalist system was to debauch the currency ... Lenin was certainly right. There is no subtler, no surer means of overturning the existing basis of society. (Keynes 1919: 148–50)[3]

The inflationary process and its undermining of the capitalist system by an arbitrary redistribution of wealth – that is, in Marxian terms, an arbitrary and out of control change in the balance between surplus and necessary labor – was at the center of Keynes' argument (Moggridge 1992: 333). Anticipating his insights on "money illusion" (Keynes 1940), Keynes denounced the fact that governments could confiscate "secretly and unobserved, an important part of the wealth of their citizens" through a "continuing process of inflation." At this stage, however, Keynes was not opposing the confiscation of resources as such, rather the fact that using this method governments 'confiscate *arbitrarily*,' thus

> [a]s the inflation proceeds and the real value of the currency fluctuates wildly from month to month, all permanent relations between debtors and creditors, which form the ultimate foundation of capitalism, become so utterly disordered as to be almost meaningless; and the process of wealth-getting degenerates into a gamble and a lottery. (Keynes 1919: 148–50)

The uncertainty in expectations, however, becomes dangerous for the maintenance of the capitalist system to the extent that class antagonism – the "popular hatred of the class of entrepreneurs" – is acknowledged a key role. Thus, these governments,

> [b]y combining a popular hatred of the class of entrepreneurs with the blow already given to social security by the violent and arbitrary disturbance of contract and of the established equilibrium of wealth which is the inevitable result of inflation ... are fast rendering impossible a continuance of the social and economic order of the nineteenth century. (Keynes 1919: 148–50)

The theme of inflationary pressures, its influence in the distribution of wealth, and *therefore* its potential in affecting the balance of power between classes are recurring themes in Keynes, as seen in his attack for a British return to the Gold Standard.

Three years after Keynes left the tables of the peace settlement with "intolerable anguish and fury" (E.A.G. Robinson 1946/1964: 34), his comments on the effects of the Treaty turned into more open optimism, only because, *ex post*, the victims of the treaty "have been patient" (Keynes 1922a: 116). A few years later Keynes admitted the political correctness of Churchill's line at the peace conference, but at the same time – for example, on the occasion of a review of Churchill's book *The World Crisis: The Aftermath*, he stressed Churchill's failure to

> see – or at least to set – in perspective the bigness of the events in their due relations, or to disentangle the essential from casual episodes ... But the Bolsheviks remain for him, in spite of the tribute to the greatness of Lenin, nothing more than an imbecile atrocity. (Keynes 1929: 54)

What is Churchill unable to grasp? Keynes seems here to stress the material power behind that "imbecile atrocity" – that is, the actual and real danger posed by the European working classes to the future of capitalism, the threat posed by what Keynes called in derogatory terms the "Party of the Catastrophe."[4]

Wage rigidity

It is not possible to separate this international dimension from the problems posed for national capital by the class struggle. In the numerous occasions when Keynes comments on the economic events and the reaction of public policy, he was able to develop the key elements which would enter into his theoretical system finally formalized in *The General Theory*. It is striking how these elements, which include both basic assumptions and policy recommendations, take shape under the continuous pressure of a change in the conditions of the balances of forces between classes and how lucid Keynes is in acknowledging this.

The first, basic implicit assumption at the beginning of any modern textbook of macroeconomics written in the post-Second World II period is wage rigidity. Keynes was forced to introduce this "assumption" in the development of his system by the concrete situation of post-war Britain. According to Keynes' biographer Skidelsky (1992: 130) "the incomplete British recovery from the depression of 1920–1922 started Keynes on the road to the Keynesian Revolution." This incomplete recovery had revealed the persistence of unemployment and *at the same time* the rigidity of real wages.

When in 1923 the economic situation stabilized, there was 10 percent unemployment which lasted for the rest of the decade until the Great Depression opened the 1930s. The increasing difficulty for British business in competing world-wide and the persistence of unemployment could be connected to two "shocks" faced by Britain between 1919 and 1922. First was a "real shock," and then a "monetary shock", both representing particular expressions of class power. The former was due to a once-and-for-all reduction in the working week at given wages obtained by labor which boosted British unit labor costs. The latter was the combination of deflation and the failure of money wages to fall to the same extent than wholesale and retail prices. "It was this deadly double-blow of a union-induced rise in the efficiency wage and a government-induced profit deflation which left expectations in the British economy too low to provide for full employment" (Skidelsky 1992: 131).

Working-class power acquired even more significance in relation to government policy which induced deflation by retaining high real interest rates through the period of falling prices in 1921–2. The policy, aimed at improving the dollar–sterling exchange rate up to the point of the pre-war Gold Standard parity of $4.86 to the pound, presupposed as a *modus operandi* the reduction of money wages through the intensification of unemployment – a mechanism, as will be discussed later, that Keynes explicitly recognized and criticized later in 1925 in his "The Economic Consequences of Mr Churchill" (Keynes 1925b) on the occasion of England's return to the Gold Standard.

Keynes recognized this rigidity of money wages in a series of four lectures he delivered to the Institute of Bankers from 15 November to 5 December 1922. In his opinion, high wages

> are compelling us to ask double for our exports when the world level of prices as measured by what we must pay for our imports, is only about 60 per cent up. It is clear that that is not a situation which can go on permanently. People will not pay us for our exports at so discrepant a price from what goods generally are worth in the world; and we see the fruits of high prices in the diminishing volume of our exports, and in our complete incapacity to employ the whole body of labor. (Keynes 1922b: 67)

While the view of the Treasury and the Bank was to pursue a further deflation to restore the pre-war Gold Standard, Keynes, alarmed by the fact that the deflation of the 1920–1 had brought Britain at the "verge of revolution," considered as a "working assumption" that "wage rates should be regarded as too rigid in the short period to adjust to the "ebb and flow of international gold credit." He therefore argued for a devaluation of the sterling, abandoning the attempt to restore the pre-war dollar–sterling parity (Skidelsky 1992: 133–4).

Although the acknowledgment of the stickiness of money wages in relation to prices was not new, what was certainly novel were the practical implications drawn from this observation. By acknowledging the new conditions of working-class power, Keynes reacted against the strategy attempting to cut money wages as "hopeless" and laid down new political hypotheses for dealing with the new level of working-class power through the adjustment of the price level and exchange rate to the going wage rate, instead of the other way round (Skidelsky 1992: 134). We have here an early formulation of what will be known later as the "money illusion" (Keynes 1940). This will define post-war inflation policies as strategies to curtail or keep in check workers' income share, strategies that will collapse after the aceleration of social movements from the 1960s to the late 1970s (Phillips 1985: 15–17), as will be discussed in Chapter 9.

Stabilization of the value of money or revolution

Keynes' reaction to deflation policies was informed by the new working assumption that these cannot function in presence of "wage stickiness." This theme will be central to the reasoning of *The General Theory* (Keynes

1936: Chapter 19). There is also another related element. If deflation policies cannot succeed in efficiently curtailing working-class income and increasing profitability, then their effect would be only the reduction of the "value of money" and the establishment of an environment which is "bad for business," the perseverance of stagnation, and the fueling of anti-capitalist sentiment within the working classes.

I noted earlier how during the polemic over the Versailles treaty Keynes was ready to acknowledge Lenin's alleged insight on the "best way to destroy the capitalist system" as that of "debauching the currency." The theme of "a modicum of price stability [as] essential for both social stability and economic progress" (Moggridge 1992: 383) is repeated other times in the 1920s especially in Keynes' polemic with official policies (Keynes 1923a: 100–1). On the occasion of a speech to the Liberal Summer School at Cambridge on 8 August 1923, he wrote that:

> Modern individualistic society, organized on lines of capitalistic industry, cannot support a violently fluctuating standard of value, whether the movement is upwards or downwards. Its arrangements presume and absolutely require a reasonably stable standard. Unless we can give it such a standard, this society will be stricken with a mortal disease and will not survive. (Keynes 1923b: 117)

These observations, which apply to both the case of deflation and of inflation, "illustrate a fundamental principle which I recommend to this assembly as likely to be of first-rate political importance in the near future" (Keynes 1923b: 117). Keynes thus argues how falling prices, and even more a "general expectation" of falling prices, must always be detrimental for business.

The point is made more explicitly in *A Tract on Monetary Reform* published on 11 December 1923 (Keynes, 1923f), which summarized Keynes' thoughts about the theory and the practice of monetary policies as developed in the previous three years. The central policy proposal of the *Tract* was to abandon – or perhaps reverse – deflationary monetary policies. Instead, the new role of monetary policies should be to stabilize the price level by stabilizing the demand for money. If deflation could not be used to reduce wages, as experience had shown, and if deflation had led to endemic unemployment as wages became sticky, and since this situation was becoming politically dangerous, then monetary policy should be directed toward the smoothing of the business cycle. The management of the supply of credit is seen by Keynes as a tool to control economic fluctuations. Along with other "monetary reformers" such as Yale University economist Irving Fisher and the Stockholm School economist Knut Wicksell, Keynes wanted to "solve problems to which socialists drew attention [the business cycle] without having to have socialism" (Skidelsky 1992: 168). In the course of 1930, after Keynes withdrew his support from the National League of Young Liberals, he actively supported Liberals and Labour politicians alike on the basis of specific political platforms (Moggridge 1992: 465). While he was ironic about those who supported the "sacredness of contract," he was warning that "the absolutists of contract ... are the real parents of revolution" (Keynes 1923d: 57).

Laissez-faire as obsolete strategy

The acknowledgment of working-class power and the suggestions of new practical policies for its recuperation informed Keynes' criticism of the laissez-faire philosophy at the heart of orthodox economic theory, and of government policies. In the context of the "despairing convulsions of revolution" (Keynes 1919: 170) the rigidities posed by the working class gave a final blow to the "self-regulating" properties of the market – that is, to the ability of upward and downward movements of what Marx called the "reserve army" to regulate and limit working-class resistance.

Keynes recognized the existence of this class constraint on the "law of demand and supply": "[t]he trade unions are strong enough to interfere with the free play of the forces of supply and demand, and public opinion ... supports the trade unions in their main contention that coal-miners ought not to be the victims of cruel economic forces which *they* never put in motion" (Keynes 1925a: 305, emphasis mine). The classic tenets of laissez-faire *are not wrong in principle*, but "belong to the days of fifty or a hundred years ago when trade unions were powerless, and when the economic juggernaut was allowed to crash along the highway of progress without obstruction and even with applause" (Keynes 1925a: 305).[5] In these remarks, Keynes thus reveals the historical and social nature of economics, the need to shape new analytical tools and new theoretical principles not in pursuit of knowledge as such, but with a clear aim in mind: the maintenance and perpetuation of capitalism *vis-à-vis* the new challenges posed by social conflict. In this sense, as Negri (1968: 19–20) has commented, questions of theoretical principle were replaced by questions of power.

This can also be seen in occasion of the General Strike[6] in 1926, which led Keynes to comment on the obsolescence of the forms of capitalist strategies to deal with class struggle. He "blamed the General Strike on muddles" (Moggridge 1992: 447). Two months after the official end of the General Strike of 1926 Keynes, during a visit to Berlin for a conference on laissez-faire, observed that the strike had been a traditional trade union answer to a traditional economic policy of capital (Gobbini 1972: 56). Instead of supporting repressing policies against the strikers, he favored an attempt to settle the dispute (Moggridge 1992: 447). Repressive policies had been called on the basis of the fact that the strikers had broken the law. "To those who clamoured that the General Strike was illegal and stepped outside the limits of constitutional action, Keynes gave a short reply: 'That may be, but so what?.'" The balance of forces has changed and "legality must be adjusted to fit the new situation" (Negri 1968: 19–20).[7]

Since the law had to adjust to accommodate the rigidity posed by the working class, so too economic theory had to renew its box of tools. As early as 1920 Robertson recognized this key point of novelty in Keynes' argument:

> Now the startling thing about this analysis of the economic structure of Europe is that it is in some respect very different from, and indeed diametrically opposed to, that of pre-war optimistic, free-trade, pacific philosophy, and resembles much more nearly that upon which, consciously or unconsciously, the edifices protectionism, militarism and imperialism are reared. (Robertson 1920: 80)

At this stage, Keynes seems to be struggling in search for ideas and practical policies to face the rigidity posed by the new social situation. Among these policies, Keynes proposed direct population control (Keynes 1923c: 124), the institutionalization of a social pact at the point of production (Keynes 1926a), and public works (Keynes 1924a: 222). Only the latter will become part of a theoretical and consistent whole in *The General Theory*. What was clear in the 1920s, and increasingly evident in the 1930s, was that social turmoil and the Great Depression exposed the inability of orthodox economic theory to give useful insights into how to deal with persistent unemployment. In 1929, Great Britain had already been suffering heavy unemployment for several years while in the United States the boom was about to turn. The theoretical apparatus of classical economics, with its embrace of laissez-faire and its prescription for non-intervention, was increasingly at odds with the needs of capitalist accumulation. In 1929, while Lloyd George was campaigning on a platform of public works, the conservative Treasury produced the doctrine according to which public expenditure could not increase employment. The argument of the famous Treasury View (Command Paper 3331: 1929) was based on the classical assumption that investment was governed by saving. Thus, an increase in public expenditure would have required a corresponding decrease in private expenditure if public expenditure needed to be financed: a case of full crowding out.

The idea behind the Treasury View was the classical belief that the causes for unemployment were to be found in too high real wages. To keep preaching laissez-faire and wage reduction in a world in which real wages were sticky in the face of deflation because of resistance of the working class as a whole became useless. Orthodox economists still maintaining the validity of Say's law with its practical implication were starting to detach their policy suggestions from the theoretical basis of economics. An example is the "round-robin" letter signed by several economists including Keynes which Pigou wrote in 1932 to *The Times* (17 October 1932)[8] in which he appealed for public expenditures as a last resort solution for the unemployment problem because the conversion of saving into investment was blocked by a "lack of confidence." Keynes has no difficulty in pointing out the incongruence between orthodox economic theory and these sorts of proposals for government intervention. In a letter to R.F. Kahn he rhetorically asked "why do they [classical economists] insist on maintaining theories from which their own practical conclusions cannot possibly follow? It is a sort of Society for the Preservation of Ancient Monuments" (Keynes 1937: 259). What was required was an economic theory which was consistent with the policy implications which were starting to become common sense and which other countries, such as Nazi Germany and the United States under the New Deal, were starting to adopt, although in different forms and contexts. *The General Theory* was written to fill this gap between bourgeois economic theory and economic policies of a new kind.

3
Keynes' Scientific System

3.1 Aggregates and time: the co-ordinates of a new capitalist strategy

In a 1937 article published in the *Quarterly Review of Economics*, after having summarized the content of *The General Theory*, Keynes concluded by defining two major areas in which his approach differs radically from the classical one. These two elements are, first, the introduction of expectations into economic discourse and, second, the use of aggregate variables. In Keynes' opinion, classical economics lacks a "theory of the supply and demand of output as *a whole*," and this also explains its failure to discuss expectations (Keynes 1937b: 223, my emphasis). The centrality of these two elements, aggregation and expectations, define the strategic terrain of modern macroeconomics.

Aggregation and the critique of classical theory

Keynes' criticism of classical theory focuses on the inability of the latter to theorize the persistence of unemployment and to formulate consistent strategies for its reduction. It is in connection with the problem of accumulation and unemployment, therefore, the problem which "the world will not much longer tolerate" (Keynes 1936: 381), that the notion of the "aggregate" needs to be evaluated.

Keynes reverses the priority of analysis of classical economics. In Keynes, the priority is placed on the social dimension over the particular, on the national economy over the particular industry, on the social determination of wages over the sectorial determination of wages, on the country's overall ability to put people to work, over the individual sectors' prospects of employment. The categories of the capitalist economy confront the individual agents and affect their expectations (Crotty 1980), and thus their behavior. The starting point is thus capital at its social level. The crisis, which is precisely the point of departure of Keynes' analysis, is primarily a crisis of social capital, within which the individual capital can be caught. The problem of the reproduction of capital as a whole, as the set of social relations constituting the web of a social fabric, is therefore posed with all its urgency as the starting point of the analysis. It is from this insight offered by Keynes that the entire building of modern macroeconomics was constructed: modern macroeconomics is founded on capitalist agony.

This prioritizing of the "social" which pervades the entire *General Theory* is then turned into working economic categories: aggregate consumption, aggregate income, aggregate investment, etc. Through "aggregation," economic theory intends to focus the attention of its analysis on society as a whole instead of individual sectors, but in so doing it also hides the constitutive elements of society: social relations as the site of conflict and struggle. Through aggregation, struggle is subsumed, hidden, and flattened out.

Keynes thus accuses classical theory of not having a theory of the demand and supply of output "as a whole," because it simply derives its general laws for society as a whole by extrapolating the laws valid for a single industry (Keynes 1936: Chapter 19). The two major examples of this criticism are found in Chapter 2 and Chapter 19 of *The General Theory*, in which Keynes challenges the possibility of a self-regulating economy through the wage mechanism. Keynes offers two points of contention.

First, there is the famous rejection of the second postulate of classical economics, which states that the marginal utility derived from wage is equal to the marginal disutility of labor (Keynes 1936: 13). This obviously means that the classical postulate at the basis of the supply of labor curve collapses. Workers cannot control the real wages for which they are willing to work. Therefore the level of employment is defined only by the labor demand curve and involuntary unemployment is logically possible. Second – and this is the argument of Chapter 19 – Keynes points out that the classical argument according to which a reduction in money wages brings about an increase in the level of demand and employment through a reduction in prices, is fallacious. Classical theorists base their arguments on working out the positive effect of a reduction of money wages on profit in a single industry and then transfer this without substantial modification to the economy as a whole. However, the method of transferring "the argument to industry as a whole" is invalid "unless we also transfer our assumption that the aggregate demand is fixed" (Keynes 1936: 259). If aggregate demand is fixed by assumption, then nobody would deny that a reduction in money wages would increase the profit level and investment, thus increasing employment (Keynes 1936: 259). However, a reduction in money wages in one industry, Keynes argues, must have a negative effect on aggregate demand, *unless* the reduction in money wages is dramatic and complete.

In both these cases, Keynes challenges the classical argument of a self-regulating economy through wage flexibility by means of a methodo-logical innovation – that is, the emphasis on "industry as a whole," on aggregates. The problem of aggregation is not posed for Keynes as a problem of derivation from individual to aggregate behavior, as in the subsequent debate on the "micro-foundations of macroeconomics" (Dow 1985), but simply as a problem of strategic perspective, as strategic starting point which requires the "laws of supply and demand of out-put as a whole." Although post-war Keynesians have engaged in arguments about the microfoundations of macroeconomics – that is, the attempt to base the pattern of aggregates on laws of individual rational behavior – this debate has never been resolved on logical grounds. Yet macroeconomics has nevertheless flourished and accepted the priority of the aggregate despite the difficulties of its microeconomic derivation. What is the social meaning of Keynes' argument? In this section I briefly discuss two aspects of Keynes' theory: the rejection of the second postulate of classical theory and Keynes' political (rather than simply theoretical) rejection of the fact that a fall of money wages cannot be used to increase employment.

The critique of the second postulate: the emphasis on real wages

In *The General Theory* the argument against the ability of the system to self-regulate itself and to lead towards full employment began with the acceptance of the first postulate of what Keynes calls classical theory (that the wage is equal to the marginal productivity of labor) and the rejection of the second postulate (that, when a given volume of labor is employed, the utility of the wage is equal to the marginal disutility of that amount of employment) (Keynes 1936: 5–6). The acceptance of the first postulate is tantamount to recognizing that the capitalist motivation for investment and production is profit and that there is a correlation between the level of employment – the number of people put to work for capital – and profit. Given diminishing marginal returns on fixed capital, an increase in employment can occur only if it increases profit and reduces wage per unit of labor. The difference with classical theorists therefore is not over the content of the capitalist relation – production for profit – but over the mechanisms which enforce this relation.

The rejection of the second postulate is at the center of Keynes' criticism of the classical theory.[1] The criticism has two components. The first, which "relates to the actual attitude of workers toward real and money wages respectively ... is not theoretically fundamental" (Keynes 1936: 8). A reduction of current money-wages could lead to a reduction in the supply of labor "through strikes or otherwise" (Keynes 1936: 8), but "a fall in the value of the existing money-wage in terms of wage-goods," by an increase in the price of the latter, would not cause necessarily a reduction in the supply of labor. The fundamental component of Keynes' rejection is the fact that the working class as a whole is not in a position to determine the real wage for which it is willing to work. The real wage is not settled as a direct bargain between labor and capitalist in a single sector, but is the result of a social process which is *independent* of the militancy of a single sector entailing the relation between money wages and prices. Therefore, Keynes identifies a weakness *both* in classical theory and in the ability of the working class to control real wages: "it would be impracticable to resist every reduction of real wages, due to a change in the purchasing-power of money which affects all workers alike; and in fact reductions of real wages arising in this way are not, as a rule, resisted unless they proceed to an extreme degree" (Keynes 1936: 14). Therefore, the "struggle about money-wages primarily affects the *distribution* of the aggregate real wage" among different sections of the working class rather than "the *general* level of real wages" (Keynes 1936: 14). If this is so, involuntary unemployment necessarily follows as a possibility. If the working class is not able directly to control the real wage, Keynes argues, it follows that there is no guarantee that the wage will equal the marginal disutility of work. Thus, the rejection of the second postulate means that the level of employment in an economy can be found at every point along the labor supply schedule below the full employment level.

It is worthwhile to notice the nature of this classification between the theoretically fundamental and theoretically non-fundamental components of Keynes' criticism of the classical school. What assumes the character of theoretically non-fundamental is the actual behavior of the working class *vis-à-vis* money wages and real wages. It is not theoretically fundamental, because even if this behavior is acknowledged by the theoretical discourse, there is nothing that theory can do to transform its nature. What becomes theoretically fundamental for economic theory goes beyond the simple recognition of the pattern of working-class struggles. Theoretically fundamental are those characteristics of the wage relation which open spaces for capitalist strategic intervention *given* working class militancy over the money-wage. Thus, the rejection of the second postulate can be interpreted within the priority given by Keynes to the "aggregate" over the "individual," to the "society" over the "factory," but this priority was expressed in order to recuperate the antagonism of the factory (Negri 1982). The priority of the aggregate must be considered in terms of the two issues informing the development of economics' fetishized categories: acknowledgment and subsumption of working-class power. *First, recognition of working-class power.* In the "more fundamental" aspect of the rejection of the second postulate the acknowledgment of working-class power is carefully qualified. Since the power of workers' "combinations" affects at most the money-wage and *relative* real wages of different sections (Keynes 1936: 14), Keynes thought that working-class power could be limited to the factory, or the industrial sector. The realm for capital's strategic intervention becomes the aggregate, society. Real wage rather than money-wage is what matters in determining the balance between surplus and necessary labor at the social level. Real wage is not simply the result of industrial militancy – that is, the result of working-class militancy in a single sector – but becomes socially regulated and determined through the interaction between this militancy (on one side) and money-wages and prices on the other. Thus, in this shift of perspective, the "economic" can become "political" and the "economic" struggles of the working class acquire a clear "political" meaning.

Second, subsumption of working-class power. The change in focus from the factory to society, from the individual to the aggregate in the terms posed by the rejection of the second postulate, opens a new strategic dimension for capital. If the working class poses a rigidity to nominal wages through its militancy, then real wages can be controlled by regulating prices through monetary policies. Thus, the "economic" becomes "political" and the price level enters the scene for the regulation of the wage relation at the social level, for the management of the proportion between necessary and surplus labor, social wages and social profit. Thus, within Keynes' framework an increase of public spending in absence of private investment is conceivable only if this key proportion is safeguarded as it follows from Keynes' acceptance of the first postulate of classical theory: "if employment increases, then ... the reward per unit of labour in terms of wage-goods must ... decline and profit increase" (Keynes 1936: 17).

Money wages cannot touch the "bottom": the political intuition revisited in the scientific system

In Chapter 19 of *The General Theory*, Keynes studied the possible effect of a reduction in money-wages on the level of employment. Here, too, Keynes' argument was based on the priority of the social, and his critique was informed by strategic considerations. In classical theory, the argument runs as follows: a reduction in money wages would have reduced the price level, and this, through the Pigou effect, would have increased the aggregate demand and therefore the level of income and employment. An alternative but consistent argument would be the one in which working-class' purchasing power would have remained the same or changed a little, but aggregate demand would have increased because of the Pigou effect on other "factors' income" – that is, rentiers'.

Following the outline in the previous chapters of *The General Theory*, Keynes refuses the "crude conclusion that a reduction in money-wages will increase employment 'because it reduces the cost of production'" (Keynes 1936: 261). An increase in employment following a reduction in money-wage can occur only *if* the marginal efficiency of capital has increased (Keynes 1936: 262) or the rate of interest has decreased (Keynes 1936: 265–6) – in other words, only if the spread between the rate of profit and the rate of interest has widened. Since the marginal efficiency of capital is "defined in terms of the *expectation* of yield and of the *current* supply price of the capital assets" (Keynes 1936: 136), only a sudden and drastic reduction in money-wages "to a level so low that none believes in its indefinite continuance" (Keynes 1936: 265) would be able to shift the marginal efficiency of capital schedule and therefore stimulate enough investment to compensate for a reduction in consumption following a wage reduction. The relation between wages and profit expectations is therefore of paramount importance. Although such a dramatic drop in wages "would be the event most favourable to a strengthening of effective demand," at the same time this is "unpractical," since "this would be accomplished by administrative decree and is scarcely practical policy under a system of free wage-bargaining" (Keynes 1936: 265). It seems therefore that the difference between Keynes and Pigou is not merely on economic principles, but on a different appreciation of political power and institutional constraint.

Keynes insists on this point a few pages later. A gradual reduction of money-wages would not have an effect on aggregate demand since "each reduction in wages serves to diminish confidence in the prospective maintenance of wages" (Keynes 1936: 265). In order to have a positive effect on investments, wages must reach the "bottom," but this is a *political* problem: "*it is only in a highly authoritarian society*, where sudden, substantial, all-round changes could be decreed *that a flexible wage-policy could function with success*. One can imagine it in operation in Italy, Germany or Russia, but not in France, the United States, or Great Britain" (Keynes 1936: 269, my emphasis).

Thus, Keynes does not reject that *in principle* a reduction of money wages would lead to an increase in investment and therefore of employment. What he is saying is that within the context of a depression, that is "weakening of the effective demand" (Keynes 1936: 265), a slow reduction of wages does not work and what would be necessary would be a sudden and drastic reduction in money-wages, but this is possible only under an authoritarian regime. This political constraint does not allow us to rely upon flexible wages as a way to restore capitalist accumulation.

It is worth pointing out that Keynes here is making a political/historical choice by opting for alternatives to regressive/repressive policies. He is making a political choice for Roosevelt against Hitler and Stalin. He is rejecting the repressive capitalist strategy in favor of what he sees can be a progressive one, one that works better. Here Keynes is in line with his general beliefs about capitalist production.[2]

3.2   Time, crisis, and expectations

Introduction

The other aspect which Keynes believed constituted the "main ground of [his] departure" from classical economics (1937: 222) was the analysis of expectations and the introduction of time in economic theory. The introduction of time in the economic discourse is the other side of the introduction of the *separation* between the decision of saving and investment – that is, in Marxian terms, the introduction of the possibility of crisis. Time and crisis are two sides of the same coin, the latter representing rupture and displacement of the (re)production of capital and the former representing the dimension in which this rupture takes place. Without the recognition of a temporal dimension in economic theory, there cannot be the recognition of crisis. In Shackle's (1968) classification of time in economic theory, "timeless models" are those which assume "pre-reconciliation of plans via instantaneous processes of information generation and diffusion" (Carvalho 1983–4: 268). Georgescu-Roegen (1971: 131) put it simply: "There could be no Time if nothing changed," whereas Dow (1985: 113) stresses how "The notion of equilibrium (and therefore of crisis) is inextricably tied up with the treatment of time. A state of rest is contrasted with a state of change, which occurs in time." It is therefore evident that "time" and "crisis" (or "equilibrium") are correspondent notions which define themselves specularly.

The classicals and the crisis

Neither the notion of crisis nor a concept of time can be found in pre-Keynesian discourse. Still, despite this absence, its theoretical framework provided insights in dealing with the capitalist crisis. Pre-Keynesian economic orthodoxy was based on Say's law[3] which rejected the possibility of crises of overproduction. The main source of demand is the flow of "factors'" income generated through the process of production. The employment of unused "resources" generates (in equilibrium conditions) an income stream by an equivalent amount. Demand is therefore generated by the increase in supply.

Say's law therefore rules out any possibility of overproduction *once* resources are employed. The mechanism which allows full employment of all resources is wage and price flexibility, through which markets equilibrate. In later formulation of Say's law, movements in the interest rate are able to equilibrate saving and investment, so that there is no possible overproduction of capital. Pigou's version of Say's law, the one directly attacked by Keynes, differs from its classical statement by its emphasis on labor market adjustment. In Pigou, overproduction is ruled out once the labor market is put in conditions of equilibrium – that is, when wage flexibility is installed.

The entire apparatus of Say's law, both its classical and Pigou's formulation, is obviously heavily apologetic in character. However, Say's law helps us to clarify how ideology is not simply an interpretation which is at odds with a presumably objective reality. Here apologetics correspond to a particular class position, capital's own, in a reality which is constituted by antagonistic class points. Here Say's law ideology becomes instrumental to providing the rationale for policies which have a class content. The pre-Keynesian interpretation of "crisis" did not regard it as the expression of the inherent contra-dictions of capitalist society but as a temporary disequilibrium which could be overcome if the wage system functioned "properly". Once the crisis, and not the temporary disequilibrium, actually occurs and is for everybody to see and experience, then the classical political economist denounced the institutional betrayal of the law of the demand and supply and invoked its re-establishment. This of course implies the repression of the working class and their newly formed organizations as they were imposing labor market "rigidities," among others. Karl Marx (1867: 793–4) observed this strategic meaning of economic theory/apology long before the Great Depression.

The absence of the notion of crisis in the classical system is accompa-nied by the absence of a dimension of time, and this is why with the analysis of expectations and the introduction of time in economic theory Keynes marks a decisive break with classical economics. In a world governed by Say's law, the process of adjustment was not a historical one and temporality – the link between past, present, and future – was conceived as having one single dimension. Expectations did not play any role in the classical model, since present and future did not constitute different entities. This is well seen in the relation between savings and investment. In the framework of Say's law, the decisions to save and to invest are not based on *future* expectations of demand, costs, and prices. In this framework therefore, the existence of profits – as well as the problem of its adequate level – *is presupposed as given*. Whatever the disturbances occurring in the economy, these will be cleared out by the market mechanism – that is, by wage flexibility, the iron law reestablishing an adequate proportion between surplus and necessary labor, social wages, and social profit. The notion of time is therefore a notion in which past, present, and future are fused together and annihilate themselves. Equilibrium is the goal, and also the starting point. It is the past and the future. The present disequilibrium is only a form of equilibrium, since the combination of the decision of investing and saving – through which the general equilibrium is obtained – is already a form of equilibrium.

With the vanishing of any dimension of time and of the differences between past, present, and future, with the vanishing of any idea of their interrelation, the end product is *eternity* – that is, *the eternity of the capitalist relation of work*. This is the bottom line which the general equilibrium framework presupposes: an implicit and Candidian belief in the impossibility of the transcendence of capitalism and the social relations of work upon which it is founded. However, it is precisely this belief that decreed its shortcomings in outlining strategies to deal with the crisis. The presuppositions of this belief were shaken by working-class movements that opened as urgent matter the question of a post-capitalist society. Keynes' introduction of time and expectation in the economic discourse, therefore, represents the acknowledgment of this urgency and the need for conventional economics to deal with it, to forge tools, insights, and strategies for its containment and its channeling into the capitalist accumulation process.

Keynes' theory as a theory of crisis

The aim of *The General Theory* is to provide a theory of the crisis in order to forge the tools for its management. The crisis as it appears from capital's perspective is a crisis of employment – that is, the interruption of the social mechanism through which capital is able to put people to work.

The first thing which needs to be noted is that in Keynes, crisis corresponds to hoarding, and this is based on the emphasis on the separation between the sales and purchase as two distinct moments, implying therefore two distinct social agents, and on the separation between savings and investment. Once this separation is brought in, an entire world of possible crises is unveiled. Crisis as money hoarding is reflected in the emphasis in the problem of demand for money. Any widening of the separation between savings and investment is reflected in the fluctuation of the demand for money and, therefore, is linked to the instability of the economy.[4]

Keynes' stress on separation between saving and investment decisions illustrated the possibility of crisis, but how might this possibility become reality? Why would hoarding come about? Given a stable consumption function and a marginal propensity to consume less than one, the amount of aggregate demand, and therefore of employment, depends on the level of investment. The latter depends on the inducement to invest – that is, on the spread between *expected profit* and interest rate. For a given interest rate determined by the banking system, or by a situation of deep crisis such as the one determined by the "liquidity trap," the level of investment is determined only by expected profits.[5] Thus, the central point is that the level of employment – that is, the ability of the system to put people to work for capital – is determined by expected profit – that is, by the *expected* degree to which the system will be able to put people to work.

In addressing the question of crisis, Keynes develops the theoretical tools for the rescue of capitalism. These essentially are, first, rejection of the absence of time in classical economics and with it of the notion of capitalism as an eternal system. By bringing into the economic discourse the fragility of the capitalist system, Keynes is able to develop the instruments to deal with the threat of grassroots struggles. Second, time is introduced in the form of expectations – that is, of *expected* profits. The current rate of profit is important only to give insights about future ones. With expected profit, not only is the capitalist relation at the center of Keynes' problematic, but also the *future* of this capitalist relation. Third, having rejected the reduction of money wages as politically unacceptable strategy, Keynes is left with two *complementary* strategies: on the side of the determinants of the overall proportion between social wages and social profit, he provides insights in the managing of real wages through the manipulation of the price level (Keynes 1940). On the side of the determinant of the level of accumulation, he favors government intervention to deal with unemployment and save the system.

A political–philosophical discussion of Keynes' critique of timeless models: "animal spirits" and historical time

The concept of time in economic theory has been discussed in several ways, which point at different meanings of the term. A major dichotomy in the representation of time in economics has been pointed out by Georgescu-Roegen (1971) and Joan Robinson (1978) in the distinction between, first, mechanical time and, second, historical time. The former is characterized by its reversibility and its independence of historical events. Qualitative changes of institutions do not affect the flow of time which can be in either direction across past, present, and future. As Shackle (1968) would say, these three moments are just moments of a known sequence (Carvalho 1983–4). Examples of this kind of interpretation of time can be found in the business cycle models of Kalecki, Samuelson, or Hicks (Shackle 1968: 223). Historical time, on the other hand, is irreversible. A third meaning of time is logical time (Termini 1981) which "does not explicitly incorporate time at all," and "uses logical precedence of variables to determine causality" (Dow 1985: 114). Fourth, Shackle introduces the concept of expectational time, "a concept relevant to the agent, the decision-maker at the moment of decision," in which "the agent 'knows' that the past is immutable and the future is to be created, as a result of the choices done in *the present*" (Carvalho 1983–4: 268).

Different authors have emphasized various notions of time in their discussion of Keynes' work. According to Termini (1981) logical time was employed by Keynes in *The General Theory*, whereas in her essay, "History vs Equilibrium," Joan Robinson points at the "very obvious fact that expectations about the future are necessarily uncertain" (Robinson 1978: 126) and therefore Keynes' analysis had to be framed within a notion of historical time.[6] Dow (1985), following Kregel's (1976) idea that Keynes' concept of equilibrium implies a combination of logical and historical time, argues there is no conflict between the two time frameworks as used by Keynes.

Joan Robinson's stress on historical time in Keynes is worth pursuing, because it opens an interpretation of Keynes' theory which makes it appear more realistic than classical theory. In so doing it therefore legitimizes Keynes' theory as a superior paradigm, in which the reference point against which evaluation takes place is "reality as it is." However, from the perspective of a political reading of economics, the realism of Keynes' historical time is a biased one, because time here is represented as an empty flow in which "events" take place. Irreversibility of course implies qualitative change, and indeed the emphasis is put on the changing conditions underlying economic phenomena. The extent of this qualitative change, however, the sense in which this time is *historical*, is constrained within a general understanding of time and history compatible with the maintenance of capitalist relations of production.

In order to give a sense of perspective and political significance, it is therefore convenient to approach the issue of time from another angle – namely, to approach another dimension of time, the one which could be better suited to the transcendence of capitalism, a dimension of time as *rupture*, as the displacement of a linearity in history, as the opening of *social*-revolutionary opportunity. It is when the present poses itself with the vision and the practice of its transcendence, of a "beyond" dimension, that one has time as rupture. All the same, the past stops simply being an object of contemplation of "what really was" as in the case of bourgeois historicism which, following Walter Benjamin "has no theoretical armature [since] its method is additive; it musters a mass of data to fill the homogeneous, empty time." What one needs is a reading of history "based on a constructive principle" (Benjamin 1955: thesis XVII). This constructive principle is a constitutive process of history, because "Not man or men but the struggling, oppressed class itself is the depository of historical knowledge" (Benjamin 1955: thesis XII). Thus, "A historical materialist cannot do without the notion of a present which is not a transition, but in which time stands still and has come to a stop. For this notion defines the present in which he himself is writing history" (Benjamin 1955: thesis XVI). To stop time is to define a moment of rupture, of a displacement, in the continuum of social relations of production. The "conception of the present as the 'time of the now'" (Benjamin 1955: thesis XVIII/A) as the time of rupture is a rebellious conception of time in contraposition to a conception of time as continuum.

In a sense, going back to Joan Robinson, the idea of rupture within the notion of historical time can also be found in Keynes, although with an important difference. Here the emphasis put on irreversibility implies of course qualitative change, and indeed the emphasis is put on the changing conditions underlying economic phenomena. Thus, for example, Joan Robinson discusses the notion of scarcity in relation to historical time:

> The question of scarce means with alternative uses becomes self-contradictory when it is set in historical time, where today is an ever-moving break between the irrevocable past and the unknown future. At any moment, certainly, resources are scarce, but they have hardly any range of alternative uses. The workers available to be employed are not a supply of "labor", but a number of carpenters or coal miners. The uses of land depend largely on transport; industrial equipment was created to assist the output of particular products. To change the use of resources requires investment and training, which alters the resources themselves. As for choice among investment projects, this involves the whole analysis of the nature of capitalism and of its evolution through time. (Robinson 1977: 8)

Although the emphasis on rupture is introduced, in this historical time, "where today is an ever-moving break between the irrevocable past and the unknown future," the sense of the "break," of rupture, is confined within the problems of capitalist accumulation, of the problems posed by the right proportions of, following Robinson's example, carpenters and coal miners. History here does not present alternatives and defines itself clearly and simply as "historical objectivism" in the continuum of the capitalist relation, as contemplation of "what really was," that is, the "irrevocable [capitalist] past," and speculations about an "unknown [capitalist] future."

In Keynes, the unknown character of this future is translated in the status of the long-run expectations of the investors which, to emphasize the difficulty of their modeling, in turn depends on their "animal spirits." In Keynes, rupture – as revolutionary, trans-cendental, rupture – exists only in the form of a threat, implicit in the theoretical apparatus, in the difficulty to endogenize variables, in the reliance on "psychological factors," on investors' animal spirits which mysteriously respond to hints of this historical rupture, in the recognition of the difficulty to model behavioral functions, etc. This threat is recognized through the status of long-run expectations of the investors. In the case of the liquidity trap, in which the infinitely elastic demand for money curve is used to portray a situation of hoarding – that is, of capital's refusal to put people to work – the threat is hanging over investors who perceive a gloomy future without hope for their profit. The truly unknown future from the capitalists' perspective, the true moment of rupture in their temporal dimension, is recognized in order to be avoided, to organize the rescue of the capitalist relation of work. For this reason Keynes is not talking about given functional relations, and is presupposing a moving marginal efficiency of capital schedule (Minsky 1975). The future is there to puzzle the investors in the present. The aim of econ-omic theory is to inform economic policy to limit the puzzle within the borders of the capitalist relation of work. Although Keynes' theo-retical apparatus is presupposing uncertainty for the future, this uncertainty is seen with the sense of urgency typical of a world in transition. In the discussion of the post-war Keynesian orthodoxy, it will be seen how this sense of urgency was lost, and the concept of time in economic theory changed, although it was far from returning to the "timeless models" of the classical period.

4
The Mass Worker and Ford's Strategy

4.1 Introduction

In Chapters 2 and 3 I have critically discussed the theoretical apparatus of the Keynesianism of Keynes. In Chapter 2, dealing with the origin of Keynes' "revolution," it was shown a direct relation between working-class struggles and the development of economic theory. In Chapter 3, I have approached the matter in more abstract terms, because the task there was to uncover the political meaning of some fundamental economic categories informing the Keynesian revolution. Post-war Keynesianism as an economic strategy presupposed a "social deal" which allowed capital to regulate the class relation or, in other terms, the balance between surplus and necessary labor. In this and in Chapter 5, therefore, I will instead deal with the historical evolution of this social conflict and I will emphasize some key institutional forms which were created or adopted as part of the strategies for its handling. I call the "social microfoundations" of Keynesianism the set of institutions and strategies aimed at the management of this class conflict. However, I regard these social microfoundations as *requirements*, as strategies, and not, as in the case (for example) of the French Regulation school or the American Social Structure of Accumulation school, as fixed and rigidly structural institutional arrangements at the basis of the Keynesian (or Fordist) period (Aglietta 1977; Gordon, Edwards and Reich 1982). As requirements, these social microfoundations attempted to provide a framework within which the dynamics of class struggles and of social movements could be contained. However, this institutional framework was full of cracks which soon will lead to the failure of the strategy. In other words, since class conflict does not occur only *within* these institutional forms, but also *against* and *beyond*, "as capital and the working class confront them as barriers to their own social reproduction" (Clarke 1988: 16), then it follows that these institutional forms (those captured by terms such as Fordism, Keynesianism, etc.) need to be considered not as synchronized, functionally required regulative forms, but rather as necessarily full of "cracks, fissures, contradictions" (Holloway 1987) precisely because they are forms of struggle.

One of the main themes of this book is how social conflict provokes a theoretical reaction in economics and a strategic reaction in policy. However, the forms, the objectives, the dynamics of social conflict are linked in turn to the ways people relate to each other in the places of production and of living in a certain historical context. For example, one thousand workers disposed along an assembly line and confined within the walls of a single large factory relate to each other and develop forms of organization that are different from, say, 10 workers behind computer screens in 100 factories spread over a large geographic area. One of the main targets of capital's strategies to deal with working-class struggles is therefore to disrupt the "class composition" that constituted the material basis upon which workers' struggles and workers' organizations were founded. These strategies, also commonly known by the term of "restructuring," lead to a historical transformation of the class composition – that is, a restructuring of what Italian historian Sergio Bologna called the "totality of socio-professional contents and its associated culture of work" (Bologna 1991: 22).

This restructuring does not eliminate conflict. It only creates the conditions for *new forms* of its reoccurrence. To each class composition corresponds a political composition of the working class, that is, "the totality of autonomous and class conscious ways of behaving and their associated culture of working class insubordination" (Bologna 1991: 22). The material power and forms of organization expressed by the working class therefore are historically specific to a particular class and political composition. Thus, for example, the struggles of what has been called the "craft worker" – which according to Bologna (1972) were at the basis of Council communism and the revolutionary waves in Europe in the aftermath of the Soviet revolution – induced capital to react through Taylorist and Fordist strategies. These substituted the craft workers with workers of a new kind, the unskilled "mass worker" (Baldi 1972; Carpignano 1973; Negri 1982).

By "Taylorism," I understand the strategy systematized and rationalized by Frederick Taylor (1903, 1911, 1912) aimed at fragmenting, dividing, and simplifying work. In political terms, Taylorism was a strategy used to decompose a working class whose strength *vis-à-vis* capital was based on skills. Fordist strategies can be seen as a direct evolution of Taylor's methods. They aimed at integrating unskilled jobs through the modern conveyor belt and attempted to recuperate the mass workers' motivation in the face of their increasing insubordination and job apathy following deskilling. With this strategy there are therefore two interlinked targets: first, the promotion of increasing productivity and high levels of growth; second, the control over the relation between productivity and wages (the balance between surplus and necessary labor) in a context of growing wages. Ford's aim was therefore on one side to control the distributive variables *and* the size of accumulation. Thus,

> whereas for Taylor wages were incentives directly linked to the position of the single worker in the enterprise according to individualistic and atomistic approach typical of Taylorian philosophy, for Ford wages became the general rate of income to be used in conjunction with the dynamic of the system. It became the general rate of capital to be injected within a framework of planned development. (Bologna 1972: 7)

The way in which Fordism attempts to reach these targets entails the company's direct intervention in workers' life not only at the point of production but also in the sphere of reproduction of labor power.

The study of Ford's experiment, the fact that it originates from the company's attempt to implement its business priorities *vis-à-vis* an insubordinate working class who despised deskilled work, the fact that Ford sets "wages" as the dynamic element of the company's growth, are useful to understand the "social deal" upon which Keynesian strategies were grounded. The original Henry Ford's attempt to deal with these problems offer here an interesting case study at a factory level of what was attempted after the Second World War at the social level with the direct participation of trade unions. This because the new class composition based on the "mass worker" allowed forms of struggles and patterns of insubordination of a new kind which then were dealt with within the institutional forms of the social foundation of Keynesianism until the struggles of the mid-1960s and 1970s made the co-optation of conflict within this institutional framework impossible.

4.2   The attack on working-class power through the elimination of the craft worker

The introduction of the chronometer in the process of production, the fragmentation of different operations into simple movements, the "scientific" organization of work, the creation of the assembly line – in a word, the creation of the modern factory and the transformation of the craft worker into a new social figure, the mass worker – meant the radical shift in the material conditions of the class conflict, its radical transformation.

When in 1903 the Ford Motor Company was founded, it consisted of eight skilled workers. In 1905 there were already 300 workers producing 25 cars a day. Unskilled workers were introduced in 1908 when the Model T began production. These workers were used to carry the parts from the storeroom to the assembly point, thus allowing increased work intensity by the skilled assembly workers by "freeing" them from movements on the shop floor. In these conditions, 500 workers were producing 100 cars per day. Finally, experiments with mechanical assembly lines, which used a rope to pull car chassis along the factory through different work stations, culminated in 1914 with the introduction of the chain-driven assembly line at Highland Park (Gartman 1979). The assembly line, it is important to emphasize, must not be understood simply as a "technological improvement." The assembly line was entirely a capitalist method of production, a capitalist attempt to impose its own organization, discipline, priorities, and plan of work:

> if we actually analyze this new so-called technology, we shall find that it is not a "technology" at all. It is not an arrangement of physical forces. *It is a principle of social order.* This was true of Ford's work. He made not one mechanical invention or discovery; everything mechanical he used was old and well known. Only his concept of human organization for work was new. (Drucker 1950: 19, my emphasis)

In other words, by pushing Taylorism (the fragmentation of the human movement) into a social dimension of production, Ford was attempting to master the productive force of social labor,[1] he was trying to impose a rhythm directly on the social co-operation of labor.[2]

This process of Taylorization and rationalization of production boosted the volume of production and the number of workers employed. However, if this process allowed Ford to take advantage of economies of scale, it did not increase productivity significantly. After one year of production of the Model T in 1909, an average of 1548 workers produced an average of 1059 automobiles. After the installation of the chain-driven assembly lines in 1913, an average of 13 667 workers produced and average of 15 284 cars (Meyer 1981: 72). Productivity, thus, increases less than the 100 percent predicted by Taylor, as is shown in Table 4.1.

At the basis of this relatively poor performance was the "human element" – that is, workers' hidden or open refusal to comply with the stricter discipline demanded by the assembly line and automated factory.

4.3   Patterns of insubordination of the mass worker

The labor problems faced by Ford in the aftermath of the introduction of automation can be classified in four categories: immigration, labor turnover, absenteeism, and labor organization. The use of the assembly line and the overall development of Detroit industry was made possible by the waves of migration which reached the city in the early years of 1900. As a sympathetic biographer of Henry Ford recalls, in the early decades of the century, Detroit "became one of the open-shop capitals of the land, where workers had to fight with flimsy weapons against well-armed employers upholding a tradition as to hours, wages and working conditions that was firmly opportunistic rather than liberal" (Nevins 1954: 512–13). Through the attack on the craft worker, the employment of newly arrived immigrants, and the use of espionage[3] and private police, Detroit's capitalists were able in this

Table 4.1   Worker productivity for the Model T Ford, 1909–13 (monthly average)

Year	Cars manufactured	Number of workers	Productivity	Productivity index (1909 = 100)
1909	1059[a]	1548	0.70	100
1910	1704	2573	0.66	94
1911	3483	3733	0.93	133
1912	6923	6492	1.07	152
1913	15 284	13 667	1.12	160

Note:
[a]Monthly average for 11 months
Source: Meyer (1981: 72).

period to enforce an open shop and avoid for a certain period any form of workers' organization within the factory. In November 1914, out of 12 880 workers, only 29 percent (3771) were American-born workers, and 9109 were foreign-born, coming from twenty-two national groups. Of this, the majority came from Southern and Eastern Europe (6790 workers or 52 percent of the total workforce) (Meyer 1981: 77). Although the presence of different nationalities allowed for a division of the working class in hierarchical terms (with the Southern and Eastern Europeans filling the lowest ranks of the wage hierarchy in unskilled positions, whereas American and German tool-makers and machinists were in the highest ranks if not in foreman positions), the cultural and language divisions constituted a problem for mass production. It has been pointed out that "the simplest lapses of communication among workers and among workers and foremen now contained the prospect of the disruption of the synchronized and coordinated flow of materials through the mechanized factory" (Meyer 1981: 77–8). The ethnical fragmentation also constituted a social problem in the industrial city, where residential segregation along ethnical and wage lines were a common factor. This was a problem to the extent that segregated residential life contributed to re-create what the factory owners of Detroit perceived as the negative stereotypical characters of immigrant workers, that is, their

> undesirable traits which affected their work-discipline and productivity in an industrial setting. These included racial hatred and jealousy, too many holidays, the drink habit, an inadequate diet for hard work, thievery, and the tendency to lie. (Meyer 1981: 79)

Ford's managers thus faced a first task of imposing a pattern of cultural conformity on the heterogeneous working class whereas the latter faced the new form of capitalist exploitation – the assembly lines – in unfavorable conditions for resisting. In these conditions, the natural form of working-class resistance which Ford had to face was *mobility* – that is, labor turnover.

In the motor industry of the time, everyone was employed day to day. There were no seniority rights and labor turnover was extremely high not only because firing policy was used as a means to control workers, but because of the extremely high quit rate: "In 1913 Ford required between 13 000 and 14 000 workers to run his plants at any one time, and in that year over 50 000 workers quit" (Beynon 1973: 19) – that is, a turnover of about 260 percent. The problems caused by this form of resistance were lamented by one of Ford's managers, Judge Hulbert, who in 1912 wrote:

> it is not at all surprising to me with our modern conditions that it is difficult to find a boy who wants to continue in employment. Our modern shops are built on such an economical plan that we get one individual doing one thing until he becomes most efficient at that one thing. It is impossible to take a child and set him one task and not expect him to chafe at that task ... Among the thousands or more boys who come to me in a year I find few that hold their positions more than three months. Generally they say they get tired of that one thing. They want to get into a shop where they get some other kind of job, one perhaps as tiresome in the end, but it represents a change temporarily. (quoted in Beynon 1973: 19)

By 1914, turnover reached 400 percent (Gartman 1979: 204). Thus, despite the large immigration influx, Ford faced a perpetual labor shortage, which was often recognized by Ford's managers (Meyer 1981: 83). At the basis of this high turnover, which was facilitated by the booming Detroit economy, was workers' search for higher wages, less tedious work, and the opportunity to develop skills. Often, workers with high turnover were people with no families ties (Meyer 1981: 79–85).

Absenteeism was the other "plague" disrupting Ford's newly automated production. In 1913, daily absences in the Highland Park plant were 10 percent of the total workforce (Meyer 1981: 80). The reasons for absenteeism were the same as those arising sixty years later in Detroit – that is, the opportunity to take a vacation from work. As in the mid-1970s, Mondays accounted for the largest numbers of absences, after a Saturday payday (Meyer 1981: 82). "Stomach troubles" were the all-purpose excuse of absence. To "lay-off" a few days without notice was a common practice in order for better-paid workers to take some vacation. For the less-paid workers, "sickness holidays" were used also for taking the time for looking for better jobs (Meyer 1981: 82–83). For Ford, labor turnover and absenteeism not only disrupted the new method of production but constituted an extra cost which Ford had to bear in order to replace those workers who quit or did not show up for work.

Turnover and absenteeism – that we could dub the typical working-class understanding of labor flexibility – were just the first signs of working-class resistance. Also, Ford was soon to be "faced by the threat of unionism and even insurrection" (Beynon 1973: 25). An atmosphere of open and organized revolt came to be felt throughout the squalid shanty towns of Detroit. The radical syndicalism of the Industrial Workers of the World (IWW), whose action spread all around the United States at that time, represented at least a possible, if not an actual, threat for Detroit's industrialists.[4] As the secretary of the Employers' Association remarked in a warning to his colleagues,

> There … is at this time more restlessness, more aggression among the workmen of Detroit and elsewhere than there has been for several years past … There is a lot of inflammable matter scattered about the plants and it is up to you … whether or not a spark ignites it, or it is cleared away before damage results. (quoted in Nevins 1954: 518)

In spring 1913, the IWW organized meetings at the gates of Ford's Highland Park plant at which sometimes a crowd of 3000 gathered. After Ford's managers withdrew workers' outdoor lunch privileges, the IWW shifted attention to other Detroit car factories. However, there were rumors that the IWW would return to Ford's gates in 1914 (Meyer 1981: 91). In this year, the IWW organized thousands of unemployed on demonstrations in Detroit and its militants were linking with the American Federation of Labor (AFL) on the question of cutting working hours (Roediger and Foner 1989: 190). Thus, Ford faced a serious labor problem: at best high turnover and tight labor market, at worst unionization and insurrection.

4.4   Ford's five-dollars day and the strategy for the subsumption of the mass worker

To cope with this "labor problem," Ford's managers attempted to implement different policies which, in the context of mass production, did not succeed. Thus, for example, piecework could not be used extensively because the "company was changing its methods of production so frequently that piece rates would have meant endless bother." Also, once the assembly line was introduced "a piecework system would have been meaningless where the new type of assembly was concerned, since the speed of the line controlled the speed of the worker" (Nevins 1954: 525).

In 1913, Ford's manager John R. Lee examined the causes of workers' "dissatisfaction and unrest" and concluded:

1. Too long hours. A man whose day is too long and whose work is exhausting will naturally be looking for another job.
2. Low wages. A man who feels that he is being underpaid will always be looking for a change in occupation.
3. Bad housing conditions, wrong home influences, domestic trouble, etc.
4. Unsanitary and other undesirable shop conditions.
5. Last and perhaps the most cause of dissatisfaction is the unintelligent handling of the men on the part of the foremen and superintendents. (Meyer 1981: 100–1)

The last point is especially important because it summarizes the breaking down of the traditional patterns of control and discipline at the point of production. The increased number of the labor force employed following the massification of production required increasing numbers of foremen with the consequent development of personal animosity and resentment against them. The latter in fact were able to blackmail the rank and file through holding extensive power on the determination of wages, promotions, etc.[5]

During the fall of 1913 Ford instituted a labor program which included the increase of wages by 15 percent, the creation of a saving and loan program, and, more important, the rationalization of the wage hierarchy, which segmented Ford's labor force in sixteen categories. The foreman was denied the authority to hire and fire workers, who instead were to expect a regular "promotion" to a higher level of the hierarchy if production targets were obtained. With this institutionalization of discipline through the wage hierarchy, "now, the worker could blame only himself when he failed to maximize his earnings" (Meyer 1981: 102).

This labor program was complemented with the famous Five-dollar day (FDD) announced on January 5. At a time when the average wage of Detroit's autoworkers was two-and-a-half dollars a day, Ford introduced the FDD, with which he sowed the seed of the social factory. This had two goals. First, it was a policy aimed at preventing any sparks of workers' resistance and dissent from igniting. As Ford's engineer Joseph Galamb puts it: with the FDD "Mr. Ford ... would lick ... the I.W.W" (quoted in Nevins 1954: 537).[6] Second, the FDD was combined with the eight-hour day, which, according to Ford, allowed maximum efficiency in running the plants.[7]

It must be emphasized that whereas the autumn's reforms concentrated on the organization of production, the FDD essentially introduced Ford's management in the sphere of workers' reproduction. With the FDD, Ford planned to tie the labor force to its factory, thus reducing working-class mobility and introducing a new mechanism for gaining workers' docility. However, "too high" wages could undermine workers' availability for work and could lead to patterns of spending incompatible with the discipline of the assembly line. The FDD thus was accompanied by measures aimed at controlling the entire life of the worker.[8] The company would intervene and dictate not only the conditions of production of manufactured commodities but also the conditions of work and life and the quality and quantity of time spent in reproducing the commodity labor power.

This was obtained, first, by subjecting eligibility to FDD to some conditions specified by the company. Not all Ford's workers could benefit from high wages. Excluded were (1) workers with less than six months of seniority; (2) youths under twenty-one; and (3) women, because Ford "hopes that all unmarried young women will marry" (Coriat 1979: 56). Second, the private life of those eligible were susceptible to the investigations of Ford's "sociological department." The following description is worth quoting in full:

Each investigator, equipped with a car, a driver, and an interpreter, was assigned a district in Detroit, mapped to contain a due proportion of Ford workers and if possible a limited number of language groups. The subjects for inquiry made up a formidable list. Naturally, each worker was expected to furnish information on his marital status, the number and ages of his dependents, and his nationality, religion, and (if alien) prospects of citizenship. In addition, light was sought on his economic position. Did he own his home? If so, how large was the mortgage? If he rented a domicile, what did he pay? Was he in debt, and to whom? How much money had he saved, and where did he keep it? Did he carry life insurance, and at what premiums? His social outlook and mode of living also came under scrutiny. His health? His doctor? His recreations? The investigator meanwhile looked about sharply, if unobtrusively, so that he could report on "habits," "home condition," and "neighborhood." Before he left a given family, he knew whether its diet was adequate; whether it took in boarders – an evil practice which he was to discourage; and whether money was sent abroad. All this information and more was placed on blue and white forms. The Sociological Department was nothing if not thorough. (Nevins 1954: 554)

The FDD was designed in the form of a profit-sharing plan. The overall wage of five dollars was explicitly subdivided into two components. One, the traditional wage earned as result of "labor," and the other a "gift" of the Ford company conditioned to workers' compliance to a certain life patterns and habits. Thus, Samuel M. Levin, an early writer on the subject, illustrates: "[the FDD] offered separate stipends to the men in this double capacity, so that a man in the lower ranks of labor might receive $2.34 per day for working ... and $2.66 for living as the company wanted him to live" (quoted in Meyer 1981: 111).

How did Ford's managers want their workers to live? They ranked workers' "sins" in four groups order of gravity: the fully qualified; those excluded because they don't fit the criteria; those excluded because of bad personal habit; those excluded because they had also unsatisfactory home conditions. Among the reasons of condemnation were an "excessive use" of liquor and gambling. Also, included were "'any malicious practice derogatory to good physical manhood or moral character.' A household dirty, frowzy, and comfortless; and unwholesome diet; a destruction of family privacy by boarders; an excessive expenditure on foreign relatives – these were among the reasons for condemnation" (Nevins 1954: 555–6).

After the classification came the judgment and the punishment. Probation was offered to the disqualified workers. Changing habits and home conditions within thirty days would have granted the worker the full sum. Sixty days would have cost the worker one-fourth of the FDD. Ninety days would have cost the workers 40 percent of the wage package, and so on. "After six months in purgatory without sign of reformation, the delinquent was cast into the limbo of Detroit, and his unearned 'profits' were used for charity. Even so, when a black sheep returned to the fold with bleats of repentance, he was usually given another chance" (Nevins 1954: 556).

Those excluded by the sentence of Ford's managers were facing a difficult situation as in comparison to their fellow shopmates; they did the same work but received half of their income (Meyer 1981: 112). They thus had three choices: they could quit and look for another job; they could continue living in this awkward situation; or they could conform following pressures of family and friends.[9]

The FDD and these forms of social control were introduced along with other important welfare innovations and administration of the social wage.[10] All together, these measures had the effect of drastically reducing absenteeism and turnover, thus providing a short-term solution to Ford's labor problems. At the same time, "The work was hard, the pace inexorable, the pressure for ever-better production insistent" (Nevins 1954: 549). In fact, the key objective of the increase in wage and the institutionalization of the control on workers' lives was to increase efficiency. The FDD represents therefore a case of "productivity deal" without the intervention of union bureaucracy. A pamphlet for Ford workers, for example, stressed that "the Ford Motor Company does not believe in giving without a fair return. So to acquire the right to participate in the profits a man must be willing to pay in increased efficiency." The latter is not only the product of good performance at the point of production, but also at the point of reproduction, as the worker "must do everything in his power to improve his standard of living and to make his environment more wholesome, both for himself and for those dependent upon him" (quoted in Meyer 1981: 118).

4.5   Workers' resistance and the decay of the five-dollar day

Apart for 10 percent of Ford workers who were not eligible, 40 percent of the eligible Ford workforce did not meet the standard set by the company and therefore did not receive the FDD (Meyer 1981: 119). The FDD was undoubtedly an object of resistance fueled not only by the natural mistrust that workers have for their bosses, but also by the excessive intrusiveness in workers' private life by Ford's investigators.[11]

The First World War demanded a deterioration of working and living conditions through intensification of work and inflationary erosion of living standard, the expansion of the authority of the national government, the repression of organized labor militancy (IWW, socialist party and others), and the subscription for Liberty Loans. However, at the same time, the tight labor markets because of the First World War and the attempt to gain working-class support for the war enabled the generalization of Ford's wage in other industries, as well as shorter hours, improved working conditions, and collective negotiations with workers' representatives. Moreover, the national drive for accumulation during the war increased discontent which, accompanied with the imagery of the Russian Revolution in 1917, caused many American and immigrant workers to refuse to comply with the requirements of the war effort.

Labor turnover increased at Ford from a low of 15 percent in 1915 to 51 percent in 1918, although military resignations accounted for only about 8 percent of the last figures (Meyer 1981: 170–1). Low productivity became a problem throughout the war, not only because of the differentiation of production for the war effort (helmet, ambulances, trucks, aircraft engines) but also because of the increase of workers' discontent (Meyer 1981: 171). Despite Ford's obstruction of industrial unionism in 1914, the war period saw an upsurge of industrial unionism at Ford and in Detroit (Meyer 1981: 171–2).

All this made Ford's FDD strategy inadequate. The strategy was disrupted by the increase in the social productivity and in the average wage outside the Ford Motor Company, by the perseverance of workers' discontent, and by the escalation of industrial unionism which challenged Ford's paternalistic policy. The level of socialization of the class relation and of the class conflict in the 1930s and 1940s forced the abandonment of individual corporate policies of integrating different moments of the (re)productive cycle and pulled the state directly into the battlefield. The management and control of the balance between surplus and necessary labor could no longer rely on a company's "sociological department" but had to be managed at the level of society as a whole and involve workers' representatives. The legitimization and the institutionalization by the state of trade unions in the form of labor bureaucracies, which were able to control the grassroots at the micro-level, became a crucial step in this direction. Through Keynesianism the state drew the elements of their strategy from Fordism, only to displace it to the level of society as a whole. In the following chapters I will show how the institutions at the core of Keynesian strategies were formed in relation to class conflict.

5

War, Class War, and the Making of the Social Microfoundations of Keynesianism

5.1 Introduction

The Second World War provided the framework within which the social institutions of Keynesianism were shaped, together with state planning. This period also witnessed the development of working-class autonomy *vis-à-vis* the union (this development continued the wave of wild cat strikes of the late 1930s);[1] the legitimization of unions by the state aimed at an active use of their apparatus for the control of working-class autonomy; the implementation of systematic growth strategies for the satisfaction of war needs; and the development of economics as discipline for macroeconomic planning together with the strengthening of its empirical counterpart via the development of national accounting techniques and statistical methods. In this chapter, I explore these developments.

5.2 Social turmoil during the great depression

In this period the economic problems at the basis of planning were the need to find ways to finance the war, the question posed by the availability of labor power in different sectors in relation to the needs of war production, the control of the general proportion of war production in relation to civilian needs, and the managing of the supply of resources such as materials, construction and facilities, and labor power. For this purpose, on January 16, 1942, few weeks after Pearl Harbor, the War Production Board (WPB) was established with the responsibility to coordinate the United States' productive apparatus to meet the quantitative and qualitative production targets required by the war. Through the different committees, divisions and bureaus of the WPB, both war production and its input requirements were planned and co-ordinated. The entire economy functioned in the plans of the WPB administrators as a huge (social) factory.[2]

However, the planning and the co-ordination of material and monetary flows, as well as flows of labor power in different sectors according to the needs of the war, required the maintenance of social peace at the point of production. It is not possible to understand the nature of this problem for capital during the war years without an examination of the development of working-class autonomy during the years of the Great Depression. The 1930s was the period in which the American mass worker forced capital to explore new strategies of regulation of the class conflict both at the point of production and at the social level. The years of the Great Depression saw the emergence of a new level of mass insubordination against capitalist mechanisms of regulating the wage relation. Both the unwaged and waged sections of the working class explored and discovered new forms of organization within which to attack capital's discipline. *Direct action* and the attempt to organize around it represented for both waged and unwaged sections of the working class a new method of struggle, although in different forms depending on their material position within the wage hierarchy.

The unwaged

The Great Depression, with its historically high levels of unemployment, did not make the American working class more docile. On the contrary, it sparked open insurrection: "Don't starve – fight!" was one slogan. Struggles spread around every issue concerning the reproduction of labor power, reproduction which was endangered by the crisis itself. Mass direct appropriation, struggle against eviction,[3] rent strikes,[4] marches forcing the passage of relief bills,[5] political demonstrations often culminating in riots, etc. gained momentum in the 1930s and threatened to challenge the social system of control.[6] In the early years of the depression organized "proletarian shopping" became a nation-wide phenomenon (Bernstein 1970: 421–3). Racist divisions were often overcome thanks to black initiative as blacks were both the hardest hit of any section of the population and also one of the most active. In the south, black and white share-croppers were coming together in the share-cropper union. Black workers started to organize in the newly formed industrial unions, something which would have been impossible in the structures of the old craft unions. Unemployed struggles saw black initiative at the forefront.[7]

The unwaged thus became a central component of the struggles of the mass worker in the 1930s. The National Unemployment Council was formed on July 4, 1930, and soon had branches and councils in forty-six states and in almost every town and city. The organization of the unemployed not only gave organizing power to the demands and needs of the unwaged, but also meant that capital could not use strike breakers against industrial action.[8]

The waged

The most militant part of the waged proletariat was composed of "second-generation workers, sons and daughters of the 1900–1920 'new immigrants'" (Davis 1986: 55). Their rebellion "owed nothing to the benevolent hand of John L. Lewis or other official leaders. The most striking aspect of the early thirties insurgency was the defiant autonomy of (usually clandestine) plant committees from any of the official apparatuses" (Davis 1986: 56). Radical leaders were "led" by the grassroots spontaneous leadership in organizing walk outs and sitdown strikes.[9]

The sitdown fever[10] started with the GM sitdown strike in winter 1937 and spread to 400 000 workers who staged 477 sitdowns as hospital workers, trash collectors, gravediggers, blind workers, engineers, prisoners, tenants, students, and baseball players. As an effect of these strikes, other plants employing 600 000 workers were forced to close down (Boyer and Morais 1955: 295 n.5). The new method of struggle was a formidable weapon, a method of struggle which enabled the mass worker to make full use of its class composition.[11] The corporations "seemed to fall like dominoes" (Davis 1986: 61).

To succeed, the sitdown was used without *notice* – that is, without any element of *mediation* and at the minimum cost for the workers. In this condition "[T]he goal of the secessionist [from AFL] bureaucrats led by Lewis and Hillman was to dam this torrent of mass militancy and to re-channel it into pacific tributaries under their command" (Davis 1986: 61). This attempt to channel workers militancy gained ground in the war period. A significant aspect of union bureaucratization was the no-strike pledge subscribed by the labor bureaucracies including the newly formed CIO and also the official organizations of the left such as the Communist Party.[12] This opened the ground in the post-war period to the role of the trade union as a mediating buffer on the shop floor in the practice of collective bargaining.

5.3 The "crisis of productivity" during the war years

In the last years of the 1930s the relief system and the bureaucratic apparatus used for its delivery brought a decline of social unrest among the unwaged (Piven and Cloward 1979: 77). The emergence of the war, by reducing unemployment, accelerated this decline. The army draft caused a dramatic change in the composition of the labor force. In the metropolitan area of Detroit almost 30 percent of the male work force of March 1940 entered military service (Glaberman 1980: 17). The official unemployment rate, which was 25 percent in 1937 and 17 percent in 1939, dropped to below 2 percent in 1943, 1944, and 1945. This involved the entrance into the labor force of new components such as women, teenagers, and underemployed farm workers. "By mid-1943, virtually anyone who wished to find a job could do so at real wages higher than those prevailing at any previous time" (Lichtenstein 1982: 110).

Women entered the metal, chemical, rubber, and aircraft industries.[13] Blacks entered auto and aircraft industries. Even though the overall rate of unionization was declining, the ranks of female trade unionists increased by 460 percent and the number of black trade unionists increased by 850 000 (Noble 1984: 22).[14] The "Little steel formula" – adopted in 1942 by the WLB during a conflict in the steel industry – froze wages at 15 percent above 1941 levels. In the war years, however, prices rose 45 percent and profits increased by 250 percent. As it will be discussed in more detail later, perhaps the most significant element of the formula was the *no-strike pledge* made by the new leadership of industrial unionism, and the related prohibition of collective bargaining and the compulsory arbitration by the WLB. The no-strike pledge was in fact to a large extent a broken promise: despite the pressure of the union leadership, the war years represented an extraordinary wave of industrial insubordination and struggle.

Faced with an organization of war production which killed 88 000 workers and injured 11 million between 1940 and 1945 (to be added to the statistics of US war casualties which counted more than 300 000 killed and almost 700 000 injured), there were 14 471 strikes involving almost 7 million workers – that is, more than in any other period including the 1930s when the Congress of Industrial Organizations (CIO) was formed. The war years saw a massive diffusion of industrial insurgency. Because of the trade unions' no-strike pledge, the struggle came directly from below. High absenteeism, high turnover (double the pre-war years)[15] and short wild cat strikes directed by spontaneous leadership, co-ordinated at the department or plant level (Noble 1984: 22) were the forms taken by workers' insubordination. Not only did the objectives of the struggle attempt to bypass control by the union bureaucrats through the institutionalization of the grievance procedure instituted by the WLB, but also the form of the struggle itself was in direct conflict with the official labor authorities.

There were in fact two things in common in these strikes. First, "They were all wildcats, that is, illegal under union rules. None of them involved traditional contract negotiations" (Glaberman 1980: 37). Second, strikes were located in those areas and industries of significant strategic importance for US war involvement: in the coal regions, Detroit, Akron, the West Coast aircraft plants and the East Coast shipyards (Noble 1984: 22). Furthermore, sympathy strikes were common. At Ford, for example, between 1941 and 1945, 10 percent of the 773 strikes were direct actions for class solidarity.

The massive entrance of women in the workforce did not limit the struggles, but instead radicalized the demands. Martin Glaberman has noted that

> In terms of behavior in the factories and on the job, what is indicated is that women were an experienced work force, that is, experienced in terms of relations with bosses and with fellow employees, although the particular traditions and practices of the auto industry may have been new. (Glaberman 1980: 20)[16]

The position of women still in charge of reproduction work had the effect of "an unwillingness on the part of women workers to subordinate themselves to the demands of management" (Glaberman 1980: 23). Women's double work load, at home and in the factory, became the condition for their everyday struggles.[17] This connection between production and reproduction work would be one of the major issues of the struggles of the 1960s which would bring on the collapse of Keynesianism.

The great bulk of wartime strikes was over control of production and labor discipline,[18] issues that directly affected management's ability to plan production, therefore limiting the coordination of war production at the social level. Strikes occurred despite the continuous presence of military officers in production plants and the strenuous war propaganda machine.[19] Many stoppages and walkouts were also the result of workers' frustration with the grievance procedure controlled by the WLB.[20] Often, the strikes were feeding on themselves, with workers expanding the walkouts to counter management's initial disciplinary reaction against stoppages.[21]

The increased power obtained through tight labor markets and the consequent reduction of fear of unemployment also enabled workers to better resist traditional disciplinary sanctions such as temporary unpaid suspension, or layoff. "Absenteeism, tardiness, early wash-up, disinterest in application to the job, lessened pride of workmanship, insubordination, and just plain soldiering" (Harris 1982: 63) were all manifestations of this increased power.

Not only control and discipline but also wages entered into the demands of the strikers, although to a lesser extent.[22] What was more of concern were issues of wage inequality, which was often perceived by the rank and file as an artificial means of division.[23]

It must be pointed out that the struggle over wage inequality was not only an attempt to circumvent the Little Steel formula and the wage freeze, but it was also symptomatic of "a larger disruption of workplace discipline and a decline in managerial authority that characterized the factory environment in the war era" (Lichtenstein 1982: 117).[24] The struggle against the wage hierarchy implied struggle against capital's "divide and conquer" strategy necessary for the valorization process. The tight conditions of labor markets which facilitated working-class militancy forced management to give in to workers' pressure over wages. They found ways to increase wages despite the prohibition set by the NWLB. Management thus was involved in "wage drift."[25]

Working-class autonomy expressed by the pattern of wartime strikes clearly was not a function of workers' impoverishment, as their financial status was better than before the war. Yet,

Workers were aware that they were bearing an unfair share of the cost of the war. There was a wage freeze that was pretty rigid, limitation of overtime pay, controls over movement to better jobs, considerably higher payroll taxes, and so on. At the same time workers were aware of skyrocketing wartime profits, no limits on executive salaries, inflationary price spirals and the like. Nevertheless, the financial status of the average worker was better than before the war. There was considerable forced overtime. Many workers had upgraded from lower-paying jobs in service and other trades, or in agriculture, to the

> relatively high union wages in defense industry. Substantial numbers of wartime workers had come off extended periods of unemployment and were experiencing relative security for the first time in their lives. And a higher proportion of working class families had more than one wage earner. (Glaberman 1980: 41)

Workers, in other words, were not reacting to their misery, but they were attacking the hypocrisy which asked them to make sacrifices when the war profits were mounting and they were using a situation of relative power provided by the labor shortage and the needs of the war to extend their own power over production.[26]

Working-class control over production was also expressed in what came to be known as the practice of "*government work.*" This was "work done on company time, with company materials, on company equipment or machines, for the personal use of the worker ... [that] involved, whether done by men or women, concealing the work from supervision and, often, a cooperative organization of the required work to make the illegal work possible" (Glaberman 1980: 23). "Government work" became widespread and reflected workers' power achieved both in the previous years of struggles and in the current situation of shortage of labor. Government work and the link between production and reproduction time brought about by women participating in the waged industrial labor force represented examples of the circulation of struggle. The development of sympathy strikes,[27] which would be targeted in 1948 by the Taft–Hartley Act, also constituted an example of the circulation of struggles over production.

To conclude, during the war years the great emphasis of the struggles of waged workers was on power at the point of production. This power would lead to what post-war managers would recognize as a crisis of productivity (Harris 1982) – that is, the fact that, to a significant extent, they had lost control of production, *not to the union, but to the rank-and-file themselves.*

5.4   Union bureaucratization and war planning

The crucial importance of autonomous struggles during the war is determined by the fact that they forced the state to shape a strategy to deal with it in the attempt to maintain war production. The key institutional element of this strategy was the bureaucratic form taken by the trade unions and their increasingly mediating role. Indeed, in this period the fundamental institutional and cultural elements of the post-war strategies were being formed in reaction to the autonomous rhythm of working-class struggles. The process of union bureaucratization and the no-strike pledge were the institutional mechanisms upon which capitalist planning had to rely, but at the very moment at which unions attempted to impose "national" priorities through the subordination of the interests of their membership, rank-and-file workers fought against companies, bypassed union leadership and attempted autonomous forms of organization.

The process of union bureaucratization was complex and it involved a strategy of co-optation of workers' grassroots organizations and recuperation of their demands. This is not the place to write such an history. However, for the present argument it is important to underline how the war allowed the process of bureaucratization to gain momentum.

After the "wild cat fever" of 1937 the control of wild cat strikes in major industries was a continuous problem faced by union leaders, companies and government (Glaberman 1980: 13). The emergency of the war and its nationalistic–patriotic rhetoric provided the context for American capital to launch a campaign aimed at the control of workers' autonomy. The basic kernel of this campaign was the role of the unions and their increased integration in the policies of the government. Thus, despite the opposition of major businesses to the greater role of the unions, these begin to work in strict cooperation with state plan.

The National War Labor Board (NWLB) was one of the main vehicles through which and by means of which union bureaucratization was promoted.[28] The NWLB, which was set up on January 12, 1942, followed the National Defense Mediation Board (NDMB), a previous attempt by the government to establish an institution for the management of labor relations on a national level. The latter was a tripartite administrative tribunal to settle all serious disputes affecting the defense program and was established after the upsurge of strike activity over wage and hour issues and union organization on heavy industries between winter 1940 and spring 1941. Unions gave voluntary pledges not to strike once disputes had been certified by the Board. Board policy was determined in equal share by labor, business representatives, and public members. This collapsed in the fall of 1941 over the demand for a union shop by mine workers, an issue on which business and unions were not able to compromise.

The NDMB proved incapable of setting the conflict. A new approach was needed. After Pearl Harbor, the new climate of urgency allowed the establishment of a new institution in the form of the NWLB which lasted until 1945. The NWLB was stronger because it had the power to impose penalties on the unions for non-compliance with its decisions. The board aimed at producing a bureaucratized, centralized, and responsible union in order to enhance and direct the machinery of a "orderly, law-bound industrial conflict" (Harris 1982: 56). In this context, management – whose approach toward industrial relations generally refused to deal with unions – had to be "educated" in their new role of negotiators with shop stewards, grievance committeemen, and union officials as mediators and moderators of discontent.[29] The difficulty of managers to comply with NWLB orders was owing to their fear that the practices of the board would have limited indefinitely their right to manage (a right that was already challenged from the shopfloor), together with the uncertainty connected with the conversion of war production into civilian production at the end of the war, with the consequent drop of orders. The latter concern would be dealt with through state subsidies on cancellation of contracts at the end of the war (Harris 1982).

The board's main difficulty however was the general "upsurge of rank-and-file unrest, directed against their employers and managers, against their 'responsible' union leaders, and against the NWLB itself" (Harris 1982: 47). This protest bypassed the unconditional no-strike pledge ratified by the CIO and AFL leaders shortly after Pearl Harbor.[30] The no-strike pledge was the act which perhaps best symbolized the union collaboration with national policies at the expense of its members' needs. It is through the pledge that it is possible to see trade unions developing as institutions for mediating, channeling, and subsuming grassroots autonomy in a way compatible to the plan of social capital.[31] Right from the start of the war, it became apparent that the unions were subordinating the interests of the rank and file to those of "the country."[32] The signing of the no-strike pledge was almost exclusively done either without advance or follow-up consultation with the rank and file (Glaberman 1980: 6) or, as in the case of UAW, using techniques of deception to sell the pledge to the membership.[33] Furthermore, the no-strike pledge was regarded as binding and irrevocable on unions. In absence of consent, the pledge was backed up by penalties and threats (Harris 1982: 47).

If on one hand such a system needed active union involvement in the attempt to displace grassroots protest; on the other hand it was evident that having signed the no-strike pledge, there was little appeal on the side of the workers to join a union.[34] It was therefore the state, through the NWLB, which actually promoted *both the diffusion of unionization in industries and union membership*. Unionization was not widespread before the war. The activity of the Board became crucial to allow the process to take place, *and therefore to prepare the institutional ground for the post-war productivity deals*. Those unions that were recognized by large corporations before the war were only acting as representative of their members or of all workers in a particular bargaining unit. Instead, during the war, union membership became a condition of employment and management had to collaborate with unions in the administration and discipline of their members (Harris 1982: 49).

The NWLB also actively promoted a new managerial culture by encouraging the diffusion of unions. The influence of the Board, and therefore of the state, extended to the shaping of the wage mechanism and the introduction of elements which would become central features in the post-war wage relations under the productivity deals. For example, the NWLB was supporting "automatic wage progression", which recognized the workers' right to expect a steadily increase in their wages given an "adequate" performance. This conflicted with the old management prerogative of rewarding individual employees on a "merit" basis. Another aspect that would inform the organization of the wage round in the post-war period was introduced during the war to meet wage pressures and centralize wage formation. Multiplant and multifirm bargaining was thus encouraged and promoted. Both the automatic wage mechanism and the encouragement of the widening of the geographical coverage of agreements represented elements of the post-war practice of wage round increases which became fundamental for the overall determination of a dynamic balance between necessary and surplus labor (Harris 1982: 49–57).

Checking-off dues were an innovation necessary to control the disaffected union membership in face of union subordination of rank-and-file needs to national priorities.[35] The "maintenance of membership" clause established by the NWLB required workers to remain union members for the duration of the contract. Employers were authorized to deduct union dues and fines from the wage of the workers and pay them directly to the unions (Harris 1982: 48).

The institutional power of CIO leadership was therefore strength-ened by the state. This represented a concession to CIO leaders who in the pre-war years had demanded union-shop contracts as a guarantee against employer attempts to weaken new unions in periods of low employment. With this concession, therefore, the state helped to enforce at the firm level, at least for the duration of the contract, the acknowledgment of a rigidity – that is, of the union as permanent institution within the firm – and by solving the financial crisis faced by the CIO as consequence of its collaboration policies, *it helped to make "cooperative union leaders somewhat 'independent' of rank-and-file pressure"* (Lichtenstein 1975: 53, my emphasis).[36]

6
War Planning and the Rise of the Keynesian Orthodoxy

6.1 Introduction

From the previous discussion it is evident that the social prerequisite of capitalist planning lies in the ability to control working-class autonomy; flows of commodities and resources for the material production of war requirements could be planned only *if* the living subjects who made these flows possible could somehow be "harmonized" and made to co-operate within the social division of labor. The key institution which enabled this was, paradoxically enough, the union. Certainly not the union understood as immediate expression of workers' needs for an organization, rather, the union understood as a particular *form* of organization, a vertical hierarchical structure which could function as an instrument of mediation and co-optation of working-class autonomy within the requirements of capital accumulation. The point which needs to be explored now is the relation between the rise of Keynesianism as orthodoxy, as a general framework within which state policies are implemented, and working-class struggles.

During the depression, the struggles against unemployment forced the state to intervene, but the set of legislative measures which were introduced were not sufficient to put people back to work.[1] Instead of curtailing the movement, the introduction of these reforms sparked industrial unionism and inaugurated the beginning of the wave of struggle of the unorganized industrial proletariat between 1933 and 1937, when the movement reached its most intense point with the sitdown fever of winter/spring 1937. As it has been pointed out, "Lacking a comprehensive blueprint for change, lacking even any clear vision of the new society, the New Deal was essentially *reactive* in character; the Great Depression had given it direction and momentum" (Brody 1975: 271).

The elements to shape "a clear vision of the new society" were not there in the 1930s, despite the fact that, in contrast with the dominant orthodoxy, some American economists had long before Keynes acknowledged the need for the state to intervene for an expansion of aggregate demand.[2] What was lacking was not only the consistent use of expansive aggregate demand to boost output,[3] and a "new dealer mentality" for economists and social planners (Salant 1988), but a proper institutional framework within which expansive fiscal polices could be viable. On the one hand, working-class power which had already refused to be disciplined by unemployment had to be constrained within the limits of accumulation. On the other hand, capital flight by managers committed to the old liberal approach had to be avoided.

The New Deal seems therefore to be the immediate response of the state to a working class that refused the crisis as a means to regulate its militancy. That response shows the developed level of political recomposition of the American working class (Rawick 1972a). This was certainly recognized by the government,[4] but it could not find a solution short of establishing a new institutional environment to control working-class autonomy. For the moment it is enough here to note the irreversible political quality introduced by the struggles of the 1930s. These struggles forced capital strategies to recognize the mass worker as a central political subject, which therefore needed to be co-opted in the accumulation process. They broke the liberal mechanism of regulation of the wage relation through the business cycle, thus introducing a rigidity in the level of wages and forcing the abandonment of the use of high levels of unemployment to reestablish labor discipline. They forced the state to intervene directly and globally in the sphere of reproduction to reestablish the political control of the working class at a social level. Through the New Deal the first elements of what has been called the "state planner" (Negri 1971) were born at experimental level in the West, and its emergence followed the birth of a new era of the class struggle.

The "beginning of respectability" of wider Keynesian principles, however, coincided with the last years of the New Deal and, mainly, with the war years themselves. Also, this respectability coincided with the process of union bureaucratization described above. Finally, the last element of this process coincided with the opening of planning and advisory roles for professional economists.

As in the case of the promotion of unions discussed above, the state also facilitated the consolidation of a new generation of social scientists in their role in planning offices. With the expansion of the NWLB in fact, its staff multiplied, and

> more and more men were called to serve as public or staff assistants. Labor lawyers and economists, sometimes fresh from college, supplied the demand for specialist manpower. One reason that the NWLB left lasting imprints on the American labor relations system was that so many of the practicing and academic labor relations experts of the postwar years gained their most important experience in its service, and absorbed its ethos. The NWLB left an ideological as well as an institutional legacy. (Harris 1982: 49)

Public members were not outright partisans of organized labor. They were for responsible unionism and *"accepted that local union stewards and grievance committeemen were often the people who defused industrial conflict*. Regional and national officers acted as 'fire fighters,' processing difficult grievances and holding the lid on local unions' discontent" (Harris 1982: 50–1, my emphasis).

Thus, while the shopfloor was targeted by union bureaucracies to create the basic social controllable conditions for planning, numerous economists started to arrive in Washington to work in strict collaboration with the military. Keynes was favorably impressed by the magnitude and the quality of the involvement of economists in the service of the American state:

> I have been greatly struck during my visit by the quality of the younger economists and civil servants in the Administration. I am sure that the best hope for good government of America is to be found there. The war will be a great sifter and will bring the right people to the top. We have a few good people in London, but nothing like the *numbers* who you can produce here. (Keynes 1941)

The usefulness of trained economists went beyond their immediate expertise. As indicated by Paul Samuelson, who became one of the gurus of the new post-war Keynesian orthodoxy, the need for planning made the economist's way of thinking more appropriate than that of any other scientists:

In the realm of decision-making itself, there seemed to be a military role which persons trained in the discipline of economics could fulfill. In one agency, units of historians and economists worked side by side: and I think disinterested third parties would agree that the economists seemed quickest to make important policy decisions. It is as if the repeated study of the imponderables of economic life – where the data are never complete and where calculated guesses have to be made – were a valuable preparation for the wartime problems. I dare say the same type of considerations are relevant to explain why, in the war-created realm of *operations research*, which involved the use of scientists to aid in decision-making, statisticians and economists often proved less paralyzed by the need to reach conclusions on the basis of incomplete evidence than were those who came from some of the "harder" laboratory sciences. (Samuelson 1959: 1623)

The ability of economists to deal with the "imponderables of economic life" – that is, with the uncertainty of the mechanisms of capital accumulation – with the ruptures brought in by the class conflict, made the economist's frame of mind better suited to contribute to the decision-making process of the war.

In the context of war planning, economists collaborated with government and gained access to a significant amount of information[5] and, in turn, demanded a more systematic collection of data.[6] In the United States this collaboration had begun – although very slowly – in the late years of the New Deal,[7] whereas in Britain, the war itself was the main factor.[8] The expanded communication between economists and civil servants injected greater operationalism and realism into the discipline.[9] The need for state planning which emerged during the depression and expanded during the war, was acknowledged and promoted. Economics had a key role to play in satisfying this need. In the words of E.A. Goldenweiser, President of the American Statistical Association in 1943, "Research in a policy-making body is for the purpose of shaping policy." "This doctrine," he continues, "may sound novel. It was not so long ago that a line was drawn between research and policy making" (Goldenweiser 1944: 312). The operational character of the discipline, its practical reason of being, was even represented by figurative images of male virility: "an intellectual eunuch, incapable of experiencing the agony and thrill of vital decisions, can not be an effective interpreting economist or statistician. This function requires a red-blooded person full of energy and creative

endeavour" (Goldenweiser 1944: 312). The operationalism of economics was connected with the need for economic forecasts: "Contrary
to a commonly held opinion that research must avoid forecasting as a
deadly sin, the basic purpose of economic and statistical analysis of
social and economic events is to make forecasts" (Goldenweiser 1944:
316). However, there would not be any need to forecast without the
need to control, to plan: "The French saying – to know, in order to
foresee, in order to control (*savoir, pour prévoir, pour pouvoir*) – is a wise
one" (Goldenweiser 1944: 316).

This emergent new attitude, would be subsequently very influential for
example, in Friedman famous essays on methodology (Friedman 1953).
Friedman defined the validity of a theory in terms of its ability to predict,
and therefore to plan, rather than explain and be of mere use for cheerful
academic chats. This emerging new attitude was accompanied by a
glossing over the differences among economists and paradigms:
co-operation between economists with different views could lead to a
softening of pre-war dividing lines and greater mutual respect (Winch
1969: 267). Theoretical controversies were reduced to the common
denominator of the practical needs of planning. It is not difficult to
discern the basis for the formation of a new orthodoxy in this intellectual
atmosphere. According to Robbins, this period

> has afforded an interval in which, our entanglement in the contro-
> versies of the past being suspended, we could consider old positions
> without that acute attachment to interested intellectual capital,
> which, in normal times, makes it so difficult to change one's
> position. (Robbins, 1947: 2)

How different these opinions are and how different the social
legitimization of economics may sound in contrast with what Alvin
Johnson had reported only a few years earlier in his presidential
address at the forty-ninth Annual Meeting of the American Economic
Association in 1937. With the American economy still in the midst of
the depression and the working class revolting throughout the
country, Johnson registered "that the intelligent public is discontented
with the economists," and that the profession is "charged with a
multitude of sins, many of which we do cheerfully and sinfully
acknowledge" (Johnson 1937: 1).[10] Johnson identified two major areas
of discontent, both of which began to find solutions with the involvement of economists in war planning. The first was that economists
were "said to disagree on every imaginable point of doctrine" (Johnson

1937: 1). The war replaced controversy with orthodoxy – that is, a debate confined within the practical needs of the planner state. Johnson could not foresee this yet. His answers to the critiques on this point were a simple twist of professional pride mixed with a naive idea of totalitarian states:

> We are said to disagree on every imaginable point of doctrine. So we do. We are freeman. Those who wish for agreement among scholars would best turn to the scholars functioning anemically under the totalitarian states, where economics is an apology for the will of a dictator, usually an ordinary man of low I.Q., magnified to a million diameters. We plead guilty to the charge of diversity of opinion. We are proud to plead guilty. (Johnson 1937: 1)

Johnson could not imagine that the "agreement among scholars" that he related to the presence of "totalitarian states" would become a character of post-war economics in Western countries, at least in relation to the fundamentals of the Keynesian revolution. The second area of discontent that Johnson identified, which at this time he recognized as serious, was the lack of practical usefulness that the general public, and in particular the "layman," saw in the discipline:

> The economic and social world was cleft and shattered by the series of events beginning in 1914. How confidently can the future historian turn to economic writings of the war and postwar periods for an illuminating analysis of the actual development of economic forces and their social political repercussion? The layman believes that the historian will find that the writings of economics offer the least fruitful material for his purposes. (Johnson 1937: 2)

Johnson thus recognized that economics had to enter the decision-making process of the government and to help shape it. Still, it was only the war that provided the favorable condition for a "paradigm shift":[11] the enforcement of a "social contract" to control working-class autonomy and keep conflict at a minimum, the great state effort in collecting and managing information, the creation of an intellectual framework of collaboration tied to practical needs, etc. All this made the "war cabinet" more suitable than MIT to set the "scientific" agenda and the conditions of development of the economic discipline: "Washington became in a real sense the centre of economic science. In some numbers economists joined the government to help solve military and civilian policy problems. So did numerous businessmen" (Samuelson 1960: 1650–1).

Furthermore, according to Samuelson, the employment of economists in war planning and the nature itself of the economic tools used by them were crucial in the balance of forces for the final victory:

> As an outsider, I can testify to the high quality of the technical wartime economics in Washington. Committee meetings were then carried on at a level that would do credit to advanced university seminars. This is in interesting contrast to what our postwar bombing surveys learned from the German records about the caliber of wartime planning in that country. Apparently all calculations had been made for a short war, and the national income and other information needed to coordinate an intense and prolonged war effort were simply not to be had in the Third Reich. In Washington, on the other hand, the general predictions of wartime economic magnitudes were vindicated by the subsequent facts – so much so, in fact, that the economic profession as a whole was becoming a little cocky. (Samuelson 1960: 1651)[12]

6.2 The "danger" lying ahead: the strategic role of economics in class war planning

The "domestic front"

By 1944, as soon as it became clear that US and allied forces would emerge victorious over the powers of the Axis, the object of debate and strategic planning became the form of the world after the war. What focused this debate was the fear of unemployment. First, it became clear that the war had enormously expanded productive capacity of the economy, and that the reconversion of the economy from war to civilian production might cause, as in the post-First World War period, massive unemployment. Second, the specter of the years of the Great Depression reminded "laymen" that it was only the enormous expansion of aggregate demand, in the form of military expenditure, which had eliminated the chronic unemployment of the American economy. Third, the struggles of unemployed and employed throughout the previous fifteen years made the mere possibility of unemployment a potentially socially explosive nightmare that had to be avoided at all costs. Fourth, and last, the potential explosiveness of high unemployment would be accentuated by the return of demobilized troops, men whose jobs seemed to provide the only means for their peaceful reintegration into society.

The impact and echoes of working-class movements in the 1930s and in the war period informed several commentators'[13] prediction of class war at the end of the war. Samuelson, for example remarks in 1944 – that is, in a year in which wild cat strikes reached a high level owing to the near-certainty of the victory and therefore the reduced impact of the no-strike pledge – that

> As this essay is written, America's most important task is that of winning the present conflict. Therefore, the difficult problems which our economy must again face when peace is at last retained have very properly been pushed into the background. The most important of these problems is that of providing for *continuing full employment.* Before the war we had not solved it, and nothing that has happened since assures us that it will not rise again. And yet it is vitally important that we win victory on this economic front. Not alone for the tremendous material advantages which full employment will bring, but also because politically a democracy cannot flourish under conditions like those of the Great Depression. (Samuelson 1944: 1429)

According to Samuelson, the experience of the war and the relative success of economic planning as demonstrated in this period should make it possible to avoid the sequence of events following the First World War.[14] Perhaps even more aware of the problems of controlling a demobilized working class were those economists and statisticians who were at the time directly involved in the research and planning bodies of the government. In 1944, for example, Goldenweiser and Hagen published an article in the *Federal Reserve Bulletin* whose title was almost self-explanatory of the worries which were circulating: "Jobs after the War." The article opened directly with the recognition of the importance and urgency of the political problem at hand: the control of a threatening working class:

> Maintenance of employment is the principal single economic objective that will have to be achieved *if the existing economic system is to survive.* It epitomizes most of the other economic aims that have to be accomplished ... The choice is between high production, high employment, and general prosperity – *and falling production, serious*

unemployment, widespread misery, and danger to our institutions. (Goldenweiser and Hagen 1944: 424, my emphasis)

The article was a simple simulation exercise in which, on the basis of different hypothetical victory-years, GNP requirements were extrapolated for different productivity levels and changes in the composition of the labor force. The object of the exercise was to forecast the different GNP levels which would be needed in order to obtain full employment.[15] There was no explicit "attempt to suggest how this goal is to be achieved" (Goldenweiser and Hagen 1944: 424), although it was clear that some form of state planning was presupposed. Instead, the aim of the paper was very limited and touched the central point: "it is only intended to point out here that a volume of output of approximately the size indicated is essential *if disaster is to be averted*" (Goldenweiser and Hagen 1944: 429, my emphasis). Strategies centered on growth and full employment gained thus increasing consensus in informing domestic policies *vis-à-vis* social antagonism. They also became the pillars of the post-war *Pax Americana*.

The "global front": the constitution of international Keynesianism

One of the main pillars of the *Pax Americana* which informed US international economic policy after the Second World War was the "politics of productivity." This strategic framework of foreign policy is clearly linked to US needs to solve domestic problems. Charles Maier's work provides an insightful analysis of "how the construction of the post-World War II Western economy under United States auspices can be related to the political and economic forces generated within American society [and] how American impulses interacted with the social and political components of the other nations, European and Japanese" (Maier 1978: 24). His analysis produced interesting links between the institutionalization of the productivity deals as a solution of American internal class struggle and American foreign policy centered on the export of the American strategy. He concludes that:

American concepts of a desirable international economic order need to be understood further in terms of domestic social divisions and political stalemates. United States spokesmen came to *emphasize economic productivity as a principle of political settlement in its own right* ... the stress on productivity and economic growth arose out of the very terms in which America resolved their own organization of economic power ... Americans asked foreigners to subordinate their domestic and international conflicts for the sake of higher steel tonnage or kilowatt hours precisely because agreement on production and efficiency had helped bridge deep divisions at home. (Maier 1978: 25, my emphasis)

Thus, US diplomatic activity during the last years of the Second World War was informed by the need to promote international trade in accordance with the politics of growth and productivity. In a detailed and well documented study of American policy during the last two years of the war, historian Gabriel Kolko showed how the problems of the pre-war economy constituted the basis for American diplomatic policy abroad and defined its military and strategic objectives:

The impact of the prewar world depression and the experience of the 1930's profoundly colored United States planning of its postwar peace aims ... [T]he United States did not simply wish to repair the prewar economy, but to reconstruct it anew. There was a remarkable unanimity in Washington on this objective, and it was by far the most extensively discussed peace aim, surpassing any other in the level of planning and thought given to it. While the United States faltered for a time in regard to its postwar political objectives, it entered and left the war with a remarkably consistent and sophisticated set of economic peace aims. (Kolko 1968: 245–6)

Given the extraordinary productive capacity obtained by the American economy, the end of the war brought a potential crisis of overproduction to which there were three possible solutions. One, the classical solution, accepted the depreciation of capital and the fall in the value of labor power which might bring higher profits and the centralization of capital. This solution was not considered a feasible alternative in face of the political dangers represented by the current political composition of the American working class. A second solution, in principle, would have been an increase in wages, and/or a reduction of working time, or any combination between the two. This would obviously have involved a decline in profitability and would have endangered the possibilities of putting people to work in the future under the capitalist relation. The vision maintained by Washington diplomats differed from both these options. At its basis there was the strong belief in the need of a reconstructed economy within which American's excessive capacity could be dampened in a profitable way:

The motives for advocating a reconstructed world economy were not at all deductive, based on the abstract premises of some logical theory, but reflected Washington's specific understanding of the problems that would confront the American economy after the war. The Department of Commerce in its first studies, published in 1943, pointed to the vastly increased industrial capacity that the economy would have to deal with during the period of transition to peace, and similar reports, many confidential, by other economic agencies followed. (Kolko 1968: 252)

The social problems facing American society once the war was over were thus the first concern of government authorities. The expansion of trade was therefore seen as necessary in order to deal with the danger of political and social instability both abroad, where the German military occupation had radicalized the population and mobilized armed resistance, and at home. In April 1944, the War Production Board calculated that the end of the war with Germany would have set free around 6 million workers, only 2 million of whom would have been soldiers (Kolko 1968: 252). In this context, foreign trade began to be regarded as a necessary condition for the creation of jobs at home.[16]

US exports to Europe grew rapidly after the war. This was accompanied by long-range success at creating a more integrated world market to sustain growth in output and employment. Institutions such as the General Agreement on Tariffs and Trade (GATT) were fundamental elements of these efforts. By 1960, US imports and exports accounted for 2.9 percent and 4 percent, respectively, of GNP and 10 percent and 16 percent of world trade. This meant that internal economic policies could be carried on as if the United States were a closed economy, without being much influenced by changes in international markets. On the contrary, the impact of the US economy and policies on the rest of the world was enormous.[17] The particular position of strength of the US economy therefore meant that American success in the management of the class relations on the domestic front had strong repercussion on the ability to manage the same relation on a world scale.

Besides GATT, the other pillar of post-war international Keynesianism was the Bretton Woods agreement signed on December 27, 1945. This outlined the overall framework within which international Keynesianism was supposed to operate. If in the case of domestic economies, state economic policy presupposed a sort of productivity deal, so in the case of international economic relations, the presupposition to international regulation was that other nation states were to promote growth, trade, and full employment.

The Bretton Woods system replaced the pre-war Gold Standard, which had led to the cycle of protectionism and depreciation during the Great Depression, with a system of fixed exchange rates. This new approach aimed at maintaining pressures for adjustment (e.g. foreign exchange reserves could provide only a short-term solution to international deficits) but allowed nation states greater flexibility in determining national economic policies. In presence of a widespread use of government control on capital movement and fixed exchange rates, pressure for adjustments of the balance of payment were put on national capitals in their ability to match or exceed standards of international competitiveness – that is to say, to the international level of social productivity of labor. However, what Bretton Woods implicitly recognized was that this could not be obtained through a deep recession in the national economy. Under the Bretton Woods system "no country was expected to suffer severe unemployment or inflation to protect its balance of payment. Henceforth, the balance of payments would become subject to national policy objectives, and not dictated by international conditions. This was a fundamental change from the way the gold standard was intended to operate" (Phillips 1980: 62–3). The political constraints are here self-evident. Furthermore, nation-states would be relatively free from external considerations to pursue domestic objectives of full employment and price stability (Phillips 1980: 63).[18]

Bretton Woods put the responsibility for marginal adjustment on the nation state, which was now equipped with Keynesian tools of economic management. The old system of international financial regulation based on gold was left more to market forces (when allowed to function) whereas Bretton Woods' system of fixed rates presupposed that the state could intervene to lower demand and stimulate supply in the case of a deficit. In other words, it presupposed that the state could affect output and the growth of the price level to manipulate relative international costs. This, of course, presupposed the state's ability directly or indirectly to manipulate class relations of power throughout the economy. It is important to point out that the international economic and monetary order in the Keynesian period was essentially based on the link among different "productivity deals," in which the IMF served for the developed countries as lender to compensate for short-term disequilibrium in the balance of payments. As it will be discussed in Chapter 9, for an individual country the real solution to this disequilibrium was based on the gaining of a competitive edge – that is, the increase in social productivity relative to wages or to increase surplus over necessary labor.

The promotion and regulation of trade and a new international monetary order established with Bretton Woods were parts of capital's general strategy of full employment and growth defined previously as acknowledgment and subsumption of working-class autonomy. Foreign aid and direct diplomatic and covert intelligence operations are other components of the same global Keynesian strategy. It is known that the Marshall Plan provided sixteen countries with $13 billion over the period 1948–51. These funds were superseded in 1951 with the Mutual Security Agency programs related to the Korean War. These funds may not have caused economic recovery, as recovery started earlier (Milward 1984). However, the role of the Marshall Plan to fuel growth and impose domestic discipline must be stressed. In Europe and Japan social unrest was becoming a serious threat to local governments and its containment was becoming difficult (Armstrong, Glyn and Harrison 1984). The massive assistance provided by the Marshall Plan helped reduce political and social pressures in Europe by increasing investment and employment without cutting consumption (Burk 1991: 13). This, together with the recognition by Western Communist Parties of the broad principles of national constitutions,[19] and therefore with their active role in the maintenance of social peace, allowed states to set the framework for the management of class relations in the context of economic growth. At the same time, the Marshall Plan induced expansion of US exports and therefore the possibility of achieving growth at home. It is not a coincidence that the Marshall Plan was announced in the same month as the Taft–Hartley Act – that is, at the time of the American government's attempt to legally circumscribe US working-class autonomy.

The global character of Keynesianism did not necessarily imply the omnipresent use of similar Keynesian domestic policies. The establishment of post-war Keynesianism represented the establishment of a principle of economic and social *management* – that is, the recognition of state involvement in the promotion of full employment and growth. This happened in conditions and contexts defined by national political and social situations. Even in the United States overtly consumer-led policies were implemented only at the demise of Keynesianism – that is, under the rhythm of massive social unrest causing the explosion of the welfare state. In countries like Britain and the United States there was the recognition of state responsibility of the maintenance of full employment. In other countries, like Italy, it would take the massive explosion of grassroots working-class struggles in the 1960s to force the state to recognize and implement minimum reforms to raise Italian welfare state in the direction of international standards of Northern Europe.[20]

7
The Institutional Features of Post-war Keynesianism

7.1 The theoretical consensus and strategic role of economics in post-war economic planning

It is now a matter of common sense to recognize a shift in the object, finalities, and tools of orthodox economic discourse after the Second World War. On a formal level, it is widely recognized that this shift has occurred in different areas, as is schematically illustrated in Table 7.1. In Chapter 6 it was shown that the war gave momentum to and legitimized the practices of state planning in the economy, especially demand management policies. After the war the "Keynesian Revolution" acquired a formal recognition through the official acknowledgment of government responsibility for a policy of full employment. This came in Britain with the publication of the White Paper on Employment policy in 1944 by the coalition government and in the United States with the Employment Act of 1946. These two pieces of legislation, although criticized by both the left- and right- wing,[1] represented the state's formal acceptance of a new era of economic policy.

Meanwhile, the role of professional economists continued to gain recognition and legitimization. In Figure 7.1, I have plotted the number of members of the American Economic Association as a simple illustration of the growing role of the discipline. The growth of the number and influence of economists accelerated dramatically in the post-war period.

The diffusion of the economic principles of the Keynesian revolution and the need for their practical implementation took place through several influential works. In Britain, Beveridge's *Full Employment in a Free Society*, published in 1944, represented the main vehicle for the spread of the new orthodoxy. It was a more radical manifesto than the

Table 7.1 Formal comparison of the economic orthodoxy before and after the Second World War

Orthodoxy	Before 1945	After 1945
Economic concepts	Not suitable for statistical verification.	Operational: economic theory is developed in terms suitable for statistical verification.
Government	Government's main concern to balance the budget. Saving considered as the basis of a well run economy, from which follows requirement to balance the budget. Economists mainly exercise an external influence on governments through pamphlets, polemics, debates, etc.	Primary role of the government is to systematize and quantify aggregates. Public and private thrift ceases to be a virtue in conditions of less than full employment income. Economists have a direct role in shaping government policies; they become direct state functionaries.
Economic policies	Stabilization of prices pursued mainly through monetary policies. These, plus wage cuts, seen as sufficient for the achievement of full employment through market forces.	Target of economic policies becomes "full employment", achieved through policy mix with particular emphasis on fiscal policy. Wages are recognized as factors affecting cost and demand. Wage cut and deflation are no longer seen as means for the achievement of full employment.

Table 7.1 Continued

Orthodoxy	Before 1945	After 1945
Role of money	Money considered to be neutral – that is, it does not affect the level of output.	Variation of cash balances are associated with variation of the interest rate which in turn affects the level of investment, and therefore of output and employment. This means that object of monetary policies becomes control of the interest rate and investment.
Focus of economic theory	Optimal allocation of resources in condition of scarcity. (Robbins 1935)	Determination of the level of output and employment. Later, it becomes the optimal (socially acceptable) combination of inflation and unemployment.

Source: My elaboration from Spiegel (1983: 611–13).

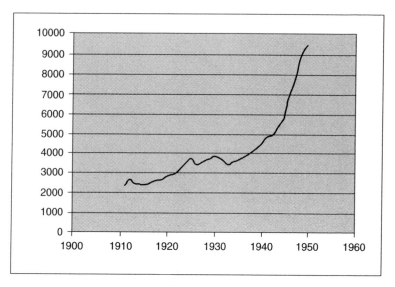

Figure 7.1   Total number of members of the American Economic Association, 1900–60 (*Source: American Economic Review*, various years)

American White Paper, which emphasized the need to overcome the chronic tendency towards a general deficiency of aggregate demand. Beveridge's book recognized the danger posed by the working class in absence of state planning and government policies of full employment. At the same time, it pointed out at the need to find ways for integrating the working class with the priorities of growth and accumulation if such policies were to be successful. In the United States, the right-wing opposition linked Beveridge's ideas (together with those of Keynes) to those of Hitler and Stalin as they fought to condemn the Employment Bill before it emerged as Employment Act in 1946.[2] One result was that the main contribution to the spread of Keynesianism in the United States came through Ackley's and Samuelson's textbooks (1966) and (1948, 1955), respectively.

Although debate continued on the Employment Act (on the effect and extent of government intervention), in the field of economic analysis a peaceful overall consensus was soon reached. By 1955, the mentor of the new economic orthodoxy, Paul Samuelson, could assert with high confidence the *de facto* resolution of theoretical controversy among different fractions and the establishment of a new theoretical synthesis:

In recent years 90 percent of American Economists have stopped being "Keynesian economists" or "anti-Keynesian economists." Instead they have worked toward a synthesis of whatever is valuable in older economics and in modern theories of income distribution. The result might be called *neo-classical economics* and is accepted in its broad outlines by all but about 5 percent of extreme left wing and right wing writers. (Samuelson, 1955: 212, my emphasis)

The post-war years accelerated, on an international scale, that process of economic consensus building. Robbins notes

Despite the sound and fury of controversy at the frontiers of knowledge – always a healthy sign – it is safe to say that at the present time, wherever a man begins his studies, provided that there is reasonable competence on the part of his teachers, he acquires a technique similar to what he would have attained elsewhere; and, if he shifts his habitation to other parts of the civilized world, he is able to talk a common language with those with whom he comes into contact. To those who can remember conditions even twenty-five years ago, this represents considerable progress. (Robbins 1956: 6–7)

Samuelson would soon echo Robbins' remark with this concern:

It is possible to argue that American economists – and Western economists generally – far from being too divided among a number of competing schools, today present a united front that reflects *too little* basic disagreement on fundamentals. (Samuelson 1959: 1629–30)

The use of a standard academic language and the declining influence of national schools were an aspect of the diffusion of the practical significance of standard economic tools. The historical roots of this universal use of the basic theoretical framework in different contexts were evidence that the nature of these contexts were not – at least in the Western World[3] – so different after all. In other words, different national governments in the West needed to actively promote economic growth and the maintenance of a stable proportion between productivity and wages, in order not only to respond to a conflict of the past, but prevent what appeared a threatened one. This recuperation of working-class conflict became the only viable strategy for different national capitals following America's tremendous economic superiority after the war and consequent imposition of the *Pax Americana*.

The basic agreement at the basis of the new orthodoxy was the belief that full employment could be obtained through proper fiscal and monetary policies. Walter W. Heller noticed that

> The basic structure of the Keynesian theory of income and employment – and even the basic strategies of Hansenian policy for stable full employment – are now the village common of the economics community. When Milton Friedman, the chief guardian of the *laissez-faire* tradition in American economics, said not long ago, "We are all Keynesian now," the profession said "Amen." (Heller 1966: 9)

At the general level, the theoretical content of this consensus was, first, Keynes' emphasis on aggregate demand (with the implied government employment policies) embodied in Alvin Hansen's "translation" of Keynes for the new generation of American economists; and, second, Paul Samuelson's "neoclassical synthesis." On the empirical side the key developments were, first, Simon Kuznet's work on GNP, which was translated in 1934 by the US Department of Commerce into national income estimates and in 1942 GNP estimates (adding quarterly estimates in 1947), and, second, the rapid development of econometric and forecasting work based on the employment of computer technology (Heller 1966: 4), which gave empirical foundations to the theory and transformed it into an operational tool for managing the capitalist economy.[4]

Within the overall framework of this paradigm, economic analyses were developed to inform government policies. At the highest point of the Keynesian era under the Kennedy and Johnson administrations it was recognized that even the President had to be educated in the language and terminology of the discipline. Heller, who had been president of the Council of Economic Advisors, defined the tasks of the economic advisor of the President as being "to analyze, interpret, and forecast; to give policy advice; to educate; and to adapt and translate" (Heller 1966: 16). Commentators were impressed by the insistence of the methodical process of education and conversion of state officials. For example "No papal emissaries worked any harder on the conversion of Constantine to Christianity than did Keynesians on Kennedy."

Paul Samuelson headed a "task force" to educate the President "to the evils of lagging growth and gave him the base for his 'get America moving again' issue" (Benks 1965: 99).

The number of economists involved received a new push under the Kennedy administration.[5] By 1965 the mutual understanding of government, business, and economic planners could be celebrated:[6]

> "Planning" is not the horrible word it once was; most major corporations have their own long-range plans, and only wish government would help them by planning its own affairs better ... And it is a fascination with the idea of management on a universe-sized scale the may have something to do with winning the support of the nation's new corporate executive. (Benks 1965: 98)

The idea of "universe-sized scale" planning bridged the ideological gap between West and East. In a speech at Yale in 1962, President Kennedy remarked: "What is at stake in our economic decisions today is not some grand warfare of rival ideologies ... but the practical management of a modern economy" (quoted in Benks 1965: 98). As the governments on both sides of the iron curtain were obsessed with the practical target of growth, economists in both blocks were united in the search for the effectivness of various forms of planning. As suggested by Winch (1968: 336):

> What unites economists today is not so much allegiance to a particular paradigm in the broadest sense. There could be no more interesting testimony to this than the growing convergence between economies as practiced in capitalist countries and the preoccupations of economic planners in European countries with communist regimes .[7]

Although many of the developments in economic analysis find their *raison d'être* within this direct collaboration of economists with the practical problems of state planning,[8] purely academic theoretical and empirical research formed the background from which economists more actively involved in government advice could draw inspiration. As Ackley (1966: 176) wrote: "The need for answers does at times propel our fine Council staff into analytical discovery. But we must inevitably rest our work on the broad base of scientific knowledge provided by you in the profession."

7.2   A struggle-pushed consensus

It has been seen how the change in perspective and practice of economics began, or at least gained momentum, within the context of the patriotic and nationalist rhetoric of the Second World War, in which the "no-strike pledge" and other forms of union collaboration aimed at maintaining peace on the shopfloor and on the social front, thus creating the social institutional conditions to permit war state planning. In these conditions production reached unprecedented peaks and unemployment disappeared to be replaced by a "scarcity of labor."[9]

By the end of the war a renewed working-class militancy erupted. The two years 1945 and 1946 saw the "biggest strike wave in history of a capitalist country" (Noble 1984: 22–3). In 1945, 3 500 000 workers were on strike; in 1946, 4 600 000 walked out. "This was more than ever before in all American labor history," wrote historians Boyer and Morais.[10]

In 1946 there were successful union national actions against General Motors, Ford, Chrysler, General Electric, and Westinghouse, plus halting of coal mining and the railroads. The main issue was wages, as the fight opposed the wage freeze of the "Little steel formula." General Motors and General Electric were forced to grant wage increases of eighteen and a half cents an hour; Westinghouse granted nineteen cents an hour; finally all three were forced to give increased union security. Most of the remainder of basic industry was forced to settle for similar raises. "Seldom had labor scored such gains in the face of growing unemployment and a threatened depression resulting from the transformation of a wartime into a peacetime economy" (Boyer and Morais 1955: 344).

What it seems to be historically significant about the post-war movement was the fact that it marked a turning point in the level and diffusion of class conflict. There was in fact a historical upward shift of industrial militancy, quantitatively considered. Whereas from 1900 to 1905 an average of 352 000 workers per year were involved in industrial disputes, in the 1920s, they were already 520 000, in the 1930s, 977 000, and in the 1940s, the number jumped to 2 310 000. Thereafter they oscillated around the figure of 2 million. In the 1950s, they were 2 198 000, in the 1960s, 1 809 000, and in the 1970s, 2 288 400. Up to the late 1970s, US capitalism had to cope with a structural widespread high level of conflict. The historical challenge for business was precisely how to continue to accumulate in the face of such a widespread and apparently irreversible movement. The 1950s were years in which US capital tried to respond to this challenge. The elements of capital's strategies were built during the war, but the massive post-war upsurge forced the co-ordination of these moments and forced many reluctant capitalists to accept new principles of industrial relations.

7.3 The social basis of keynesianism and its limits: the social "microfoundation" of macroeconomic policies

The viability of Keynesianism was thus based on the co-optation of these struggles within the mechanism of capitalist growth. This was based on the implementation of productivity deals. The latter were achieved through an "efficient" control of industrial action by official unions. On the other hand, if the government had to abandon expansionary policies to concentrate on anti-inflationary policies, this meant that the institutions presiding over the productivity deals were malfunctioning. "Anti-inflationary policies" here essentially meant that the government intervened at the macro-level because the institutions at the micro-level were not working. In addition, income policies and direct state intervention in the renewal of social institutions represented a further attempt, outside the realm of fiscal and monetary policies, to control the overall gap between productivity and wages. Thus, the degree to which government intervention could concentrate on the determination of the level of growth was directly proportional to the degree to which this set of social institutions was able to control working-class autonomy and maintain a stable balance between productivity and wages.[11] In other words, the management of the parameters of profitability at the micro-level, through a new arrangement of industrial relations, was the central prerequisite of Keynesian strategies. This was obtained through the legitimization and promotion of industrial bargaining, the establishment of the productivity deals, and their diffusion in society through the practice of the "wage round." In Marxian terms, this meant targeting the balance at the social level between surplus and necessary labor in society as a whole. Government intervention through fiscal and monetary policies could thus target a certain level of accumulation and employment for a *given* social rate of exploitation.[12] Some of the main analytical expressions of this co-optation will be discussed in Chapter 9 and 10 in the case of the fiscal multiplier and the Phillips curve.

7.4   A general illustration of the social "microfoundation" of macroeconomics

The basic logic of the productivity deals was that wage increases could be granted only in return for increases in productivity. This meant that in exchange for higher wages, workers had to accept changes in the conditions of work. State legislation such as the Taft–Hartley Act and the institutional role of unions were designed to bind workers within this arrangement.

The centralization of bargaining and the increased centralized power of the labor bureaucracies *vis-à-vis* local unions meant, first, that grievances and resistance organized around job control were taken away from the shop floor and given to central bodies. This process of centralization can be seen as a response to working-class struggles during the war years organized around job control issues. Second, and more important, the setting of pay increases at the national level meant that there was no direct connection between wage determination and local work rules (Katz 1985: 37). Thus, the connection between income and work was *planned* via the mediation of central bodies such as the union and management.[13] This disjunction between local work rules and central pay settlements created the possibility that productivity and wages would not follow the pattern planned. This was a possibility which affected the economy as a whole, because of the practice of the "wage round" which socialized over most of the corporate sector of the national economy a given balance between productivity and wages increases, through the mechanism that will be discussed in the next section. This opened the possibility for state intervention in the form of "fine tuning" fiscal and monetary policy and later of income policies, that can therefore be understood in terms of the readjustment at the social level of the balance between income and work, between necessary labor and surplus labor.

The GM–UAW 1948 agreement established a pattern in the American labor relations which influenced the entire dynamic of capital accumulation for about twenty years, and had even more influence on the way of thinking of economic and political intelligentsia. The productivity deals spread in other industries through the set of union institutional links or through the threat of unionization. Piore and Sabel (1984: 80–7) provide a clear description of this process, which I use as a guide for the following few pages.

The automobile settlement spread throughout the major unionized sector via the institutional links of the unions. Also, because the automobile industry was an important source of demand for other major industries such as steel, rubber, and plate glass, the latter industries' ability to resist workers' pressure rose and fell with automobile demand. Thus, the balance of class forces in the automobile industry influenced the settlement in other industries, allowing contract settlements in different industries to move together. Outside mass production manufacturing, union organization was present in such industries as construction, trucking, large retail establishments, mining, and communications. In these industries, economic conditions were not tied to those of the automobile industry, nor were the unions historically or institutionally closely tied to the mass production unions. However, the settlements in mass production industry set standards for every contract.

The large non-union share of the private sector was forced to follow union wages by the threat of union organization. Ununionized Du Pont, IBM, and Texas Instruments paid wages equal to those in organized sectors, while elsewhere wage increases tended to follow those of the unionized industries. "Had [they] failed to do so, the differential would have risen, making nonunion firms an increasingly attractive candidate for a union election under the auspices of the prounion (or at least not antiunion) National Labor Relations Boards" (Piore and Sabel 1984: 81).

The public sector, which had historically low levels of unionization, saw in the postwar period a significant increase in union members. The increased militancy of this expanding sector of the national economy linked the wage setting movements in the public sphere to those in the private sector. Despite the difficulty in measuring and implementing productivity increases in the public sector, the high level of organization and spontaneous autonomous actions allowed the diffusion of wage increases along the private sector pattern.

The determination of wages through a "wage round" thus tended to foster an upward wage mobility throughout the economy. This resulted in an increased rigidity of relative wages and relative prices. Fisher (1981) has shown that the variability of relative prices falls dramatically in the Keynesisan era – that is, between 1950 and 1970.[14] Piore and Sabel (1984) use the variance in the rate of change of average hourly earnings to measure the degree to which the rate of change of wages differed in different industries. The authors show that in the post-war period both relative wages and relative prices were stable. In other words, relative wages and relative prices were not suitable to provide the "signals" necessary to guarantee a "proper" allocation of resources to highly profitable trades. This rigidity, together with the upward trend of the average wage determined by the practice of the "wage round," was an expression of the reduced overall cyclical movement of the economy as regulator of the class relation through the movements of the reserve army. The flexibility of labor power required to compensate the discrepancies of capitalist development and accommodate unavoidable market and productive imbalances was provided by the large reserve army which was accumulating through the massive process of automation of US agriculture. In this context, the minimum wage legislation sanctioned a wage differential between the reserve pool of the South exempted from the minimum wage and the rest of the country. The minimum wage thus created a reserve army available to work in the manufacturing sector at the wage rate prevailing in mass production. Internal promotion was used to fill the higher levels of the job segmentation.[15] Thus, corporations did not have to use high wages to attract new workers (Piore and Sabel 1984: 85–7).

7.5   Recognition and co-optation of working-class autonomy: the Taft–Hartley act

The institutionalization of the conflict presupposed the creation of institutions able to control working-class autonomy. This meant also being able to identify and attack those people whose struggles would have threatened the productivity deals. This was also possible through the dismissal of those activists that arose from the workforce during the years of the war and in the immediate post-war period. Corporate policies were favoring "superseniority" to veterans and generally encouraged and promoted hierarchy. This, together with the change in gender and racial composition of the labor force brought about by the return of veterans, made possible the expulsion of those workers and stewards who formed the more militant stratum of the working class during the war.[16]

Another factor representing a direct attack on working-class autonomy, but also embodying elements of mediation, was the Taft–Hartley Act. The "Slave Labor Act" – as labor militants called the 1947 Taft–Hartley Act – was "the most important piece of antilabor legislation in US history" (Roediger and Foner 1989). "'The bill was written sentence by sentence, paragraph by paragraph, page by page, by the National Association of Manufacturers,' said Representative Donald L. O'Toole of New York" (Boyer and Morais, 1955: 347). Among the repressive measures against labor militancy, the bill reinstituted injunctions, gave courts the power to fine for alleged violations. It established a sixty-day cooling off period in which strikes could not be declared. It outlawed mass picketing. It provided for the suing of labor for "unfair labor practices." It denied trade unions the right to contribute to political campaigns. It abolished the closed shop, went far toward building the conditions for a return of the old open-shop days that preceded the CIO. It authorized employer interference in attempts of his employees to join a trade union. It prohibited secondary boycotts. It authorized and encouraged the passage of state anti-union, "right-to-work" laws. (Boyer and Morais 1955: 348)

According to the same authors, in a matter of months the bill

had brought the trade union movement to a complete standstill in organizing, afflicted it with paralysis, subjected it to the loss of literally millions of dollars in damage suits and fines, paved the way for union raids against each other, and subjected an increasing number of union leaders to indictment and imprisonment. (Boyer and Morais 1955: 347–8)

The most important aspects of the Act were, however, the attack on the circulation of working-class struggle through the repression of sympathy strikes, which originally constituted the basic strengths of the 1930s' and 1940s' movement, and the repression of working-class autonomous action to control production and limit the working day. This resulted in the increased bureaucratization of the conflict on the shop floor and thus the shift of the power from the rank and file to the labor bureaucracies. Roediger and Foner (1989), for example, point out that the Title 3 of the law, "perhaps … least appreciated part of Taft–Hartley,"

facilitated the legal enforcement of collective bargaining agreements by making unions liable for violations. It codified the employer's decisive remedy for wildcat strikes and slowdown through lawsuits against the entire union. This effective attack on informal protest over conditions encouraged shop stewards and paid union officials to participate in causing rank-and-file workers to accept what David Brody has called "the workplace rule of law."

It reinforced wartime tendencies among workers to see unions as cooperating with management in maintaining shopfloor discipline and solidified the accompanying tendencies to not press capital issues or to press them outside of union channels. (Roediger and Foner 1989: 267)

Another crucial target of the Act which became interiorized by the "logic" of the post-war capitalist strategies was the containment of grassroots struggles against the length of the workweek. According to the same authors, the same section of the Taft–Hartley Act "contributed most to the decline of protest over the length of labor" (Roediger and Foner 1989: 267). The authors also point out that the secular trend in reduction of working time stops in the 1940s, the workweek remaining just above the 40 hours. In the 1980s, this trend moves upward. If, as Juliet Schor (1991) among others, argues, working time should be understood to include also unwaged work, then the upward trend begins after the Second World War, and accelerates in the 1980s.

The Taft–Hartley Act represented a decisive contribution to the post-war strategy since it repressed and reduced the spaces of resistance against work and promoted the use of the union as the institution devoted to channel and control bottom-up autonomous resistance.[17] The Keynesian strategy prevented the increases in productivity from being translated into a reduction of the workweek.

7.6 The union contract

The practice of the productivity deals was introduced in 1948 with the UAW–GM agreement which served as a model for the subsequent series of contracts. The key element of this deal was the establishment of a wage rule which included an annual improvement factor (AIF) and a cost-of-living adjustment escalator (COLA). The AIF increased wages at 2–3 percent per year, whereas the COLA automatically raised the hourly wages along the increases in the nation-wide consumer price index. The AIF, which originally was three cents and later 3 percent a year, was chosen so as to match the rate of productivity increase under-way in the general economy (Katz 1985: 20):

The other aspect of the 1948 and subsequent deals which regulated the auto industry and other major corporations was the growing weight of fringe benefits (pensions, health and life insurance, paid

Table 7.2   The growth of fringe benefits, 1955–87 (expressed as a percentage of wages and salaries)

1955	17.0
1965	21.5
1975	30.0
1986	35.5
1987	36.2

Source: Schor (1991: 67).

vacation, etc.) as a proportion of the overall wage. In the postwar periods these acquired an increasing share relative to the money wage as it is possible to see in Table 7.2.

Fringe benefits create a strong incentive for the firm to perpetuate long hours. This is because they are paid on a per-person basis; therefore it is more profitable for a firm to hire a smaller number of people and make extensive use of overtime than hire more workers who should also be paid benefits. (Schor 1991: 66)

Fringe benefits also represented a disincentive for workers to quit, as Ford had learned from the experience of the 1910s (Chapter 4).

Unemployment benefits were also of importance. These payments were on top of state unemployment insurance payments. In the case of laid-off autoworkers, they represented 95 percent of net pay for up to fifty-two weeks (Katz 1985: 23). The *raison d'être* of unemployment benefits was the maintenance of a stable class relation, since their availability and size served as buffer for compensating the social problems arising by layoffs. In this way they also permitted a reduction in the pressure to cut wages in response to cyclical declines in the industry (Katz 1985: 23).

The union contract represented the central institution around which working-class power was acknowledged. At the same time, however, that power was subsumed within the pattern of accumulation. With the Taft–Hartley Act and the elimination of sympathy strikes, the state struck at grassroots organization. The contract form enabled the marginalization of grassroots activity and the bureaucratization of workers' claims.

Historian Martin Glaberman has provided a brilliant analysis of the role of the contract in its function of containment of working-class autonomy, which I briefly discuss below. The first contract from General Motors, obtained in 1937 after a sit-down, was one mimeographed page. "Foremen, for the first time, *asked* the steward how much production the department would get so he could plan accordingly" (Glaberman 1952: 11). From the one-page contract of 1937, that still enabled the rank-and-file to set the pace of the initiative on the shopfloor, the contract developed into a complicated set of rules which defined in detail the role of operations and grievance procedures. The single most important achievement of the contract from business' perspective was the establishment of a mechanism which took the control of production away from workers:

> A contract is a compromise. That establishes that, no matter what union gains are recorded, the rights of the company to manage production are also recorded. And in the grievance procedure it takes the power out of the hands of the workers and puts it in the hands of the stewards and committeemen. The union officials become the enforcers of the contract and the union becomes the agency by which the worker is disciplined and tied to the machine. (Glaberman 1952: 20)

Through the contract, victories were recorded but so were the rules to limit workers' autonomy.[18] As a result the rank-and-file became increasingly alienated from labor leaders.[19]

An example of how the contract embodied this twofold meaning could be seen in the case of the grievance procedure:

> The heart of the contract is the grievance procedure. Through it is established a certain measure of control over production. An especially severe penalty against a worker may be lessened or very unjust one eliminated. But basically the right to discipline remains. And that is cause for most of the friction, the humiliation, the dissatisfaction in the shop. It is a steady grievance. (Glaberman 1952: 20)

The main function of the grievance procedure was to delay and reduce direct antagonism between rank-and-file and foremen through the mediation of union officials. Even though a worker won a case, this "victory" could not prevent that the same grievance from occurring again. Another example is the introduction of seniority:

> It was necessary protection against discrimination; against men being laid off and hired at the whim of the foreman; against having to get the foreman presents or doing work for him to keep your job;

against being forced out when you get too old to suit them. But at the same time, so long as capital dominates production, it is a means of keeping the worker tied to his particular job. He cannot go to another plant to try for something better because his seniority is too important to lose. It puts the younger worker at the mercy of the slightest change in the economic scene, subject to frequent layoffs and insecurity. It prevents the men from using their ability and even from gaining experience and knowledge. (Glaberman 1952: 23)

The workers recognized this contradictory character of the contract and resisted. Wild cat struggles generally exploded right after the closure of a contract.[20]

Capital's attempt to regain control of production lost during the war years is well documented and acknowledged by many radical economists and historians of the Social Structure of Accumulation School (Gordon, Weisskopf and Bowles 1987). The main problem of this interpretation, however, is the way it fails to differentiate between workers and union bureaucrats. It regards the loss of power on the shopfloor as the price that workers had to pay in order to obtain higher wages. The phenomena is understood in terms of a "capital–labor accord," in terms of a "truce" between classes. However, there was no truce between capital and the working class, even though there was one between capital and the labor bureaucracies. It was this truce that grassroots protest increasingly attempted to overcome. These struggles matured and developed in the midst of the Keyenesian era and continuously undermined the "accord" suggested by the Social Structure of Accumulation school. Thus, for example, the number of grievances increased in this period:

> The grievance procedure became virtually worthless to the workers. In 1955 at the termination of a contract presumably designed to provide a grievance procedure, there were in some GM plants as many as *10 000 unresolved grievances*. GM complains that the number of grievances in its plants has grown from 106 000 in 1960 to 256 000 in 1969 or 60 for each 100 workers. (Glaberman 1975: 24)

The increase in the number of grievances is a good indication of the rejection of work and work practices by the workers. Since grievances involve production standards and quality of life in the plant,[21] their growing number becomes a good indicator of the opening cracks within the microfoundations of the Keynesian era, within the social fabric of the Keynesian capitalist plan. Because "The fact that they are called grievances helps to conceal what they really are – a reflection of the total dissatisfaction of the workers in the way production is run and of the desire of the workers to impose their own will in the factory" (Glaberman 1975: 25).

7.7   The link between work and revenue among unwaged workers

Statement of the problem

The creation of institutions able to control the proportion between surplus and necessary labor at the micro-level was relatively simple, at least in principle, in the case of waged workers. The profitability of the company gave a proxy of the success of this strategy in relation to others in the market. However, there was no direct way to measure the degree of control over productivity and wages (work and revenue) in case of public sector workers and unwaged workers. This absence of measurement translates into a deficiency in control. In the case of the public sector, there was no direct correspondence between increases in wages (given by the practice of the "wage round") and increases in productivity. The difficulty of measuring the latter in absence of accountable profits and of measurable "product" (i.e. services) reduced the possibility to control workers in this sector.

In the case of unwaged workers, on the other hand, the problem of the link between work and revenue has been even more concealed by the fact that women, students, the unemployed, etc. are generally understood as non-workers simply because they are unwaged. In the context of society as a whole, however, the activities of these sections of the population were targeted as if the overall parameters of accumulation of society were central in the distribution and administration of the transfers to these sections of the population. Grants, subsidies, and other forms of transfers began to be dispensed in ways and forms which attempted to secure (at least) a corresponding increase in work. The end net result was obviously unmeasurable in the short run, since capitalist society does not provide a formal evaluation of the value contribution of unwaged labor. However, in the long run, if the growth of transfers and welfare benefits exceeded the capacity of the welfare bureaucracy to squeeze living labor out of the recipients, then the overall dynamic balance of accumulation between social productivity and social wage would be affected. In what forms is it possible to squeeze living labor out of welfare recipients and, more generally, unwaged workers? In what follows I provide few examples.

A brief illustration

The first example is provided by the role that women played within the structure of the nuclear family. As pointed out by Dalla Costa (1983), among others, governments' expansionary policies during the Keynesian era could promote development only on condition that workers could consume in such a way as to reproduce themselves as physically efficient and psychically disciplined labor power. Workers consumption thus presupposed the work of reproduction mostly carried out by women. This invisible work, because it is unwaged, creates a labor power able to cope with the intensified rhythms of work of the Fordist period. Women's domestic labor, therefore, "is the primary means through which the income distributed by the state, or wages, can be translated into greater productivity increases" (Dalla Costa 1983: 12). The productivity deals that assured a higher level of income in exchange for productivity increases are rooted in the intensification of domestic labor despite the wave of technological innovation entering the household in this period.[22]

Another example is in the realm of the administration of unemployment benefits. One of the problems faced by US capital in achieving, or at least promoting, a policy of full employment concerned the management of the increasing reserve army generated by the wave of automation in agriculture, in the industry, and in mining. As automation can be understood in terms of capital's effort to recuperate control of the working class at the shopfloor level, the automation of agriculture can be understood at a broader level as well – that is, in terms of capital's attempt to meet the demand of a metropolitan working class for cheaper and plentiful food.[23] The latter required a significant increase in farm productivity which farm workers would refuse to generate without a protection of farm income through state price support. Furthermore, food acquired a fundamental strategic meaning in the hands of American capital, as the Marshall Plan and other foreign food aid were used to manage class relations at the international level. Hence, the strategic importance of agriculture and the magnitude of its transformation. Price supports, mechanization and the use of chemicals helped mainly large farmers. The great majority of small farmers and farm workers were forced to leave the land and emigrate into the urban areas. In all these cases, automation expanded the reserve army.

However, since high unemployment had become by now politically intolerable, it was required that the state took action in two directions. First, to provide a policy of full employment and at the same time to provide a "safety net" for those still outside employment. Second, to make sure that those benefiting from the welfare state could make a contribution to the overall accumulation of capital. In the case of the unemployed, this meant that the welfare system put in place was geared toward the enforcement of low-wage work.

Piven and Cloward (1972) have described and convincingly documented the different methods to enforce low-wage work through the welfare system in the early post-war period. They concluded that

> the structure of the American public welfare system meshes with and enforces the work system, not least by excluding potential workers from aid. The "fit" of the welfare system in a stable but diverse economy is assured by varying the pattern of exclusion in accord with regional differences in labor requirements. Furthermore, harsh relief practices also maintain work norms by evoking the image of the shamed pauper for all, especially the able-bodied poor, to see and shun. And so it is that if the justification given for welfare restrictions is usually moral, the functions these restrictions serve are typically economic. Those who exploit the cheap labor guaranteed by these practices can take comfort not only in their godliness but in their profits as well. (Piven and Cloward 1972)

In this way, from the point of view of capital accumulation, the "productive" (for capital) function of the unemployed welfare recipients corresponded to active competition on the labor market with other workers. Real wages could be depressed through the proper functioning of competition among workers, but competition among workers entailed work in the form of active job search.[24] Struggles in the mid-1960s organized around the welfare system and challenged this link between revenue (in the form of transfers, etc.) and work (in the form of competition among unemployed workers); this would prove to be a crucial factor for the crisis of post-war capitalism.

Another example of how control over the proportion between surplus and necessary labor played a strategic role for capital in the case of unwaged workers is provided by education. The growth in the reserve army soon proved to be unmanageable simply through the policies of work enforcement of the welfare system. The relative low accumulation rate of the domestic economy in the 1950s and the beginning of the struggles around welfare issues and the continuous waves of mechanization in agriculture and other industrial areas such as the mine fields in Appalachia added to the difficulty of capitalist absorption of labor power.

As a result the investment in "human capital" emerged as a way to accommodate also the demands coming from those better-paid sections of the working class who wanted their sons and daughters to escape the discipline of the factory. The human capital strategy was theorized in terms of its contribution to economic growth in a way that paralleled traditional theorizing about the contribution of physical capital. Public expenditure investment jumped from $1 billion in 1960 to $7 million in 1970. The relative size of expenditures per student also increased (Caffentzis 1975). Investment in "human capital" was nothing but the investment in human beings for business needs, and therefore it attempted to plan what Marx called "variable capital," its quality and quantity, alongside the planning of constant capital. As has been suggested, "investment in human capital arose when capital had to begin to take into account in an explicit way the whole social circuit of capitalist society in which labor power is produced, qualified and reproduced" (Caffentzis 1975). The planning of variable capital therefore constituted the missing link for the plan of the entire social circuit of capitalist production.

The strategy was based on the general upgrading of the workforce and the replacement of skills made obsolete by the waves of mechanization. This not only allowed a better technical upgrading of the labor force in line with the needs of accumulation but also put people to work directly in the form of schoolwork, whose hierarchical structure provided a natural training ground for the hierarchical system of waged work. Grade structures, selective criteria, testing, etc. parallel the wage structure and provide a mechanism of selection to locate people into different ranks of the social hierarchy. Thus the school system offered not only an upgrading of the working class, but also the means to manage its divisions.[25] Obviously, the payoff for the human capital strategy was directly related to the degree of student adaptation to the hierarchical structure of education, etc. In the late 1960s, the demands and aspirations of the student movement broke the link between grants and other forms of funding and schoolwork, thus challenging the role that education was supposed to have for capital accumulation. This of course would have an impact on the overall circuit of capital accumulation and the balance between necessary and surplus labor.

7.8   Conclusion

The process of integration and planning of human capital is only one aspect of capitalist planning of reproduction *as integral part* of the accumulation process. Whereas the productivity deals in the "core" sector of the economy meant a further movement toward automation, for the society as a whole it meant the reorganization of all life around work. In other words, the struggles of the mass worker in the 1930s and 1940s forced capital toward the social factory – that is, capital's strategy of coordination of all aspects of life, of planned coordination of the moments of production and reproduction. The social factory finds full expression in the state's attempt to subsume every aspect of life as a moment of the capitalist relation of work. This subsumption means essentially that every aspect of life became the target of a strategy which had a twofold character, first, the determination of the level of work, second, the control of the proportion between surplus and necessary labor – that is, the basis of Keynesian strategies as discussed in previous chapters. Once capital becomes *social* capital and the factory a social factory, the classical distinction between waged and unwaged workers no longer distinguishes between those workers who enter the capitalist relation and those who do not. This distinction informs us only about the form of the capitalist relation, and the relative position of power of different sectors of the same working class defined *vis-à-vis* social capital.

8
The Theoretical Features of Post-war Keynesianism

8.1 Introduction

I regard the passage from Keynes to the Neo-classical Synthesis as a refinement of the theoretical tools provided by economics corresponding to a historical situation in which new institutions for the management of the class conflict were set up. The original theoretical apparatus of Keynes and the refined one of *Keynesianism*, or the Keynesian *orthodoxy* in the form of the Neo-classical Synthesis, differ because of the changing conditions of the class relations. Keynes was writing at a time in which the problem of working-class autonomy and its channeling was urgent and social experiments for its control such as the New Deal were relatively new. In the post-Second World War era, the practices of social regulation theorized and experienced earlier became a central feature of the capitalist regime. A gravity center for the class struggle was established through the productivity deals and the establishment of a reference point against which to measure the social proportion between surplus and necessary labor. Thus, whereas in the theoretical apparatus of Keynes, the subsumption of working-class autonomy is assumed as political *project*, in that of Keynesianism it is assumed as a fundamental institutional *condition*. This obviously had the limitation of any capitalist strategy of subsumption, founded on the belief that social conflict can indeed be frozen and the newly established institutions of capitalism are able to deal once and for all with the contradictions of the capitalist mode of production. The basic pillar of the Neo-classical Synthesis, the IS–LM model, assumes a concept of aggregate and a concept of time and equilibrium that corresponds to this new class situation.

8.2 The analytical framework of the neo-classical synthesis: the IS–LM model

The analytical framework used by the Neo-classical Synthesis was, as it is well known, grounded on the IS–LM model originally introduced by John Hicks' famous paper "Mr Keynes and the 'Classics'" in 1937. Further development attempting to integrate Keynes' analysis into the Neo-classical framework within the IS–LM model saw the contribution, among others, of Franco Modigliani (1944), Lawrence Klein (1947), Don Patinkin (1948), and Alvin H. Hansen (1953). The IS–LM model became not only the main tool through which economic theory was popularized in intermediary textbooks, but also the framework to organize and develop economic thinking[1] as well as empirical research and operational techniques.[2]

The effort to integrate Keynes in the equilibrium framework resulted in the formulation that long-run persistent unemployment can be generated if one of the following three conditions holds (Dow 1985): (1) investment demand is inelastic with respect to the interest rate; (2) the economy is caught in a liquidity trap; (3) money wages are downward rigid. Pigou (1941) was more restrictive, arguing that the first two conditions would have been neutralized by a fall in the general level of prices following a downward shift in aggregate demand below the full employment level for a given aggregate supply. With lower prices, real money balances would rise, thus increasing wealth and consumer demand. The only condition therefore which should be seen as responsible for keeping the long-run state of the economy below full employment was the rigidity of money-wages. Patinkin (1956: 65) was able to show the existence of a value of the general price level corresponding with a level of aggregate demand that was consistent with full employment. This assumed a given supply of money, the stability of key functional relationships of the system, and the independence of their position from the path toward equilibrium.

As a result of this analytical refinement, Keynes' theory of income determination and its emphasis on aggregate demand was framed in a general equilibrium model, a "Grand Neo-classical Synthesis" (Arestis 1992). In this model, there is an inherent tendency toward a stable equilibrium of full employment in the absence of wage rigidity. However, in presence of this rigidity, there will be disequilibrium on the labor market. Working-class power is thus recognized at the same time that its subsumption is modeled.

The number of analytical uses offered by the reduction of the entire economy to the simple relationship between interest rate and income is enormous, as every student of economics knows. It is not the aim of the present work to enter in the details of this analysis, nor to discuss its internal logic[3] or the limitations of the IS–LM models within the planners' tool box.[4] Instead, the purpose here is to discuss the foundations of the analytical apparatus of the Neo-classical Synthesis, and to highlight its political meaning.

In order to appreciate the strategic shift of post-war economic orthodoxy it is worthwhile to compare it with the orthodoxy before the so-called "Keynesian revolution." Table 8.1 offers such a schematic comparison between the two economic paradigms.

The comparison is carried on metaphorically in terms of a temporal and spatial dimension, as well as in terms of the direction, the engine of economic growth. By "temporal dimension," I understand the concept of time – and therefore of equilibrium – which is characteristic of the two orthodoxies. By "spatial dimension," I understand the level of spatial aggregation which is chosen to inform particular economic strategies. The object of the comparison is *economic orthodoxy*, defined as a broadly accepted set of beliefs which informed the economic discourse and the economic/political strategies of capital in a given period. In this sense, therefore, Keynes' own work enters into the picture only in so far it has influenced the formation of post-war economic orthodoxy.

Table 8.1 represents synthetically an understanding of the "Keynesian revolution" which is different from conventionally accepted ones. The latter identifies a "paradigm shift" in terms of ruptures occurring in internal presuppositions of the theoretical analysis. I instead follow the criterion of identifying a "paradigm shift" in economics in terms of the concrete ruptures in the role of economics as capital's strategic weapon. Thus, the three rows of Table 8.1 represent the three co-ordinates, the three theoretical dimensions, of this strategy. In this sense, the "revolutionary" character of Keynesianism is defined in relation to change in the paradigm of control – i.e. the methods of managing the capitalist relation of work. The radical break in economics occurred primarily in its strategic dimension. In the first place, before the Keynesian revolution, the role of economics was mainly confined to a legitimization of capitalism and of laissez-faire practices to control the working class. Its immediate practical relevance was mostly in relation to advice concerning sectoral problems of individual capital. For example,

Table 8.1 Political comparison of mainstream economic paradigms before and after the Second World War

	Before	After
Spatial dimension	Focus on microeconomics. The strategic problem of decision-making and policy advice was about sectorial problems of individual capitals.	Focus on macroeconomics. The strategic problem becomes accumulation of the capitalist social relation as a whole.
Temporal dimension	Timeless models Pre-reconciliation of plans, and therefore the implicit assumption of the eternity of capitalism.	Introduction of time – that is, recognition of the fragility of the capitalist relation. In the form of "adaptive expectations," the future presupposes the reconciliation with the present "habits" or set of "conventions" (Shackle 1968).
Strategic variable – that is, engine of growth	Saving, thrift – that is, capital's ability to extract a mass of surplus labor to use to put people to work.	Demand, needs – that is, capital's ability to respond to working-class needs without however upsetting the proportion between surplus and necessary labor. The latter, in the "pure" Neo-classical Synthesis, is presupposed as given and regulated by Keynesian institutions or becomes the object of inflation policies.

in case of a business slump, "An economist's job was to help intelligent businessmen to manage their businesses in such ways that they suffered a minimum of damage" (Robinson 1946: 92). After the Second World War the framework of reference changes radically. Macroeconomics constitutes the main focus of theoretical investigation. The strategic problem moves its focus from the individual capitalist to aggregate accumulation, to the reproduction of the capitalist relation of work at the social level. However, the aggregate is no longer, as in Keynes, the starting point of the critique of the classical strategy, but appears immediately as the dimension of capitalist management.

This strategic dimension is reflected in the concept of time embodied by the new orthodoxy. In the wake of *The General Theory* time becomes an explicit element of economic modeling. This is tantamount to saying that economic theory has interiorized the separation between decisions of saving and decisions of investment which constituted Keynes' critique of classical economics. However, as discussed earlier, the introduction of time, in whatever form, as a dimension of temporality challenged the optimistic vision of capitalism held by classical economics. With the introduction of time in economics the implicit postulation of the eternal character of capitalism is lost. At the same time, however, as will be discussed later, the concept of adaptive expectations through which time is used enables the recuperation of the future as capitalist future, to discount it on the basis of the current expectations based on "habits" and "conventions" (Shackle 1968) – that is, on the basis of a stable class relation. With respect to Keynes, the "class situation" has changed, and the future, as capitalist future, appears on the horizon to assuage capitalist fears.

Finally, the third element of the radical change in economic discourse was the implicit perception of the dynamic principle of capitalism. In pre-Keynesian orthodoxy, accumulation was strictly linked to the capitalist capacity to command a large mass of surplus value. After Keynes, demand constituted the driving principle – that is, capital's ability to respond to working-class needs without losing control over the proportion between surplus and necessary labor. This ability lies either in a set of institutions that forward a "social contract," or in economic policies aimed at the management and control of inflation levels, and therefore the overall balance between necessary and surplus labor, or in a combination of the two.

8.3   Aggregation, wage rigidity, and working-class power

We have seen that the introduction of the question of aggregation in Keynes corresponded to the recognition of capital at its social level, of crisis as crisis of the capitalist society as a whole, crisis of the reproduction of the capitalist relation of work. Keynes was able to think in terms of aggregate quantities through the introduction of a common measure, wage-units, with which he measures output, consumption, investment, money supply, etc. Hicks (1974) exposed the issue simply and elegantly. "Wage-units" depended on a principle which he called "wage-theorem":

> When there is a general (proportional) rise in money wages, says the theorem, the *normal* effect is that all prices rise in the same proportion – provided that the money supply is increased in the same proportion (whence the rate of interest will be unchanged). It is not maintained that the wage-theorem will be true in all conditions; ... But Keynes clearly thought that it was usually true. It is because of the theorem that investment, and income, and money supply are measured in wage-units; for it follows from the theorem that when so measured, they are *independent* of the level of money wages. (Hicks 1974: 59–60)

The use of wage-units is consistent with the assumption of the constraint posed by the class struggle over wages. "The wage-unit as determined by the bargains reached between employers and employed" represents an "ultimate independent variable" (Keynes 1936: 246–7), together with the "three fundamental psychological factors" and "the quantity of money as determined by the action of the central bank". Haberler (1962: 291) stresses how this list of the "independent variables" is, one may say, overdetermined, since

> the Keynesian theoretical system proper (apart from the discussions of related matters and of the hints and asides that can be found in profusion in the *General Theory*) depends on the assumption of wage rigidity. If that assumption is not made, the Keynesian system simply breaks down or, to put it differently, it loses its distinctive and differentiating quality which sets it apart from what is loosely called the "classical" system. (Haberler 1962)

Thus, ultimately, aggregation is carried out *given* a particular balance of forces between classes, as the wage-unit is an independent measure determined *exogenously* outside the model.

If with wage-units all strategic variables of macroeconomic models are independent of the level of money wages (Hicks 1974: 59–60), it followed that "the wage-theorem could not be understood until one had grasped the rest of the theory; yet the rest of the theory (when expounded in the way Keynes expounded it) could not be understood without the wage-theorem" (Hicks 1974: 59–60).

In Keynes' method of aggregation through wage-units, therefore, there was an element of circularity. Wage units were an expression of an abstract, social definition of the wage – that is, a definition of the wage which was not referred to a particular sector, a particular wage of a particular category of worker. In this sense, aggregation presupposed wage units, which in turn presupposed "aggregation," but to establish the independence of investment, income, etc. from the level of money wages meant to establish at the theoretical level the independence of investment, national income, etc. from the struggles over money wages, struggles which occur at first in the individual sectors. It meant to displace conflict from the level of the sector (in which struggles for money wages occur) to the level of society as a whole (dominated by the interaction of prices and money wages, resulting in real wages). The concept of the aggregate is thus defined by means of the presupposition of a social definition of the wage. This is the class meaning of the "circularity" present in Keynes. This element of circularity, however, does not offer easy ground for exposition, and Keynes' circularity is "resolved" in the post-war Keynesian assumption of fixed wages:

> We had to find some way of breaking the circle. The obvious way of doing so was to begin by setting out the rest (multiplier, liquidity preference and so on) on the assumption of *fixed* money wages. Then, with that behind one, it was fairly easy to go on the wage-theorem. That is, what we did – I still think that it was what we had to do. (Hicks 1974: 60)

The assumption of wage rigidity was at the basis of the popularization of the Neo-classical Synthesis.[5] The famous Keynesian cross diagram was popularized in Samuelson's *Economics* (1948), and for several editions was shown on the front cover. The basic insights of Keynes' theory was maintained – that is, the acknowledgment of working-class power through the rigidity of wages. It is true that different authors have analyzed the property of the Keynesian economic system in case of flexible prices and wages.[6] Also, the assumption of fixed nominal wages by Keynes and early Keynesian models was later relaxed with aggregate demand and aggregate supply models in favor of slow adjustment of prices and wages to market conditions. However, in terms of conventional wisdom this was not seen as modifying substantially earlier conclusions since the "Pigou effect" was not believed to have a significant role[7] and therefore government policies were at center stage. Samuelson could, for example, develop his multiplier–accelerator model as a simple fixed price model without arising the kind of reactions to its microfoundations that would be generated of few decades later. As Stanley Fisher recalled:

> When asked recently his view of the causes of wage and price stickiness, [Samuelson] replied that he decided forty years ago that wages and prices were sticky, that he could understand the behavior of the economy and give policy advice on that basis, that he had seen nothing since then to lead him to change his view on the issue – and that he had not seen a pay off to researching the question. (Fisher 1987: 239)

8.4   Wage rigidity, productivity deals, and state planning

The assumption of the rigidity of wages and prices presupposed of course an implicit conceptualization of the relative balance between classes, in which the balance between necessary and surplus labor at the social level was conceptually frozen at a given level and an increase in public spending could be seen as increasing the level of employment (accumulation) *without upsetting that balance*. In other words, the Neo-classical Synthesis implicitly presupposed a class relation which was regulated at the micro-level through the set of productivity deals. It is this fundamental stability that allows the writers in this tradition to model government planning. Although in different terms, this has been observed by Alan Coddington where he refers to the Neo-classical Synthesis as "hydraulic Keynesianism":

> This designation reflects the view that the natural and obvious way to regard elementary textbook Keynesianism is as conceiving of the economy at the aggregate level in terms of disembodied and homogeneous flows. Of course, *conceiving of the macroeconomy in this*

way will be fruitful only to the extent that there exist stable relationships between these overall flaws. It is my contention that *the central characteristic of "hydraulic Keynesianism" is the belief that such stable relationships do exist at the aggregate level.* (Coddington 1983: 102, my emphasis)

The belief in stable relationships between flows is at the basis of demand management policies. The flows involved here are obviously flows of expenditure, income, and output. Coddington noted that neither output nor prices makes an independent appearance but "appear inextricably in the contribution each makes to the overall flows of spending and receipts" (Coddington 1983: 102). The author also contended that the belief and the attempt to establish stable relationships between aggregate flows were inconsistent with the pre-Keynesian paradigm – or, as Coddington called it, with reductionism:[8]

> For any reductionist programme must give a crucial role in its theorizing to *prices as such* (not to the contribution they make to overall spending flows). The grounds for this are that it is prices as such which provide the incentives that individuals face in making the choices on which the whole scheme is to rest. (Coddington 1983: 102–3)

The emphasis on prices and wages here can be read in terms of their role as incentives, as tools, to enforce the relation of work. In Keynesianism – or hydraulic Keynesianism, as Coddington calls it – this central role of relative prices has disappeared.[9] The shift from pre-Keynesian economics therefore is strategically crucial and fundamental: it entails a shift in the perspective through which capital's strategies are laid down, and its acceptance depends upon its adequacy to the new "class situation."

The abandonment of the role played by prices "as such" entails the underplay of the fiction of rational agents making choices. If the "allocation of resources in the presence of scarce means" – that is, the formula within which movements in wages are interpreted to function as tools to overcome disproportions (crises) – is no longer central, then diffused, constrained choices are no longer seen as able to guarantee the development of capital. The "work–leisure choice" of a worker (based on the level of wage and the balance of utility obtained through leisure and the wage on one side, and the disutility of work on the other), was at the basis of pre-Keynesian strategies. It was of course a constrained choice, in which the constraint took the form of "enclosure" – that is, of a separation of the workers from the means to satisfy their needs (the initial "endowment" which forces the "choice" is socially determined by capital). In Keynesianism, the flexibility of prices, affecting diffused "choices," is no longer the central theoretical category that represents the enforcement of the capitalist relation of work. The market loses its predominance as a tool to reestablish the "right" proportion between surplus and necessary labor. This proportion is determined outside the model by a given balance of forces. Individual, constrained choices cannot any longer be the central vehicle for capital's strategies. What is left is only one act of choice, that of state planning and managing the level of accumulation. Here, Coddington's analysis is again instructive: "contrary to the viewpoint associated with reductionism, hydraulic Keynesianism is a scheme in which there is only one agency making deliberate acts of choice; that one agency is 'the government'" (Coddington 1983: 103).

The theoretical basis for this, however, is essentially the assumed stability among the overall flows. "It is the belief that there are indeed stable relations among the various overall flows in the economy which provides a basis for the government to pursue its policy goals regarding the overall level of economic activity and hence, relatedly, of the level of employment" (Coddington 1983: 103). The *stability* of the overall flows is the framework within which Keynesianism can operate as paradigm to inform economic policies.

8.5 Time and expectations: endogenizing "animal spirits"

The paradox of Keynesianism is that although the state intends to plan, it can plan only in so far as there is stability at the point of production. The social basis of this stability was the constitution of a "social contract," the productivity deals. This predictability was therefore an expression of a concept of time which was different both from the timeless models of pre-Keynesian economics, but also from what Robinson attributes to Keynes as "historical time."

It was pointed out in Chapter 4 how with Keynes the introduction of time represented the acknowledgment of the limits of capitalism, in contraposition to equilibrium models in which the absence of time presupposes pre-reconciliation of plans and the eternity of the social relations which make up the capitalist mode of production. Keynes' theory of output and employment was based on the assumption of the exogenous character of capitalists' long-run expectations, these being governed by unpredictable "animal spirits."[10] In Joan Robinson's words:

> The uncertainty that surrounds expectations of the outcome of a plan of investment, of the course of technical progress, of the behaviour of future prices, not to mention the effects of natural and political cataclysm, cannot be reduced to a "calculated risk" by applying the theorems of mathematical probability. (Robinson 1978: 126)

Thus, an autonomous shift in long-run expectations can determine a gap between effective demand and full employment output, in order to require government intervention if full employment is to be achieved. How is it possible to interpret in the light of this shift the apparent return of the Neo-classical Synthesis to the concept of equilibrium?

It is known that the Neo-classical Synthesis revises the treatment and role of expectations as used in Keynes. In particular, the role of "animal spirits" is played down, and the exogeneity of expectations is transformed into endogeneity. Although there were some logical reasons for this,[11] I want to emphasize that the orthodox framework which has endogenized the animal spirits of Keynes' investors has done so still maintaining one crucial innovative character of Keynes' analysis, the introduction of time and expectations. Obviously, the analytical and theoretical importance that these latter two acquire in the Neo-classical framework may be somewhat different than in Keynes, but with respect to the pre-Keynesian orthodoxy there is a strategic shift. It is this shift which needs to be understood in political terms.

8.6 Adaptive expectations, productivity deals, and state planning

As early as 1936, in his review of *The General Theory* Hicks recognized "the method of expectation" used by Keynes as the most revolutionary thing about the book. The innovative character of this method was to consider expectations among the data of the system. In a retrospective view, Hicks wrote:

> I recognized immediately, as soon as I read *The General Theory*, that my model and Keynes' had some things in common. Both of us

fixed our attention on the behaviour of an economy *during a period* – a period that had a past, with nothing that was done during the period could alter, and a future, which during the period was unknown. Expectations of the future would nevertheless affect what happened during the period. Neither of us made any assumption about "rational expectations"; expectations in our model were strictly exogenous... Subject to these *data* – the given equipment carried over from the past, the production possibilities within the period, the preference schedules, and the given expectations – the actual performance of the economy within the period was supposed to be determined, or determinable. It would be determined as an equilibrium performance, with respect to these data. (Hicks 1983)

An equilibrium position is obtained subject to these exogenous expectations. In Keynes, each period has its own history and it is not possible to determine values of the economic variables in the long run. In Keynes, there are no values to which the economic system tends towards in the long run. The capitalist long run is undetermined, a question mark. In Keynes, the instability of the system is based on the unstable nature of expectations: both those of speculators (necessarily linked to the volatility of the stock markets) and those of capitalists tied to their "animal spirits." If expectations are not stable, then, investments are not stable, and thus the instability of the level of real income and employment.

In Keynes, therefore, it is not possible in these circumstances to lay down a theory of intertemporal expectation formation or to envisage a "theory of endogenous expectations revision" (Begg 1982: 22). The first attempt toward the direction of linking different short-run equilibrium positions come with adaptive expectations, which postulate that economic agents use information on past forecasting errors to correct current expectations.

Adaptive expectations, originally introduced by Cagan (1956), did not properly represent a return to orthodox economics in the sense that the recognition of time, and therefore the instability of capitalism, is maintained. The difference is the potential degree of threat put on the stability of the system. In Keynes, the psychological reactions of capitalists with respect to their expectations of the future were unpredictable. With the capitalist world slipping under their feet, uncertainty was absolute and expectations could only be exogenous, a variable that could not be planned, that could not be managed. In the

Neo-classical Synthesis, the sustainable character of capitalism is recuperated, contradictions are believed to be manageable, and long-run expectations become endogenous.

Adaptive expectations, in which a variable is a lagged function of itself and tended toward an equilibrium value, amounted to a notion of temporality certainly different from that of Keynes, in which the future was mostly a matter for uncertainty, but *a dimension of time nevertheless*. As I have argued in a previous section (p. 31), in the context of Say's law the *existence* of profit is presupposed and any dimension of time disappears, since past, present, and future have the same qualitative character, as three forms of "equilibrium." With the vanishing of time the end-product is the *eternity* of the capitalist relation of work.

In the Neo-classical Synthesis, there is a difference. Saving is equal to investment only *ex post*, after a mechanism of adjustment has occurred. Certainly, it could be argued that this amounts to the reintroduction of Say's law because it introduces the notion of equilibrium, but this argument ignores the role of the process of getting to equilibrium. Say's law presupposes the understanding of the capitalist relation of work as eternal, immediate, with not even the mediation of time, of a *process*. In the Neo-classical Synthesis there is faith not in the capitalist relation as such as in pre-Keynesian economics, but in the *mechanism of adjustment*, in the process that allows the capitalist relation to reproduce itself – that is, in lagged asymptotic movements toward equilibrium. Here savings and investment are separated *ex ante* and *crisis* is an *ex ante* condition of the system. The crisis, therefore, the rupture, the displacement of the class relation, is something that economic theory now acknowledged with the Neo-classical Synthesis, but it did this in the bourgeois way, seeing it as automatically overcome. Thus, *ex post*, equilibrium is regained. In between there are adaptive expectations. The presupposition of the elements of crisis, however, thus supported the notion of non-full employment equilibrium and the necessity of state intervention. Thus, a link was established between crisis and the need for the state to intervene.

There are two key fundamental and apparently contradictory characteristics at the basis of adaptive expectations. First, the presupposition of stable relations. As described above, within the framework of adaptive expectations, long-run expectations (and therefore current decisions of investment and consumption which are a function of them) depend on the present and the past, but the asymptotic character of responses to external shocks is there to say that past and present operate as tranquilizer, that the capitalist class relation is not, after all, in danger, and that after a period of adaptation the system recuperates its long-run equilibrium path. At the basis of this tranquilizing effect there is implicit assumption that class relations can actually be stabilized.

Second, the introduction of given expectations in the Neo-classical Synthesis is fundamental. It blasts open the general equilibrium framework, introduces the state planner and the faith in an institutional environment able to govern the stability between productivity and wages. It therefore heals the open wounds represented by the recognition of time in economic analysis. The equilibrium now is not a "given," but a *result*, and the conditions of this result are rooted in the assumption of a stable set of relationship among variables, stable sets of habits and conventions, stable consumption functions, etc. – that is, a stable overall *settlement* of the class struggle.[12] It goes without saying that this is precisely only an assumption.

Adaptive expectations presuppose passivity, habits, and conventions. In other words, they presuppose the idea that working-class autonomy can be confined within the borders of a linear time, in which the possibility for disruption is acknowledged but only within the necessity of its subsumption. The passivity presupposed in adaptive expectations is formulated in relation to the reaction of investors to external shocks and in relation to working-class consumption patterns. In both cases, the current amount demanded by the two classes is the result of an expected future which – in the long run – appears certain and reassuring. In the case of capitalists, the long run is the capitalist future in which investment can claim profit, whereas for Keynes this was not entirely certain. In the case of the working class, time appears in the form of a steady growth in income and therefore in a particular consumption pattern. The long run appears therefore as a multiplication of current income, appears as plentitude projected in the future, appears as dimension of hope in the form of consumerism. The future can therefore be easily discounted to obtain the value of current consumption as in the permanent income hypothesis (Friedman 1957), but this implies the *adaptation* of working-class needs to a given and stable proportion between necessary and surplus labor. In the real world, the degree to which this "adaptation" occurs is of course the result of the balance of power between classes. It is capitalist management which attempts to "adapt" working-class needs and aspirations into stable proportions. The theoretical discourse therefore presupposes conflict, as well as capital's ability to settle it. The adaptation and passivity implicit in the context of "adaptive expectations" *presuppose therefore again their opposites – that is, the activity of the state planner attempting to control the activity of the struggling working class.* "Stability" therefore is full of cracks. The stability presupposed in the simple Keynesian model (for example, in the multiplier analysis discussed in Chapter 9) will be followed by a less rosy picture, one in which the balance between productivity and wages is not entirely externally given and stable, and therefore requires the help of policy adjustment to regulate it (as is discussed in Chapter 10 in the case of the other analytical pillar of post-war Keynesianism: the Phillips curve).

9
Economic Modeling and Social Conflict: 1 – The Fiscal Multiplier

9.1 Some methodological remarks

If there is a correspondence between class relations and economic theory, are we able to see it? Can economic models reveal their class nature to the critical eye? Can economic modeling reveal its nature as a set of conceptual devices that represent class relations in a mystified way, and therefore help strategies for the enforcement of capitalist accumulation *vis-à-vis* various social patterns of resistance?[1] The difficulty resides in the fact that by its very nature economic modeling presents itself as a *technical* discourse. A "technical discourse" is one that is apparently free of value judgments about the object of investigation. The fetish-like character of technicism lies in the way it abstracts from the social nature of its object of inquiry, from the fact that capitalist society is pervaded with clashing oppositions. It is only through this abstraction, it is only by "forgetting" the character of the social roots of our condition, that one can claim to be able to embrace objectivity and impartiality in an economic discourse.

In this chapter I show how one of the main tools of post-war Keynesianism, the fiscal multiplier, assumes, without making it explicit, what indeed post-war Keynesianism had to implement: productivity deals. I can show this by reading the simple Keynesian multiplier through Marx's lenses. My objective is to make explicit, for the Keynesian multiplier, what from a Marxian perspective should be made explicit in any discourse about the capitalist economy, namely the role of the social relations of production.

To avoid any misunderstandings, I must here make explicit what this chapter is *not* about. This chapter is not about Marx being right and

Keynes wrong, or vice versa. Neither is it about comparing, contrasting or integrating different theories, or functional relations, or causality propositions in the two approaches. For this reason, I will not discuss the abundant neo-Marxian literature that has attempted to integrate the two approaches with the aim of developing new models.[2] Instead of aiming at an integration, this chapter's main aim is a *translation*, and the insights we can gain through it.

This operation of course requires a "translator", a mapping device that enables us to read analytical categories in ways that are different from those originally intended and which became common in the community of professional economists. I will try to make the basic analytical tool of Keynesianism – the fiscal multiplier – intelligible and understandable in terms of Marx's categories. Since Marx's main concern is the exposition of social relations behind economic categories (Marx 1867: 169), here my focus is to search for the role played by social relations in the Keynesian multiplier. However, since in given historical period social relations are expressed in institutional forms, my analysis also gives some general insight about the basic institutional requirements assumed within the Keynesian framework, requirements without which the Keynesian multiplier could not be operational. This latter insight is of course not entirely new, since the writers in the Social Structure of Accumulation and Regulation traditions have often pointed out how institutions which enable harmonious capital–labor relations were fundamental for the governance of the macroeconomy during the Keynesian era.[3] However, what to my knowledge has never been pointed out within these traditions is that embedded in the *very analytical tools* used by post-war macroeconomics was the assumption of a stable and given balance between classes in society, an assumption that was never made explicit. This means that a translation of the Keynesian multiplier in terms of Marx allows us at the same time to uncover at least part of what Gunnar Myrdal called the "inherited normative system" (Myrdal 1953: 22)[4] of economics, and therefore to discern some hints of the "political element" of macroeconomics of mainstream Keynesianism.

Since Keynes' *General Theory*, the consumption function has become one of the pillars of modern economics. Every textbook of economics starts with this basic concept as the building block of the entire edifice of macroeconomic theory. Its importance resides in the definition of the fiscal multiplier and in the mirrored relation to the savings and consumption functions. These are concepts which assume a strategic meaning as far as the explanation and regulation of economic activity are concerned. Therefore the proposal of policies that attempt to influence the growth rate of an economy and, in the old days of Keynesian orthodoxy, the achievement of full employment, are based on some understanding of the quantitative side of these expressions.

Yet, the concepts built on the definition of the consumption function accept a basic interpretation of reality which is in line with the methodological individualism of neoclassical economics. "Aggregate" consumption is by its very nature a concept which lumps together "individual" consumption decisions by simply adding them up independently of the different social roles that different consumption activities may fulfill. A central characteristic of this is of course that the individuals making these decisions are regarded in isolation from each other both as consumers and as producers. *Homo economicus* is believed to be not only rational, but also a self-sufficient atom.

The translation of the multiplier into Marxian categories requires that we translate this discourse based on methodological individualism into one in which individuals are understood in terms of their sociality. For Marx, whatever is the mode of production, individuals are not atoms but *social* individuals (Marx 1845: 120). This essentially means that, for example, their individual consumption activity is at the same time a social act. Within the capitalist mode of production, this sociality not only implies certain kinds of production relations, but also is itself the presupposition of another round of accumulation and therefore of the reproduction of those social relations of production. For example, in satisfying their needs by consuming commodities, workers not only reproduce themselves as human beings, but at the same time they reproduce themselves as labor power – that is, as human beings who stand in particular social relations of production with each other and with the owners of the means of production.

In Marx's framework therefore, profits and wages are the forms, acquired in everyday life, of surplus value and variable capital. The last two categories are defined not simply in terms of distributive criteria, but in terms of the social role they acquire in the reproduction of the social relations of capitalist production. Profit is defined not in terms of capitalists' unlimited wants in search of satisfaction, but as surplus value – that is, in terms of the unlimited drive of profit-making (Marx 1867: 254). Furthermore, in this fashion reinvested profit implies the reproduction of the set of class relation of production defining the capitalist system. Through the analysis of surplus value therefore, Marx regards profit not simply as the income of the capitalists, but as the result and precondition of the maintenance of an historically defined system of production. Individual capitalists are only the bearers of this more fundamental historically specific social function, which consists in being the active agents of accumulation (Marx 1867: 92). In this sense, the *specific social agents* which in actual historical circumstances are responsible for the implementation of this profit-making activity are secondary as far as the general analysis is concerned. So, too, in the case of wages the theoretical priority of social relations of production over income distribution is evident. As variable capital, the wage is not just the income of labor, but the value of labor power, meaning that it corresponds to what is necessary, in given social and historical circumstances, to reproduce workers and their "race of peculiar commodity-owners" (Marx 1867: 275) for another day, month or year of work within the given set of capitalist social relations of production.

The primary role of social relations of production in Marx leads to the interpretation of economic categories that arise from everyday practice and their integration in economic theory, not as wrong categories, but as fetishized representations of these social relations of production. This insight of Marx (De Angelis 1996), enables us to move beyond the often sterile Marxist criticism of orthodox economic theory which labels it simply as wrong and ideologically biased. If there is a correspondence between fetishized categories and social relations of production, the task is to investigate *how* this correspondence is played out. In other words, if we recognize the standard economic categories as fetishes, the role of critical theory is not to dismiss them as such, but to investigate what lies behind the fetish in order to show how the analytical tools of economics are themselves the expression in thought of alien forms of social processes and how, precisely for this reason, they can inform strategies for the furtherance and maintenance of those alienated social interactions. This task is made relatively easy by the fact that their fetish-like character originates from the actual relations of production, so that the categories used by the economic discourse may want to speak for themselves. Indeed, as we will see, just a few basic algebraic steps are sufficient in order to turn the basic Keynesian multiplier into a formula that may be recognizable by a critical eye.

The discussion thus far implies that the translation of the Keynesian multiplier into Marxian categories is an operation that is quite different from those several attempts to devise a multiplier which would recognize classes and the role of income distribution in the determination of output and employment. Traditional attempts like these have their roots in Kahn's original (1931) formulation of the employment multiplier which depended on distributive variables and described the amount of secondary employment that would result from the employment of an extra worker. Other authors have used different versions of the traditional multiplier in order to highlight the role of distribution and class relations. Writers in the Post-Keynesian tradition such as Kalecki (1943), Kaldor (1956) and Pasinetti (1962), for example, have introduced classes into the analytical structures of their models in order to discuss the role of income distribution at the level of economic activity. Their effort thus represented a return to the roots of pre-Marxian classical political economy, as their analysis is devoid of a critical insight into what Marx calls the "imaginary expressions" of economic categories which "arise ... from the relations of production themselves." In other words, for these authors economic categories are not "categories for the forms of appearance of essential relations" (Marx 1867: 690). Their analysis is an attempt to model reality, not an effort to show how class relations are represented, in a mystified form, in economic categories.

Finally, there is a strong tradition of writers who, building upon Kalecki and others, have consciously tried to integrate the Marxian and Keynesian approaches. Models originally developed in the United States by the writers in the Social Structure of Accumulation tradition and in France by those of the Regulation school, have raised the issue of capitalist governability and macrostability on the basis of indicators of harmonious capital–labor relations. In these models the integration of Marx and Keynes is obtained by an eclectic juxtaposition of what are thought to be the key features of a Marxian and Keynesian approach.[5] As suggested in the Introduction, my enterprise is distinct from these approaches as it does not aim to integrate Marx and Keynes, but to translate what has become a standard analytical tool of mainstream economics into categories that are understandable in Marxian terms. Consequently, my enterprise is distinct from these analyses for at least two reasons. First, I show that there is no need of adding the "class struggle" insight into the Keynesian approach because the latter already embeds such an insight, although in a mystified and hidden form. Second, precisely because it embeds such an insight, its exposure opens the way for us to critically evaluate the analytical tools of modern macroeconomics and the macroeconomic strategies that spring from them.

Besides the specification of the translation device, our enterprise necessitates the specification of the object of translation. The traditional income determination model can be defined in terms of a wide range of characteristics depending on a wide range of levels of specification. Depending on their level of analytical complexity, economic textbooks teach us that there are multipliers with or without taxes, in a closed or open economy, with endogenous or exogenous investment spending, etc. Since the aim of this chapter is not the development of a more or less realistic model but the translation of the basic model into Marxian terms, I will deal with the simplest formulation of the multiplier. This formulation treats the economy as a closed economy, with no public spending and in which investment spending is entirely exogenous. These simplifications will serve to emphasize that the crux of my argument stands *whatever* is the relation between investment and income, and however the level of investment is determined. Indeed, we shall see that whatever the level of aggregate demand is and however this is determined, its effect on the level of employment through the multiplier mechanism depends entirely on variables at the core of the determinants of capitalist accumulation, namely the extension of working hours, labor productivity, and the wage rate. In this way, our attention can focus entirely on the multiplier itself and its meaning. In section 9.7 and 9.8, I will then discuss the case of the multiplier with public expenditures and in an open economy, respectively.

9.2   The dissection of the simple income determination model.

Textbook macroeconomics starts with the so-called "income determination model". This is built starting from a macroeconomic equilibrium condition that the sum of expenditures must equal the money value of aggregate output. In a closed economy, the equilibrium condition is

$$Y = C + I + G \tag{9.1}$$

in which Y is aggregate consumption, C is aggregate income, I is aggregate investment and G is public expenditure.

For reasons of simplicity, let assume there is no public expenditure, so (9.1) becomes

$$Y = C + I \qquad (9.2)$$

Consumption is assumed to be a simple linear function of income:

$$C = A + bY \qquad (9.3)$$

so that substituting into (9.2) we obtain:

$$Y = \frac{1}{1-b}(A + I) \qquad (9.4)$$

Assuming again for simplicity that autonomous consumption A is zero, (9.4) turns into

$$Y = \frac{1}{1-b}I \qquad (9.5)$$

The fraction $1/(1 - b)$ is the Keynesian multiplier. A stable marginal propensity to consume b gives, *ceteris paribus*, a stable multiplier, and therefore a predictable effect of a change in aggregate demand (e.g. I) on the level of income and therefore employment. One could argue that a stable multiplier is the key for the successful management of the economy by the government. As was seen, Coddington (1983) has pointed out the stability of income and expenditure flows as a basic assumption of what he calls "hydraulic Keynesianism." Here I want to reinterpret the Keynesian multiplier and its stability criterion as a strategic variable rather than as a result. This is done by reinterpreting the denominator of the Keynesian multiplier in terms of the spread between productivity and wages. I will do so by rewriting the standard national income identity with a few modifications. National income Y can be expressed as

$$Y = \pi L \qquad (9.6)$$

in which π is labor productivity (Y/L), and $L = Nh$, where N = number of people employed, h = average hours worked (daily, weekly, etc.). (9.5) can therefore be expressed as

$$\pi L = \frac{1}{1-b}I \qquad (9.7)$$

or

$$L = \frac{1}{\pi - \pi b} I \qquad (9.8)$$

In general terms, (9.8) gives us the amount of labor put in motion by a given level of investment. In order to understand this relation, however, we have to investigate the meaning of the denominator of (9.8) and, in particular, of the product between productivity and the propensity to consume.

Let us start with the unit of measurement. The propensity to consume is a pure number, with no dimension, as it relates the change in consumption (in money units) to the change in income (in the same money units). As productivity is expressed in terms of money units per hour of labor, the product between productivity and the propensity to consume can be interpreted as the proportion of the hourly product that goes to consumption – that is, consumption per hour of work. It is at this juncture that we can introduce Marx's framework of interpretation.

Along with Marx (1858, 1867), the wage is the form taken by the more substantive category of the value of labor power. The latter is defined in terms of the labor necessary for the reproduction of the commodity labor power, and it presents itself in its objective form as the bundle of commodities that are necessary for this purpose. The reproduction of labor power entails not only the reproduction of those currently employed, but also their families, the unemployed, the retired, etc. – in short, the reproduction of the working class as a whole. The Marxian definition of the value of the labor power implies that first, from the workers' standpoint, savings represent postponed consumption, and not a means for enrichment,[6] it does not represent the basis for an "unceasing movement of profit-making" (Marx 1867: 254). Second, even if workers formally save, this saving serves, in the hand of *today's* capitalists, as part of an advance of capital for production.[7] Thus, since for Marx what is important is capital as a social relation of production, and accumulation as accumulation of a social relation,[8] it is irrelevant whether some of the financial resources for investment are *formally* owned by workers. To the extent that they finance investment which is controlled by capitalists, these resources act as capital *vis-à-vis* the workers. Thus, at any given point in time, whatever workers consume represents in aggregate what is necessary to reproduce them as labor power, which takes the form of wage. In this light, the product between labor productivity and the propensity to consume, which we have interpreted as consumption per hour, can be interpreted as the social wage rate.[9]

It is therefore possible to rewrite (9.8) as

$$L = \frac{1}{\pi - \omega} I \qquad (9.9)$$

in which $\omega = \pi b$ is what I call the *social wage rate*, the difference $\pi - \omega$ is the profit per hour, and the ratio $1/(\pi - \omega)$ is what I call the *social multiplier*. By "social wage rate", I understand the wage rate, in a given time period, that is necessary to reproduce society as a whole for another round of capitalist accumulation.[10] By "social multiplier", I understand the Keynesian fiscal multiplier understood in terms of the spread between productivity and the social wage rate.

Empirically speaking, however, the definition of the social wage rate is of course a numerical proxy, because the consumption of capitalists is also taken into account in the calculation of the propensity to consume b. However, three points need to be considered. First, if we want to translate Keynesian categories into Marxian ones, rather than bringing from the outside the assumption of classes, this difficulty is unavoidable because the Keynesian categories, and indeed all aggregate categories of modern macroeconomics, lump together what for a Marxian perspective may be theoretically distinct. Thus, this difficulty may be considered as the necessary cost of a translation between two distinct paradigms which are based on two distinct methodological foundations. However, second, since the proportion of property income over total national income is very small, in considering πb as the social wage rate, we may be only slightly over-estimating it.[11] Finally, there is an advantage in this small empirical problem in that it allows us to concede Marx's central insight that the critical issue underlying a capitalist economy is not so much the distribution of income between capitalists and workers (distribution out of which capitalist consumption is derived), rather it is the boundless *drive of profit-making*, the fact that the capitalist society is a society geared toward accumulation for accumulation's sake (Marx 1867: 254).

The definition of the consumption per hour of work as the social wage rate, allows us to understand $\pi - \omega$ as profit per hour of work, that is the money value (per hour of work) of what is not consumed by society as a whole and thus becomes available for enforcing another round of capitalist accumulation and alienated social relations. Defining the product between labor productivity and the propensity to consume as the social wage rate – understood, in Marx's terms, as a money representation of the labor necessary for the reproduction of labor power as a class per hour worked[12] – allows us to locate within the simple multiplier, what for Marx is one of the fundamental hubs of the capitalist economy. The relation between wages and productivity is a relation that not only defines profit margins and therefore, ultimately, the entire *raison d'être* and motivation of capitalist production, but also uncovers the political and social dimension behind the veil of pure economics.

Within the standard income determination model, the social multiplier defined above plays the same role as the traditional fiscal multiplier. The only difference is that we are now able to envisage the role of class relations within the traditional transmission mechanism. As the standard fiscal multiplier defined the increase in output for a given change in aggregate demand, the social multiplier, being a simple transformation of the fiscal multiplier, defines the increase in employment for a given change in aggregate demand. While in the case of the fiscal multiplier the size of this depended on society's propensity to consume (and therefore to save), the social multiplier depends on the spread between productivity and the social wage – that is, the profit per hour worked. In the case of the fiscal multiplier, an exogenous change in aggregate demand leads to a change in the same direction in output (and therefore employment), which in turn induces a change in consumption demand which affects output, and so on. The net final change in output (and employment) which depends on both initial and induced changes in aggregate demand, is regulated by the size of the multiplier. In the case of the social multiplier, an initial increase in aggregate demand leads to a change in the same direction in total hours worked in the economy (and therefore output and, for a given working time, employment), which in turn induces a change in consumption (that is, demand) which affects L, and so on. The net final change in total hours of labor worked (and therefore output and employment), which depends on both initial and induced changes in aggregate demand, is regulated by the size of the social multiplier.

It is clear that the higher the spread between labor productivity and wage rate – that is, the higher is the profit per hour worked – the lower the social multiplier. Thus, a given initial increase dI in aggregate demand, will induce an initial increase in total labor hours of $dL = d(Y/\pi)$ which will then induce an increase in demand of $\omega dL (= bdY)$, and so on. So, *ceteris paribus*, the higher is π the lower is the initial increase in employment following an increase in aggregate demand; the higher is ω, the higher is the induced increase in employment. Thus the net effect, in a given period, depends on the spread between labor productivity and the social wage.

9.3 The Keynesian multiplier and Marxian categories: rate of surplus value and rate of profit

It is useful to spend some space on the meaning, in Marxian terms, of the spread $\pi - \omega$, the profit per hour, and of the social multiplier. The profit per hour can be read in terms of Marx's category of the rate of surplus value, or the rate of exploitation, or the balance between surplus and necessary labor for society as a whole. This is defined as s/v, where s is surplus value – that is, the monetary expression of the amount of surplus labor for society as a whole, and v is variable capital, or the monetary expression of necessary labor (assuming the monetary expression of labor – or "value of money" – constant).[13] Dividing both numerator and denominator by L, the rate of exploitation s' is

$$s' = \frac{s/L}{v/L} = \frac{\pi - \omega}{\omega} \tag{9.10}$$

Thus, for a given wage rate, if the profit per hour increases, the rate of surplus value increases. If wage rate and productivity grow at the same rate – as in the case, for example, of the productivity deals of the Keynesian period – then the profit per hour also grows at the same rate, thus leaving the balance between surplus and necessary labor (rate of exploitation) constant. If productivity grows more than the wage rate, the profit per hour increases more than the wage rate, and thus the balance between surplus and necessary labor increases.

It must be pointed out that from the point of view of capital there is a minimum level of productivity growth which is compatible with a non-declining profit rate. The latter is in fact defined as

$$r = \frac{s}{c+v} \tag{9.11}$$

in which r is the rate of profit, s the total amount of surplus value (profit), c the price value of fixed and circulating capital invested (assuming one-year turnover), and v variable capital (wages). Dividing both numerator and denominator by L, (9.11) can be rewritten as

$$r = \frac{\pi - \omega}{k + \omega} \qquad (9.12)$$

in which k is the capital–labor ratio. Thus, if productivity grows in line with the wage rate, and if increases in productivity are obtained through increases in the capital labor ratio k, then from (9.12), in order to maintain a non-declining profit rate, $dr/dt \geq 0$, it is required that $d(\pi - \omega)/dt \geq d(k + \omega)/dt$. Thus, the higher the increase in the capital–labor ratio following technical change or an increase in wages, the higher *must* be the increase in the spread between productivity and wages in order to maintain the same degree of profitability. If this does not occur, the profit rate falls.[14]

9.4 Implicit assumptions and implications of the dissected income determination model: wages and productivity

Assumptions

The transformed multiplier makes clear that the validity of the standard Keynesian argument that an increase in aggregate demand will lead to an increase in national income (and therefore employment) depends on the following two crucial assumptions:

1. The multiplier is, in the very short term, *given*, that is, it depends on the assumption of a given spread between labor productivity and the wage rate and, for a given wage rate, a given rate of exploitation in the economy. In Marxian terms, this means that what is assumed as given is a particular balance of forces between classes at the point of production (π)[15] and in the labor market (ω).
2. In a growing economy the social multiplier is *stable* and *predictable*. It is only to the extent that this stability condition holds that the Keynesian multiplier can be used as an analytical tool for the design and implementation of growth strategies.[16] However, the social multiplier also tells us that the effectiveness of these strategies depends on the *actual* stability and predictability of the social multiplier. This means not only that Keynesian policies rely heavily on institutions able to negotiate a social deal among representatives of workers and capitalists. These policies also presuppose that these representatives are actually able to implement and deliver these deals. These deals are obviously essentially

productivity deals, in that they entail growth in labor productivity and in the wage rate. As the growth in productivity depends on the introduction of technical change and therefore affects the labor process, the organization, and rhythms and patterns of work, the Keynesian multiplier implicitly presupposes the ability to govern not only income distribution among classes, but also the very core of class relations at the point of production.

Furthermore, in a context of growing productivity and productivity deals that link increases in wages to increases in productivity, the social multiplier tends to decline. This makes the employment effect of expansions of aggregate demand smaller and smaller, requiring larger and larger investment outlays to maintain a given level of employment growth.

Implications

The assumptions of given, stable and predictable class relations thus form the core of Keynesian income determination theory through movements of aggregate demand. The exposition of these hidden assumptions makes it relatively simple to envisage the effects of movements in productivity and the wage rate on the employment impact of a given level of investment within the framework of this dissected Keynesian multiplier:

1. Technical change and process innovation, together with increases in labor intensity, increase labor productivity and thus reduce the employment impact of a given level of investment.
2. A more relaxed working life – that is, the reduction of labor intensity (which by no means implies the reduction of technological change) – reduces labor productivity and increases the employment impact of a given level of investment.
3. The employment impact of a given level of investment is positively related to movements in wage rates, increasing when the latter increase and vice versa. However, it is clear that increases in wage increases and reductions in labor intensity would not only increase the employment impact of a given level of investment, but would also have a negative effect on the level of investment, as capitalists would see that their profit been eroded. The classical contradictions of capitalist production is thus hidden within the Keynesian multiplier.

9.5   Implicit assumptions and implications of the dissected income determination model: extension of working time

Assumptions

Another crucial assumption of the standard income determination model is a given extension of working time. We can rewrite (9.9) as

$$Nh = \frac{1}{\pi - \omega} I \quad \text{or}$$

$$N = \frac{1}{h(\pi - \omega)} I \tag{9.13}$$

where h is the average working time, and N is the number of people employed. Equation (9.13) shows that for a fixed working time and predictable growth of $\pi - \omega$, investments can have a predictable effect on employment N. We can thus see that the stability condition that we have encountered in relation to the spread between productivity and wages is now applied to working time, as this has an effect on the social multiplier. As the productivity deals were the institutional framework regulating the post-war spread between productivity and wages, so one of the most remarkable stylized facts of post-war accumulation has been the ending of the secular downward trend of working time. This trend occurred through a series of successive "shocks" brought about by cycles of struggles for the reduction of working time (Roediger and Foner 1989).[17] The stability in the social multiplier required by the post-war Keynesian strategies led to the devising of an institutional environment able to prevent the occurrence of these shocks as discussed in Chapter 7 (p. 86).

Implications

One clear implication of the introduction of working time in the model is the negative relation between working time and the employment impact of a given level of investment. A lower h means, *ceteris paribus*, a higher multiplier and therefore a higher employment effect of a given change in aggregate demand. Again, as in the previous cases of wage rate increases and reduction in labor intensity, a lower extension of working time means a fall in profitability, and therefore one would expect a consequent fall in investment.

9.6 The social meaning of the Keynesian strategy of employment creation

We are now in a position to explore the meaning of the Keynesian strategy of employment generation within the framework of the dissected multiplier. From (9.13) it is possible to see that a predictable positive effect on employment depends on a stable social multiplier. By letting the denominator of the social multiplier be

$$P = h(\pi - \omega)$$

that is, the total profit per worker per period of working time, we can calculate the total differential of N by applying conventional rules of differentiation, and set it greater than zero:

$$dN = 1 / P^2 (PdI - IdP) > 0 \tag{9.14}$$

After few algebraic steps, we find that an increase in employment therefore is only possible if

$$dP / P < dI / I \tag{9.15}$$

(9.15) spells out the essential conditions for an increase in employment. This condition of course acquires a different meaning in terms of the necessary investment to generate employment depending on whether dP/P is greater, equal or less than zero. Keynesian economics assumed a short run stable and given multiplier, which in terms of our translation means that $dP/P = 0$ in the short run. Employment generation can thus follow an expansion of aggregate demand. However, the short-run given and stable multiplier here presupposed in terms of (9.9) and (9.13), implies that in society there are productivity deals that are functioning and are allowing a stable balance between productivity and the social wage rate for a given extension of working hours. As we have seen in the previous chapters, in the United States this has been obtained through the institutionalization of unions, especially after the Second World War the active involvement of their bureaucratic apparatus in practices of control of grassroots militancy as well as the establishment of wage rounds of collective bargaining across the economy.

The spread between productivity and the wage rate can also be targeted with the practice of income policies. These have the same aim as productivity deals, although while the latter are established at the microeconomic level, from which they then spread throughout the economy, income policies move from the macroeconomic level. Income policies were often attempted when productivity deals failed to keep in check the spread between π and ω.[18] Furthermore, as mentioned before, (9.12) indicates that in a context of an increasing capital–labor ratio, capitalists are under increasing pressure to increase the denominator of the social multiplier (numerator of the rate of profit) in order to set up counter-tendencies to the fall in the rate of profit. This of course further depresses the social multiplier and further reduces the employment impact of a given level of investment. To maintain the goal of full employment in a context of institutional regulation of the spread between productivity and wages requires that this same spread is continuously tuned upward in order to compensate for the increase in the capital–labor ratio, thus allowing a non-declining profit rate and therefore sustaining investment demand. However, from the perspective of employment generation, this policy is self-defeating, as the employment impact of a given level of investment falls.

Since in this framework reasonably stable accumulation occurs only to the extent that productivity deals are successful, this strategic option has collapsed with the collapse of the "golden age" of post-war capitalist accumulation in the late 1960s and early 1970s. This was brought about by waves of struggles of different movements and the consequent collapse of the institutional conditions supporting the stability condition.[19]

9.7 The social multiplier with public expenditures in a closed economy

For reason of completeness, in what follows I want to add public expenditures to the translation of the traditional multiplier. I will not, however, discuss the new social multiplier obtained. Its meaning should, at this point, be straightforward and does not differ from the general meaning of the social multiplier without public expenditure. The latter only introduces a wider dimension in the definition of the social wage rate.

The introduction of public expenditures necessitates the introduction of some hypotheses concerning the use and social meaning of government outlays. Traditional literature and common practice distinguishes between public expenditures as consumption and as investment. Within Marx's theoretical framework, this same distinction would be made in terms of public expenditures as advances of *variable* capital or advances of *constant* capital at the level of society as a whole. For example, unemployment benefits would count as advances in social variable capital, as they serve for the reproduction of the working class as a whole, while subsidies to industries aimed at the restructuring of their production process would count as social constant capital. Often public expenditures acquire a twofold meaning, and the classification proposed becomes blurred. For example, expenditure in road maintenance can be interpreted as investment in both social constant capital and social variable capital, to the extent that roads are used for both business and leisure purposes.

To take into account this twofold role of public expenditures, let us write the national income identity in terms of

$$Y = b(Y - tY) + \alpha G + \beta G + I \tag{9.16'}$$

or

$$\pi L = b(\pi L - t\pi L) + \alpha G + \beta G + I \tag{9.16''}$$

in which

b = propensity to consume

π = labor productivity

α = percentage share of public expenditures going to reproduction of labor power – i.e. social variable capital

β = percentage share of public expenditures going to finance capital accumulation and social constant capital.

L and I are defined as above as the total amount of labor and investment, respectively.

t = tax rate.

Since $\pi L = Y$, $b\pi L = C$, and $\alpha + \beta = 1$, $t\pi L = T$ (tax revenue), (9.16'') is nothing but the familiar expression of national accounting identities $Y = C + G + I$.

By multiplying αG by L/L, (9.16''). can be written as

$$\pi L = b(\pi L - t\pi L) + \alpha g L + \beta G + I$$

in which g = public expenditures per hour of work (G/L).

Rearranging, we obtain

$$\pi L - b\pi L - tb\pi L - \alpha g L = \beta G + I \quad \text{or}$$
$$L(\pi - b\pi + tb\pi - \alpha g) = \beta G + I$$

Solving for L and rearranging, gives:

$$L = \frac{1}{(\pi - \omega + t\omega - \alpha g)}(\beta G + I) \tag{9.17}$$

The introduction of public expenditures allows us here to further clarify the meaning of the social wage rate. I call $\omega_n = \omega - t\omega$ the *net* private consumption per hour of work, while αg is public consumption per hour of work. Their sum therefore gives us what society consumes per hour of work, what I called before the social wage rate, ω_s:

$$\omega_s = \omega_n + \alpha g$$

Thus (9.17) can be rewritten as

$$L = \frac{1}{(\pi - \omega_n - \alpha g)}(\beta G + I) \quad \text{or} \tag{9.17'}$$

$$L = \frac{1}{(\pi - \omega_s)}(\beta G + I) \tag{9.17''}$$

9.8   Social multiplier in the open economy

The social multiplier can also help us to shed light on the social meaning of the post-war Keynesian strategy in a framework of an open economy. From national accounts we have the usual open economy identity

$$X - M \equiv (S - I) + (T - G) \tag{9.18}$$

where $S - I$ is the macroeconomic balance, and $T - G$ is the government deficit (surplus). From this identity it is clear that any deficit in the balance of trade means that either $I > S$ or $G > T$, or a combination of both. It also means that in order to equilibrate a balance of trade, $S - I$ and/or $T - G$ must grow. For the country in deficit the cost of not adjusting the trade balance through changes in $S - I$ and $T - G$ is a spiraling trend toward recession. But this mechanism is not a politically neutral mechanism. Again, by introducing the social multiplier, we can have a clearer picture of the meaning of a trade deficit and the social cost of its adjustment. To do so, I rewrite (9.16'') so as to include the external sector:

$$\pi L = b(\pi L - t\pi L) + \alpha G + \beta G + I + X - M \tag{9.19}$$

which can be rewritten as

$$X - M = \pi L - b\pi L - bt\pi L - \alpha g L - \beta G - I \qquad (9.20)$$

$$X - M = L(\pi - \omega - \omega t + \alpha g) - (\beta G + I) = L(\pi - \omega s) - (\beta G + I) \qquad (9.21)$$

From (9.21) it is evident that, *ceteris paribus*, the higher is the profit per worker the higher must be the balance of trade. It also means that in case of a trade deficit adjustment can be obtained either through a reduction in social investment (I and/or βG) and/or increase in the social profit per hour. Thus, while a trade surplus represents a golden condition for capital accumulation via expansion of social investment (I and βG), a trade deficit represents for capital a golden stimulus to restructure production and social spending in order to increase the condition of profitability and competitiveness. It must be pointed out that this is true independently of the regime of financial regulation and international transactions. Different regimes of international finance only concretize in historical terms *how* this adjustment occurs, what are the instruments and social pressures which make it occur and the particular strategy used. It is possible to express equation (9.21) in terms of Figure 9.1.

In Figure 9.1 any point below the line 00' expresses a deficit of the balance of trade and vice versa, any point above it is a surplus. Line CA_1 is the graphical expression of (9.21). Its intercept is given by the level of social investment $[-(\beta G + I)]$, while its slope reflects the conditions of profitability for society as a whole $[(\pi - \omega_s)]$. The economy starts at a deficit at point a on line CA_1. Graphically, a deficit could be eliminated by moving along the line and positioning the economy at x, using L_x quantity of labor. However, there is no inherent mechanism in the economy that would guarantee this movement. An increase in L occurring under *ceteris paribus* conditions would imply a society positioned on a general trend towards more labor intensive techniques. As a movement along the CA line would imply given factor costs, there is no economic reason for an increase in L, unless profit *expectations* are on the rise. If this was the case, we would also expect the increase in L (either due to an increase in working hours – "h" – or an increase in employment – "N" – or a combination of both), accompanied by a corresponding increase in investment. In turn, this would presuppose an increase in the conditions of

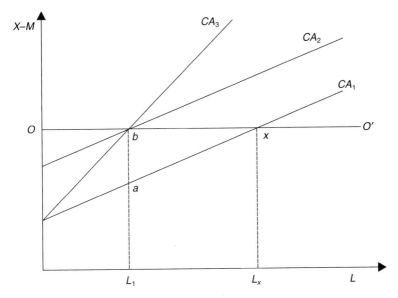

Figure 9.1   Class relations and balance of trade: 1

profitability. In the first case, line CA_1 would shift to CA_2, and in the second, it would rotate, thus preventing any "pure movement" along CA_1 itself. Thus, any solution of a deficit in the trade balance lies between a pure fall in investment given the conditions of profitability, or an increase in profitability for a given level of investment. This is shown in Figure 9.1. by lines CA_2 and CA_3, respectively. It is clear, however, that these two extremes are in fact related to each other. Often, a fall in investment and a corresponding increase in unemployment is a necessary condition to weaken the working class and thus impose stricter work discipline and/or lower wages.

   Thus (see Figure 9.2.), a deficit in the balance of trade, is initially generally followed by a fall in investment that would reduce the level of labor expended from L_a to L_b, which in turn would lead to a rotation of the line until c is reached on CA_3. Of course, the degree of rotation between CA_2 and CA_3 depends on social and political factors. The higher is the "rigidity" posed by the working class to labor, wage conditions and public spending, the smaller is the rotation of the CA line, thus more difficult it is for capitalists to re-establish a balanced trade

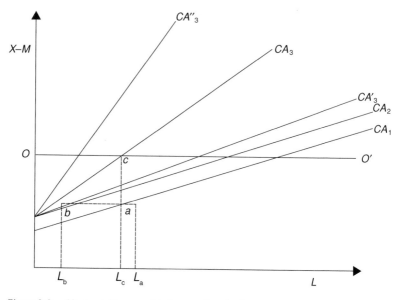

Figure 9.2   Class relations and balance of trade: 2

account in conditions of competitive profitability. Capitalists would therefore deepen the conditions of recession (which would easily turn into a depression) by furthering the decrease in investment and therefore widening the shift of CA_1 to CA_2, thus also increasing unemployment (increasing distance between a and b). A balanced account of course can occur at any level of employment, right or left of point c as indicated by lines CA'_3 and CA''_3.

It goes without saying that there is not a unique solution to a problem of trade deficit in the balance of payments, although the capitalist requirement of accumulation would imply a unique direction to different strategies of adjustments. In what follows, I will briefly compare, in the context of (9.21), the pre-Keynesian and the post-war Keynesian strategies to deal with a deficit in the trade balance – that is, the Gold Standard and the "dollar standard" of Bretton Woods.

The gold standard

In case of a deficit in the current account, there would be an outflow of gold, and a reduction in money supply, credit, etc. that would

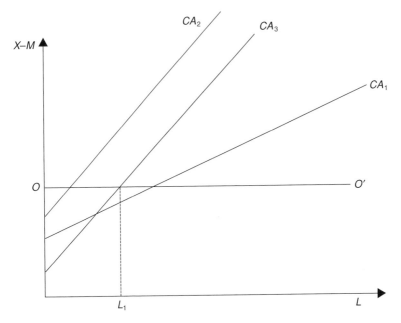

Figure 9.3   Adjustment under the Gold Standard

enforce a recession, which would shift upward and rotate CA_1 to CA_2 (Figure 9.3.) and enforce worse wage and labor conditions. This, in combination with cheaper exports, would increase investment thus shifting downward the line to CA_3. Crisis occurs when the working class "refuses" to allow sufficient rotation (profitability) to the CA line.

Bretton woods

The pattern is the same, but the transmission mechanism is different. Temporary balance of payments deficits are financed by the IMF and reduction in investment (and thus the shift of the CA line) is milder than in the case of the Gold Standard. However, this presupposes the presence of a set of institutions at the micro-level that push up productivity higher than wages so that CA_1 moves to CA_2 in Figure

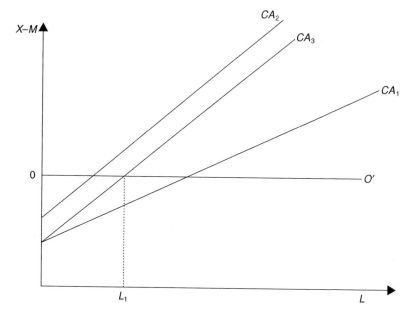

Figure 9.4   Adjustment under Bretton words

9.4. The consequent increase in social investment leads to a shift from CA_2 to CA_3. Crisis occurs when the working class "refuses" to accept a given relation between productivity and wages – that is, a given productivity deal. Inflation is the consequence of this situation.

10
Economic Modeling and Social Conflict: 2 – Inflation and the Phillips Curve

10.1 Introduction

The basic assumption of the Neo-classical Synthesis in its simplest form was fixed wages and prices. This assumption allowed a simple method of aggregation and put emphasis on government policies to manage the level of accumulation for a given balance between necessary and surplus labor. However "the consequences of doing it were serious" (Hicks 1974: 60). The consequences Hicks is referring to are those related to the lack of a proper theory of inflation, or the relation between wages and inflation:

> For when Keynes' theory is set out in this text-book manner (as I shall call it) it is bound to give the impression that there are just two "states" of the economy: a "state of unemployment" in which money wages are constant, and a "state of full employment" in which pressure of demand causes wages to rise. So "full employment" is an "inflation barrier." As long as employment is less than full, even if it is only marginally less than full, there should be no wage-inflation. So all we need do, in order to have "full employment without inflation," is suitably to control demand. (Hicks 1974: 60–1)

Hicks recognizes that this textbook version of Keynes' economics "is by no means clear that it was Keynes's own," also because "it is hard to see that in his book he has *any* theory about the causation of changes in money wages" (Hicks 1974: 61). Economists thus started to worry about inflationary pressures in the economy, beginning with the immediate post-war period. If (relative) prices were kicked out of the door of economic theory they were allowed to reenter by the window in the form of the price level. If the assumption of constant real wages and prices presupposed a social constraint at the micro-level in which a balance between necessary and surplus labor was assumed as given, with the analysis of inflation this balance became the target of economic policy. Ever since Keynes, economic thinking about inflation always had an immediate political meaning. Indeed, the more or less hidden agenda in most theories of inflation starting from Keynes is to investigate the relation between price level and a particular "distribution" of income, or, in Marxian terms, a particular balance between necessary and surplus labor.

When at the beginning of the Keynesian era critics started to denounce Keynesian economists for their shortsightedness with respect to inflation, Joan Robinson (1958; 1974) pointed out how Keynes wrote extensively on inflation and on how indeed inflation ought to become a proper target of economic policy. Indeed, she was right. Keynes' assumption of the second postulate of the "classical" theory – that is to say, that capitalists always realize their choices – meant that in order to increase the level of employment (accumulation) an initial increase in aggregate demand would have to bring about a reduction of real wages. If nominal wages were rigid downward, then prices had to increase. An increase in the price level could be obtained through a flexible monetary policy which would be a more politically acceptable option than one of wage cuts called for by classical economists (Keynes 1936: Chapter 19). In Keynes' opinion a flexible monetary policy and a flexible wage policy were alike, as both were instruments to reduce real wages. Furthermore, as monetary policy was already in the hands of the government and easily manipulated, "only a foolish person" would not favor a flexible monetary policy. In "How to Pay for the War" Keynes (1940) was very explicit in proposing a manipulation of prices as a strategy to shift the balance in favor of surplus labor. In the context of the war economy, inflation was viewed as the result of high purchasing power and high expenditure and the reduced availability of consumer goods caused by war production. Thus inflation was viewed as the result of a rise in demand in conditions of full employment. On this occasion Keynes reintroduced what in the "Treatise on Money" (Keynes 1930a) he calls the "widow's cruse" theory.[1] According to this, output and expenditure were brought into balance through a shift in the distribution of income towards profit by means of a rise in prices.

10.2   The Phillips curve and capital's strategies

In the literature before 1958, the year of the appearance of the Phillips curve, theories of inflation could be classified into two broad categories, "demand-pull" and "cost-push" theories. The basic common factor in all these theories of inflation is the fact that inflation is seen as a monetary phenomena which has real effects on the overall balance between surplus and necessary labor and that an equilibrium can be established such that a proper and stable balance can be obtained only through curbing working-class power in one form or another (De Angelis 1995: Chapter 7). What these theories did not offer, though, was a coherent box of tools able to inform economic policy on two fronts simultaneously: the management of the *social balance* between surplus and necessary labor (the relation between productivity and wages) and the *level* of accumulation. Demand-pull and cost-push theories in fact treated wage increases and the level of accumulation (unemployment) as two independent and unrelated variables. This meant that they were considered non-conflicting goals of economic policy. For example, in the Keynesian case, economists could distinguish between two mutually exclusive conditions: below full employment, where wages and prices were stable, and full employment with inflation. In the case of the cost-push theories inflation is the product of union strength, which is assumed to be independent of the level of unemployment.

The British economist A.W. Phillips (1958) studied the empirical relationship between the rate of increase of money wage rates and the level of unemployment. He took British data for the period 1861 to 1913 on which he fitted an empirical curve. The result was a downward-sloping curve showing an inverse relation between the two variables. In the same fashion, he derived a curve that interpolated also the data for the intra-war and war periods. Lipsey (1960) incorporated Phillips' empirical work within standard theory by considering wage changes as proportional to excess demand for labor and using unemployment as a proxy for excess demand. Lipsey's contribution helped to explain the position and the shape of the Phillips curve (Santomero and Seater 1978). The Phillips curve was introduced in the United States by Samuelson and Solow (1960) within the context of anti-inflation policies. Following this introduction in the United States, the Phillips curve became the object of an enormous empirical literature attempting to account for the negative relationship between inflation and unemployment. The distinction between cost-push and demand-pull inflation became unnecessary (Backhouse 1985: 340), as the Phillips curve could provide a framework within which to account for both of them by simply adding variables into the Phillips equation. Hines (1964), for example, introduced unionization as a measure of "union power" in the Phillips curve. This sparked much research in the 1960s and 1970s regarding the appropriate measure of working-class power in wage bargaining (Backhouse 1985: 340).

The inverse relationship between the rate of increase in the wage rate and unemployment was not a novelty. The original contribution of the Phillips curve was to show that inflation could coexist with unemployment. This result had important policy implications. If inflation and unemployment were mutually exclusive, as assumed in the Keynesian framework and in demand-pull and cost-push theories, policy-makers could target a level of unemployment without inflation. However, if they were shown not to be mutually exclusive, the idea of simultaneous achievement of full employment with no inflation had to be abandoned in favor of the notion of a trade-off between these objectives.

While the original Phillips curve related unemployment to wage changes, economists started widely to use a transformed Phillips curve, which related unemployment to price changes.[2] The reason for this was that such a transformation would be of much more use for policy-makers, as they tend to designate policy goals in terms of price changes rather than change of wages. The derived Phillips curve after all is a simple transformation of the original one, in which $p = \dot{w} - \dot{\pi}$, that is, inflation level p is equal to the gap between the rate of change in money wages $\dot{w}$ and the rate of change in productivity $\dot{\pi}$ (which is assumed to be constant). It is clear, therefore, that inflation has the economic function to erode every increase in real wages above the increase in the level of productivity. The higher is the pressure of necessary labor to gain a larger share of the total product to the detriment of surplus labor, the higher are inflationary pressures. Inflation in this model offers policy-makers a proxy for class power. This is seen in Figure 10.1., in which the curve *aa* shows the rate of increase in money wages associated with different rates of unemployment, and curve *bb* shows the rate of increase in the price level associated with different rates of unemployment (in all figures p = rate of change of prices; $\dot{w}$ = rate of change of money wages; U = unemployment rate). Curve *bb* is obtained by subtracting the rate of increase in productivity from the rate of increase in the money wages at all possible unemployment rate levels.

Thus, the lower is the unemployment rate, the greater the underlying power of workers to push wages above the rate of increase of

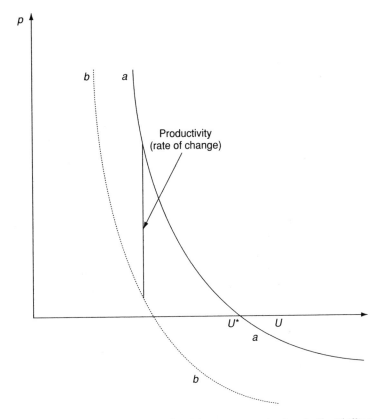

Figure 10.1   Relation between productivity, wages, and prices in the Phillips curve

productivity, and the higher will be inflation. Inflation level will be zero if wage increases match productivity increases. This will happen only at a relatively high unemployment rate, U^* – that is, at relatively low conditions of class power. That level of unemployment therefore corresponds to a particular level of capital accumulation, which allows maintenance of a certain balance between surplus and necessary labor. Now, the key point is that *any combination between prices and unemployment along the transformed Phillips curve describes a given balance between necessary and surplus labor at the social level, between productivity and social wage rate, as wage increases in excess of productivity increases are eroded away by price increases.* In other words, the Phillips curve expresses the same basic given assumption that lies behind the fiscal multiplier. Within the logic of the Phillips curve, the policy options offered to economic policy are constrained within a determined trade-off between unemployment and inflation. However, the real constraint is the same overall balance between necessary and surplus labor in correspondence of any of such combinations.

The political meaning of the Phillips curve is thus twofold. first, it offers a possible menu of choices for state planning through which to target a particular balance between surplus and necessary labor at the social level through a particular level of inflation *and* of the level of accumulation and employment. Second, it reflects the fragility of productivity deals. In other words, the Phillips curve makes evident that the government can no longer rely only on the social contract at the shopfloor to guarantee a certain balance between necessary and surplus labor, but that it has to intervene through the targeting of the price level in order to regulate that balance at the social level.

This second important point concerning the political reading of the Phillips curve resides in the fact that it indicates the continuous presence of a social threat posed to the capitalist establishment by the working class. As was seen above, within the framework of the early Neo-classical Synthesis and the simplest formulation of the income determination model, this social threat was presupposed as totally subsumed once wage rigidity was assumed into the system. However, within the context of the Phillips curve, a dynamic element is introduced and the price level is explicitly recognized as the social mechanism having the function of eroding what the working class has gained. If the early version of the Neo-classical Synthesis optimistically indicated that a level of accumulation (employment) could be obtained through state demand management policies while the overall balance between surplus and necessary labor was maintained by the social contract instituted at the micro-level (the simple income determination model), the Phillips curve indicated that this is no longer possible. The social contract at the micro-level is loose and fragile. The level of accumulation and consequent level of employment affect workers' power and therefore the breakdown of a particular balance between necessary and surplus labor. In order to determine a particular level of accumulation, the state now must intervene also on that balance. Social engineering now involves a delicate trade-off between inflation (necessary in order to maintain a particular balance) and unemployment (to which corresponds a particular level of accumulation).

Given the trade-off, economists and social planners could use the Phillips curve to "choose" a combination between the two. The choice of this combination could be done either in relation to a "social

welfare function" or through the definition of a "zone of socially tolerable outcomes." The latter point provides a simple illustration of the
political meaning of the Phillips curve.

The "zone of socially tolerable outcomes" (Peterson 1988: 466n 3;
Humphrey 1973) or "feasible range" is the area included between a
maximum "socially tolerable" inflation rate–that is, the highest inflation
rate before generating negative future expectations likely to increase the
instability of the investment function or before causing capital flights –
and a maximum "socially tolerable" unemployment rate – that is, the
highest unemployment rate before people start to rebel and the social
fabric is seriously threatened with disintegration. In Figure 10.2. this is
represented by the shaded area. The important point here is the fact that
the planning instruments of the economists are openly including the
threat of political instability.

Now, in terms of the management of the economy, a range of
possible combinations of unemployment and inflation is defined if the

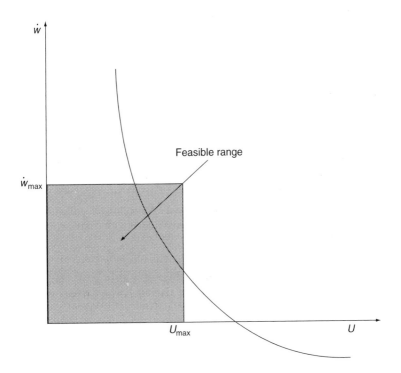

Figure 10.2   Feasible policy targets constrained by the class struggle

Phillips curve lies within this area. However, if the Phillips curve lies above and on the right of the "feasible range" area, then there is no socially tolerable combination of unemployment and inflation. At the level of this analysis, the solution is to shift the Phillips curve to the left. This means that productivity deals at the micro-level have reached their limit and a direct social deal fixing the social balance between necessary and surplus labor must be implemented with the direct intervention of the state, the official unions, and the organizations representing the capitalists. This could be done either through "income policies" or, as Samuelson and Solow point out, through direct anti-working class legislation:

> the important question [is] what feasible institutional reforms might be introduced to lessen the degree of disharmony between full employment and price stability. These could of course involve such wide-ranging issues as direct price and wage controls, antiunion and antitrust legislation, and a host of other measures hopefully designed to move the American Phillips' curves downward and to the left. (Samuelson and Solow 1960: 194)

The extent to which one or the other policies could be pursued must obviously depend on the balances of forces within society.

From the previous discussion, it is clear that the level of accumulation the Keynesian state can target is subjected to many considerations of political nature. It is also clear that there is no uniquely determined direction of causation between the level of accumulation and the level of social antagonism. The Phillips curve approximately indicates that the higher the level of unemployment, and therefore the lower the level of accumulation, the lower the level of inflation. On the other hand, economists have also pointed out the risks involved in this case. A too low level of accumulation and too high level of unemployment may fuel "class warfare and social conflict" (Samuelson and Solow 1960: 193).

10.3 From cracks to wreckage: class struggle, the crisis of Keynesianism, and the collapse of the Phillips curve

The period in which the Phillips curve gained acceptance in the United States was the early 1960s. Social unrest was starting to mount, as in the case of steel strikes in 1959 and the civil right movement, and there was increasing need to manage the productivity deal at the social level. The Phillips curve was able to offer a simple and practical instrument for thinking about the management of the trade-off between unemployment and inflation. With the increase in struggles during the 1960s and 1970s, economists noticed the Phillips curve dangerously moving away from the "zone of socially tolerable outcomes" in an apparent uncontrollable spiral.

It is widely recognized that since mid-1960s a serious crisis – or, better, serious *crises* – have beset major capitalist countries. At the level of economic relations, there have been crises of accumulation, of productivity (Weisskopf, Bowles and Gordon 1983), of profitability (Shaikh 1987), and a fiscal crisis of the state (O'Connor 1973). At the level of political–juridical relations, there has been a crisis of democracy and democratic institutions and a crisis of representation and participation (Crozier, Huntington and Watanuki 1975). At the level of society at large, there has been a crisis of the nuclear family and a crisis of education. At the level of the ecosystem, there has been a crisis of world ecology. At the level of economic orthodoxy, there could not be other but a crisis of Keynesianism.

From the mid-1960s many basic economic indicators showed a turning point. Investments that were flourishing in the 1950s and 1960s turned sour and worsened after the 1974 oil crisis. Business and manufacturing investment collapsed (Clark 1979). Industrial profit rates began their downturn in the mid-1960s (Duménil, Glick and Rangel 1987). Inflation began to approach double digits by the late 1960s. The welfare state appeared to crumble under the weight of increasing deficits and exponential increase of the public debt. All these trends could be translated into DM, lire, or pounds because the turning point was more or less evident in all major capitalist countries and resulted in the collapse of the mechanism of their international coordination, the Bretton Woods system (Phillips 1985). Furthermore, if the "golden age" had seen an impressive increase in productivity growth, the subsequent period suffered what numerous observers have called the "productivity slowdown." What is more important, productivity in most OECD countries grew less than money wages, thus leading to inflationary pressures as business tried to restore profit margins.

Behind the changes in these indicators was the crumbling of the institutions which had contributed to the miracle of the post-war period. In 1975 the Trilateral Commission produced a study of the condition of Western democracy (Crozier, Huntington and Watanuki 1975). The result for Western Europe and the United States was unanimous: despite the differences among these areas, "democracy" – that is, the political–juridical system which held together the social, economic, and ideological fabric of Western societies – was in deep crisis. One of the most important factors responsible for this crisis was a change in people's attitude toward authority. One basic area in which this change in attitude was manifested was work. The document of the Trilateral Commission recognized the political importance of work as a form of social control (governability) within Western capitalism, and therefore pointed to the challenge faced by Western political elite.

The different movements of the 1960s basically undermined the capacity of the state to plan. The social factory was based on the fragile interconnection of production and reproduction, interconnection and coordination through the managing of a balanced growth between revenue and productivity, through the relation between income and work at the factory and at the social level. In this context, the various social movements of the 1960s and 1970s undermined in practice this "balanced growth" by focusing on wage and welfare claims *and* by questioning authority and work: the combination of demands for higher wages *and* the questioning of labor discipline and authority by both waged and unwaged was bound to become a social time bomb. Such a danger was anticipated by economic theory in the treatment of inflation within the Phillips curve.

Samuelson and Solow (1960) introduced the concept of inflationary expectations into the Phillips curve, by arguing that an economy with high unemployment would reduce inflationary expectations and there-fore shift the Phillips curve to the left. However, it was not until Phelps' (1967) paper and Friedman's (1968) presidential address to the American Economic Association that the introduction of inflationary expectations into the Phillips curve became the basis for a fundamental critique. These contributions represented the foundations of a critique of the short-run Phillips curve, the introduction of the long-run Phillips curve, and the consequent undermining of theoretical support for demand management policies. These contributions introduced a vertical long-run Phillips curve corresponding to a natural rate of unemployment (NRU), thus emphasizing the relation between the rate of growth of *real* wages and unemployment. With the long-run Phillips curve economic theory sanctions the acknowledgment of the failure of the strategy based on the "money illusion." With Friedman's critique, what is acknowledged is the fact that the working class cannot be fooled – or, at least, not in the "long run." It is precisely this power of the working class which is seen at the basis of the failure of economic policy. The basis of social engineering of state planning consisted in maneuvering and controlling the balance between surplus and necessary labor through the maneuvering of the real wage by means of the inflation rate. The working class broke the direct relation between real wage–that is, the qualitative and quantitative level of its needs – and employment – that is, the amount of work – and in so doing disrupted at its roots the foundation of the Phillips curve along which that relation is stable.

Friedman criticized the Phillips curve for being misspecified, in the sense that supply and demand for labor depended on the growth rate of real wages and not on nominal wages. Table 10.1 and Figure 10.3 illustrate his argument. An increase in aggregate demand (e.g. in money supply) will lead to an initial and a final effect described in Table 10.1.

The initial effect will be to increase the level of employment (1) as workers are attracted by higher money wages. However, as soon as they realize (5) that their real wages will remain the same because of the effect of higher prices ((2), (3), (4)), they will demand further increase in nominal wages so that real wages will increase (6). Through a depression in profit, unemployment will increase and this will lead to the return of real quantities to the level existing before demand management policies were introduced (7). The repetition of the mechanism leads to the long-run Phillips curve corresponding to the NRU. Therefore, the actual level of unemployment differs from this NRU only in so far as people make mistakes in their inflationary expectations. Low and high unemployment

Table 10.1   Initial and final effects caused by an increase in aggregate demand

Initial effect (movement *a–b* in Figure 10.3.)	Final effect (movement *b–c* in Figure 10.3.)
1. Increase in output and employment	5. Increase in expected prices Because of adaptive expectations, workers begin to expect an increase in prices
2. Workers expect higher real wages e.g. there is an increase in *ex ante* (real wages)	6. Rise in real wages
3. Selling prices of goods increase more than prices of factors of production	7. Real quantities return to the level existing before demand management policy
4. Fall in *ex post* real wages	

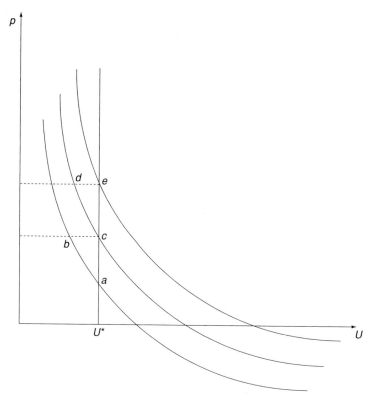

Figure 10.3   Shift in the short-run and long-run Phillips curve

would be the result of inflation being underestimated and overestimated, respectively.

From Table 10.1. it is evident therefore that Friedman emphasizes the fact that the NRU is a real phenomenon determined by other real phenomena. Purely *nominal forces*, such as anticipated inflation, cannot change the natural rate. In other words, expected profits and/or wages can influence the behavior of economic agents, but when expectations do not match with reality, then investment decisions tend to return to the previous level. If raising the rate of inflation once and for all only lowers the unemployment rate temporarily, then the only way to keep the unemployment rate permanently below the natural rate is through a continuous increase in the rate of inflation – i.e. by accelerating prices. If this critique is correct, then the idea of a trade-off between unemployment and inflation is wrong, and with it the possibility for the government to choose a combination between the two. The idea of a trade-off, Friedman argued, is valid only in the short-run.

The conclusions of this critique are therefore the following: (1) the level of employment/unemployment can be affected by aggregate demand policies only in the short -run; (2) in the long -run the NRU prevails (or the "non-accelerating inflation" rate of unemployment, NAIRU); (3) inflation is a byproduct of government expansionary policies; (4) inflation can be stabilized through stable and predictable monetary growth so that there is no gap between *ex ante* and *ex post* variables; (5) inflation can be reduced through restrictive monetary policies; (6) the NRU can be reduced through supply-side policies. The latter is the key point. Friedman's critique provides a justification for what will become supply-side policies in the late 1970s and 1980s. It is important to underline the fact that these policies are based, at least at the theoretical level, on the acknowledgment of working-class power. This power has forced capital to change radically the form of its strategy.

The introduction of the long-run vertical Phillips curve meant that the planner state cannot any longer affect the level of accumulation. In the early Neo-classical Synthesis, this was possible by simple management of aggregate demand for a given contract at the point of production. With the Phillips curve, the determination of the level of accumulation became constrained by the ability to control a certain balance between surplus and necessary labor through monetary and fiscal policies. With the long-run Phillips curve, the state planner can affect the level of accumulation only by shifting to the left-hand side of the vertical curve – that is to say, by reducing the NRU. This may happen only through direct intervention on the supply side. This point is important. The NRU depends, according to Friedman, on three main factors: (1) technology; (2) social institutions; and (3) shocks. Apart from the latter, the first two combined determine the balance between productivity and wages – that is, the overall balance between necessary and surplus labor. Only changes in these factors or the appearance of shocks in the labor and commodity markets could change the level of the "natural rate." The first two factors became in 1980s the targets of supply-side policies mostly aimed at reestablishing the link between wages and productivity, through massive restructuring and consequent changes in the class composition at the factory and social level to weaken the working class.

11
Conclusion: Looking Ahead

11.1 The general features of this book

This book has studied the relation between social conflict and the rise, establishment, and collapse of an economic paradigm. We have seen not only that the economic strategies proposed by this paradigm have a political meaning, but also that its own theoretical categories and analytical framework can be interpreted in a way that reveals the strategic character of the economic discourse *vis-à-vis* social movements. Indeed, a logically coherent link between theory and policy seems to have been a necessary requirement for the spread of the Keynesian orthodoxy since, as indicated, pre-Keynesian economists reached Keynes' same policy conclusions in the midst of the Great Depression, thus contradicting their own theoretical framework. However, consistency between theory and policy is not a sufficient condition for the establishment of an economic paradigm. To serve as a consistent strategic tool and to be *operational*, Keynesianism required an institutional arrangement able to guarantee a relationship between classes that was stable, predictable, and under control. I have argued that, so far as the analytical apparatus of post-war Keynesianism was concerned, this stability was a *given*, an assumption that reflected the post-war institutionalization of trade unions and the recuperation of social conflict into a mechanism of accumulation. The analytical apparatus of post-war Keynesianism interpreted this stability in terms of such concepts as time, equilibrium, expectations, and the fiscal multiplier. The analytical recognition of cracks in this assumption, which reflected cracks in the actual stability of class relations, came with the Phillips curve. Thus, the Keynesian economic orthodoxy revealed its dependence, as a theoretical/strategic option, on the flesh-and-blood conditions of social relations. The collapse of Keynesianism thus corresponded to the massive social turmoil of the 1960s and 1970s that shook every aspect of life and disrupted the stability and predictability of class relations.

These movements encouraged inflationary pressure and threatened the intertemporal stability of contracts needed for capital accumulation. In the workplace, the strong grassroots organization of the 1970s implied that the trade union apparatuses could no longer contain the struggles. Local unions were gaining increasing autonomy from the central offices concerning actions and priorities.

The social movements of the 1960s and 1970s, whose demands were largely based on the separation of revenue and work in various spheres of society, contributed to making the concept of the short-run Phillips curve useless for economic planning and instead promoted the conceptualization and diffusion of the long-run vertical Phillips curve. In this framework, the only solution for capital was the inversion of economic policy priorities: the state had to intervene with supply-side policies to adjust the overall balance between the parameters of accumulation (represented by a shift towards the left of the long-run Phillips curve) and to subordinate the problem of the level of accumulation (employment) to that of low inflation. In the early 1980s, supply-side policies aimed at shifting the relations of power among workers and employers in favor of the latter through the contribution of labor market deregulation, publicly subsidized production restructuring, and anti-union laws. Also, the welfare state became the target of neoliberal strategies around the world, with deficit reduction policies aimed at cutting social spending and restructuring rights and entitlements won at the dawn of the Keynesian era. In a word, all components of the social wage were targeted.

The level of accumulation itself became the object of restrictive monetary policies. Strong grassroots organization had shown that growth can turn very easily into inflationary growth, thus giving credence to Kalecki's suggestion (1943: 351) that full employment under capitalist relations of production brings political instability. The experience workers and welfare state claimants had of moderate inflation during the 1950s and 1960s taught them the meaning of the "money illusion," and what it could do to their pocketbooks. Once the trick was uncovered, inflation could no longer serve the purpose of eroding workers' and claimants' income, and the wage–price spiral started to explode. At the same time, those sectors of society which were not initially part of productivity deals – such as minorities, women, public workers, etc. – but which were nevertheless supposed to perform various forms of unwaged work necessary for the reproduction of the system as a whole, began to organize and scale up their demands and aspirations. The result was an explosive price–social wage inflationary spiral. It is common to attribute the "blame" for the two-digit inflation of the 1970s to workers and claimants. However, given the conflicting nature of social relations in capitalism, such blame could be as easily cast on the profit-earners, who were not willing to accept lower profit margins. In any case, the lesson learned by economic theory, which found expression in supply -side, monetarist and neoliberal policies from the late 1970s to the present, was that inflation embodied a threat of the displacement of power from capital to labor (in all its forms), and that full employment was a dangerous nurturing ground for this power. Anti-inflationary policies, which often fuel recession, thus became the top priority of economic policy.

Yet, at the time this book is being completed, the first signs of a new widespread global crisis seem to be appearing on the horizon. After the world economy was hit by the shock waves of social, economic, and political turmoil coming from East Asia and Eastern Europe, the defenders of the neoliberal dogma began to voice their worries loudly in the columns of the *Financial Times*, *The Economist*, the *Wall Street Journal* and *Business Week*. They worry that the neoliberal ideological, cultural, and political hegemony may be over (see section 11.4, p. 155). From their perspective, there is indeed much to worry about, as this latest crisis has begun to expose *ad hominem* the implications of free-wheeling global markets, and thus started to undermine their legitimacy. Although this is not the place to analyze the last twenty years of neoliberal policies and the processes of financial, production and trade globalization that led to the current crisis, I will offer a few observations here.

11.2   The new crisis and the process of globalization: general characteristics

In the first place, the process of globalization that has occurred in the last twenty years cannot be viewed in isolation from those social conflicts that brought Keynesianism down and that were setting remarkable constraints on capital accumulation. Despite the effort of the conventional wisdom to portray the process of globalization entirely as a spontaneous development of market forces, there is clear evidence to suggest that post-1970s' governments, in collusion with powerful corporate and financial groups, in fact promoted financial integration and deregulation, trade liberalization, and the internation-alization of production.[1] Unsurprisingly, the basic rationale of these various aspects of globalization does not differ greatly from the general character of the policy implications of the long-run vertical Phillips curve discussed in Chapter 10, as each of these aspects of globalization contributes to the management of the fundamental parameters of accumulation.

Financial integration and liberalization allows capital mobility to serve as a disciplinary device to limit the scope of any concessions by individual governments that could harm national competitiveness and to present "adjustment" in terms of cuts in welfare spending and entitlements as a necessity posited from outside. In other words, the globalization of finance can be read in terms of a mechanism for the regulation of the balance between necessary and surplus labor at the global level. In the countries of the North, capital mobility has the same function as IMF structural adjustment policies in the South, the only difference being that the former appears as an impersonal and objective reality. Of course, global financial deregulation also fuels speculation and contributes to bringing about instability and sudden crashes.

The globalization of trade, increasingly pursued in the 1980s and 1990s and now institutionalized with the creation of the WTO, offers the possibility to widen the scope for competition across countries, and therefore to increase the pressure on each national civil society to raise productivity and production standards, to innovate, to reduce costs, and to moderate monetary demands in terms of wages, public services, etc. This insistent, blind promotion of competition across the globe is of course accelerating the threat to indigenous cultures and local networks of production and subsistence and it is promoting the commodification of every aspect of human life.[2] It is also contributing to rolling back gains obtained at national levels in terms of environ-mental and labor standards by allowing the WTO to overrule national and regional laws that were implemented as a result of pressures from below, thus subverting, instead of promoting, the democratic process (Nader and Wallach 1996).

Finally, the globalization of production is shaping and reshaping the international division of labor, and coincides with multinational corporations' drive to reduce production costs and reach and create new markets. In the chemicals, automobile, electronic and textile sectors, among others, plants have been closed in some regions of the North and reopened in regions of the South. For those relatively labor-intensive sectors such as textiles, capital mobility could be further utilized to react to increases in production costs in emerging markets as soon as they reach "uncompetitive" new levels, owing, for example to pressures brought about by a newly unionized workforce. In this case, plants could shift to another "emergent" economy. This pattern, which initially had disastrous effects on the unskilled labor force, has subsequently reached skilled workers, who are increasingly exposed to global competition (Reich 1991). However, one of the most striking effects of globalization on labor markets is the dramatic increase in global poverty and the increasing role of various forms of modern slavery within the international division of labor (Chossudovsky 1997).

11.3   Globalization and new social movements

This set of neoliberal strategies of global integration did not occur in a vacuum, but *against* a set of social forces opposing it. Mainstream economists and many other social scientists often forget the oppositional nature of capitalist society, as well as the dynamism of the forms of these forces. The fact is that throughout the neoliberal 1980s and 1990s struggles have often posed limits to the forces of globalization and forced setbacks in the implementation of the international economic institutions' agenda. Consider the drive towards the integration of the South of the world into the global economy, which used debt as the main tool for enforcing market dependence. Yet the history of debt in the Third World is a history dotted with "IMF riots" (Walton and Seddon 1994), which often forced the IMF to "allow" national governments to repeal some of the most socially devastating conditionalities imposed by IMF loans. Another example is provided by the campaign against Multilateral Agreement on Investments (MAI) – that is, the negotiations among OECD countries to allow multinational corporations more freedom to roam the world, by lowering public and legal restraints. In April 1998 the ministers involved were forced to interrupt negotiations for six months and rethink their strategy, after the growing group of "network guerrillas" publicly exposed the secret negotiations and revealed the MAI's potentially devastating social and economic consequences (de Jonquières 1998).

Also, the character of social movements and struggles against neoliberalism and the effects of globalization have evolved since the beginning of the 1980s. In the countries of the North, for example, neoliberal strategies were at first met with the resistance of social subjects whose main socioeconomic characteristics and political/ organizational imagery were typical of the class composition of the Keynesian era. These struggles were mostly reactive in nature and mainly defensive of rights and entitlements threatened by the new neoliberal policies. But with the passing of time and particularly the unfolding of the 1990s, this defense of rights and entitlements of the Keynesian era has been paralleled by a process which, although still at an embryonic stage, is leading to the formation of new oppositional alliances. These alliances have started to develop new political and organizational imageries and to define new claims, new rights, and new entitlements. To an observer endowed with a stereotypical radical cynicism, the long period of neoliberal hegemony starting in the early 1980s may appear simply as a long period of working-class defeat. Certainly, many entitlements and many rights have been lost. However, to an observer who takes an historical perspective, these last twenty years cannot be synonymous only with defeat. A process of the *recomposition* of radical claims and social subjects has been underway, a process that is forcing every movement not only to seek alliances with others, but also to make the struggles of other movements their own, without any prior need to submit the demands of other movements to an ideological test. Unlike the times when communist and socialist organizations provided the hegemonic ideological frame of reference for many struggles, today the ideological frame of reference seems to be the ongoing *result* of the process of recomposition among different social subjects. The premise of this process of recomposition is the multidimensional reality of exploitative and oppressive relations as this is manifested in the lives and experiences of the many social subjects within the global economy. On its own, the heterogeneous character of this premise is not able to effectively confront the hegemonic and monolithic *pensée unique* that legitimizes neoliberal strategies. But the interaction among these social subjects on the various occasions of struggle creates an alternative mode of thinking, which is increasingly able to root the multidimensionality of human needs and aspirations in the universalism of the human condition. In a word, the process of social recomposition against neoliberal hegemony is creating a new philosophy of emancipation.

Indeed, the globalization of trade and production has contributed to widen the scope of the political aspirations of movements around the world (Waterman 1998). This can be seen in at least two major developments. In the first place, the great variety of movements in the last few decades, and the resistance within each movement against being subsumed within the neoliberal ideological discourse, is forcing the formation of new radical ideas and practices that attempt to encompass the basic aspirations of all movements. It is now impossible to define the basic elements of a progressive paradigm without testing it against the issues raised by the struggles of a great variety of social movements. The relief of poverty does not justify blind environmental destruction (thanks to the environmental movement); environmental protection does not justify the unemployment of thousands of workers (thanks to the labor movement); the protection of jobs does not justify the production of arms, instruments of torture, and yet more prisons (thanks to the human rights movement); the defense of "prosperity" does not justify the slaughter of indigenous peoples and their cultures (thanks to the movement of indigenous peoples); and so on with the movements of women, blacks and students, among others. The visibility of a great variety of contentious issues and aspirations leads of course to inevitable contradictions, the transcendence of which is the object of daily political practice, communication among movements, and the continuous formation of new alliances, which is helping to shape new political visions. For example, the acceleration and promotion of dialogue between grassroots labor activists and militant environmentalists, human-rights groups, women, etc. is shaping new political weapons. Activists are learning, for example, that cuts in the welfare state can be resisted on human rights grounds, thus leading not only to broader coalitions,[3] but also to shaping a more sweeping sense of what the movement is for, and imbuing it with a richer philosophical perspective.

In the second place, the globalization of trade and production has contributed to widening the scope of international alliances, bringing together the needs and aspiration of a great variety of social subjects across the globe. This was seen in the various movements that in these latest years opposed the processes of neoliberal globalization. These movements not only grew into increasingly organized and effective international networks of resistance against individual neoliberal strategies, but also initiated a social process of recomposition of civil society across the globe based on priorities that are not compatible with those of global capital. At the same time as capital's strategy of globalization is increasing the interdependence of different peoples around the world by heightening their vulnerability, movements are transforming their practice and transcending the distinction between national and international, making it less definite, less important.[4] Also, as more and more state functions are transferred to supranational state bodies, so too the struggle against these bodies (IMF/WB/WTO, etc.) is blurring the distinction between national and international.

The configuration of this new wave of international organizations was perhaps first recognizable in the struggle against the North America Free Trade Agreement (NAFTA). The Anti-NAFTA campaign represented the coming together of these different souls, forcing the official US labor bureaucracies to distance themselves from support of US foreign policy for the first time in history. The traditional AFL–CIO failure to back progressive movements and unions in Latin America and other Third World countries allowed US employers to pit workers in these countries against those in the United States.[5] Other international networks which combine both a greater scope for internationalism and the overlapping of different issues include: the "for humanity and against neoliberalism" network promoted by the Zapatistas, the insurgent indigenous people of the Mexican region of Chiapas;[6] other interfacing networks such as Peoples Global Action against the World Trade Organization (PGA), and the Action for Solidarity, Equality, Environment and Development (ASEED);[7] the networks against IMF, the World Bank and Third World debt;[8] the network against the proposed Multilateral Agreement on Investment (MAI) – which forced the OECD countries to postpone negotiations on global investment liberalization;[9] and the broad cross-issues and international alliance that brought about the collapse of the WTO millennium round in Seattle in December 1999.[10]

11.4   The current crisis and neoliberal opportunism

Within the context of the current global crisis, some governments and several commentators previously known for their "free market" stance appear to be desperately distancing themselves from their former positions, or at least from their most blatant rhetoric, and are now promoting either various forms of indigenous capitalism de-linked to various degrees from the global economy or policies with a Keynesian flavor. Thus, for example, in autumn 1998, the Malaysian government decided to move towards the imposition of capital controls, a policy that only a few months earlier would have been unthinkable. Similarly, "[a] number of ultra-free marketeers, formerly keen proponents of shock therapy, such as Jeffrey Sachs [*El Pais* 2/8/98], are now suggesting [that] in order to counter the immediate danger, ... [Japanese] banks should be nationalized!" (Ramonet 1998: 1). The dogma was cracked not so much by the "failure" of the neoliberal policies to provide prosperity, but by the fear that the resulting crisis could spin out of control and turn into a major socio–political problem of global proportions. Thus, by the beginning of September 1998, right after the Russian crisis, *Business Week* urged a plan of action not only for economic reasons, but for "geopolitical reasons," as

> The American model is under attack everywhere as the free market system is rolled back. Hong Kong, the epitome of laissez-faire capitalism, is intervening in the stock market to prop up the stocks of real estate tycoons. As a result, the government owns 10% of some of the biggest companies there. Taiwan effectively makes its currency nontradable as the government bails out businesses and intervenes in the stock market. Russia is toying with capital and currency controls, while Malaysia actually imposes them. Tokyo moves away from a market solution to its banking crisis and pressures Toyota Motor Corp. to bail out Sakura Bank Ltd. Everywhere the free market is increasingly perceived as the enemy of growth. Increasingly, nations are opting out. (Nussbaum 1998: 14)

Although the main neoliberal orthodoxy has not been dethroned, the specter of a global depression (and not only recession) is having its impact. Suddenly, even the bastions of neoliberal market rigor are finding suitable exceptions to the rule of capital mobility, to high interest rates that hold down inflation, to moral hazards that in principle would not justify the government spending billions of US tax dollars to finance bankrupted hedge funds and banks, to the rule of privatization for privatization's sake, etc. However, this is not a movement away from neoliberal ideology. Rather, it is the official declaration of neoliberal *opportunism* as the governing economic ideology. Like Nassau Senior, the liberal economist who justified state intervention on the basis of expediency,[11] or like Pigou who, despite the theoretical roots of his laissez-faire policies, promoted public expenditure in the midst of the Great Depression (see Chapter 2), modern neoliberal economists seem to be promoting some non-orthodox policies for a limited time to exorcise fears of a global economic collapse, and to limit the dangers that neoliberal practices could be blamed for the collapse itself.

11.5   The current crisis and the Keynesian alternative to neoliberal strategies

If neoliberal ideology is for the time being still strong, the persistence of the crisis will certainly promote an environment for useful discussion about the possible alternatives. The crisis will give those interested in limiting and threatening the cultural and political hegemony of *pensée unique* an almost epochal opportunity. I obviously cannot review here all the alternatives to the dogmas of neoliberal ideology. Since this book has discussed the historical evolution of Keynesianism and some of its basic features, and since the crisis has mobilized the memory of Keynes and the Great Depression in the columns of many commentators, I will here briefly discuss the question of the viability and desirability of a new Keynesianism at the dawn of the new millennium.

The viability of Keynesianism today

In the Introduction of this book, it was asked whether the Keynesian post-war experience could be repeated in the context of the current crisis. The retrospective analysis presented in this book suggests that Keynesianism (understood as an organic whole of coherent policies, rather than one or another aspect of these policies) would face enormous difficulties in the modern global context. Broadly speaking, in a closed economy, Keynesianism relies on at least two interlinked institutional pillars: expansionary demand policies to promote growth and employment creation, and a predictable and secure institutional environment making it possible to recuperate social conflict and to manage the spread between labor productivity and wages. In an open economy, a third pillar must be added to these two – that is, restrictions on capital movements.

If any of these parameters is missing, Keynesianism cannot be viable. However, the real issue comes down to the last two, which are the necessary *conditions* for systematic demand-led growth promotion policies to be viable. For example, if a government promotes full employment policies by increasing aggregate demand without at the same time utilizing a mechanism that disciplines the labor market, cost-push inflation will be the natural result (probably promoting Kalecki's political instability). In a context of open capital markets, the simple announcement of a government's Keynesian intentions may well be sufficient to bring the government to its knees via a massive capital outflow. It seems to me that there are at least two main constraints to the viability today of any Keynesian policies. The first is the existence of capital movements, and the second the nature of the labor market and the composition of the labor force.

Capital movements

It was seen in Chapter 9 that one of the rationales of capital movements is to bring a disciplinary device to bear on the spread between productivity and wages. Capital controls introduced by different countries in the context of global Keynesianism made sense (from the perspective of capital accumulation) precisely because in each country there was an alternative mechanism to regulate that spread, based on productivity deals. However, once this latter proved no longer sufficient to maintain stability, governments around the world tended to replace the promotion of labor bureaucracies with the promotion of financial capital deregulation.

The last twenty years have been characterized by a tremendous increase in the amount of money capital that has floated around the financial markets of the North. Also, the guardians of neoliberalism such as the IMF and World Bank have placed enormous pressure on the countries of the South to liberalize their financial markets and promote local stock markets and capital inflow. In 1995, while world exports of goods and services totaled about $6.1 trillion, the *daily* foreign exchange market turnover amounted to about $1.2 trillion – that is, about 50 times as much annually. Tables 11.1–11.3 give an indication of the remarkable size reached by international financial capital movements.

Table 11.1 shows that the flow of foreign portfolio investment has been staggering, even in relation to foreign direct investment (FDI) flows. Table 11.2 indicates the remarkable growth of non-residents' holdings of public debt, and Table 11.3 shows the steep increase in cross-border transactions in bonds and equities as a percentage of GDP. While in 1975, during the crisis of Keynesianism, cross-border transactions in bonds and equities were a negligible percentage of GDP (ranging from 1 per cent in the case of Italy to 5 percent in the case of Germany), in 1997 these have reached phenomenal levels: in the case of Italy, more than six times greater than GDP.

All these data are clear indications of the degree of financial integration reached and therefore of the full exposure of national economies to the whims of financial markets and to security owners with no particular "national allegiance." No government can afford to upset speculators with policies that are not compatible with the priorities set by international capital.

Table 11.1 Gross and net flows of foreign direct and portfolio investment, 1970–97[a]: major industrial countries

	1970	1975	1980	1985	1990	1995	1996	1997
Gross flows								
Foreign direct investment	14.45	34.25	82.82	75.94	283.24	369.01	357.53	448.32
Portfolio investment	5.26	27.10	60.58	233.44	329.63	764.34	1182.64	1040.19
Net flows								
Foreign direct investment	-4.05	-9.98	-8.14	-12.66	-59.58	-33.18	-87.14	-92.60
Portfolio investment	1.42	8.53	16.02	25.03	41.36	186.53	287.37	272.51

Note:
[a]Group of Seven Countries.
Source: International Monetary Fund, *Balance of Payments Statistics Yearbook*, and Institute of International Finance (1998).

Table 11.2 Non-residents' holdings of public debt, 1983–97[a] (percent of total public debt)

Year	USA	Japan	Germany	Italy	UK	Canada	Belgium
1983	14.9	...	14.1	...	...	10.7	13.2
1984	15.4	...	14.6	...	7.2	11.3	14.6
1985	15.2	3.7	16.3	...	7.0	12.4	13.9
1986	16.1	3.3	20.1	...	8.0	16.1	14.7
1987	16.6	3.3	21.2	...	10.7	15.5	15.5
1988	18.4	2.0	20.7	...	12.2	15.7	17.5
1989	20.8	3.0	22.1	...	13.7	16.3	19.2
1990	20.1	4.4	20.9	4.4	14.7	17.4	19.3
1991	20.1	5.8	23.1	5.2	15.2	19.0	22.7
1992	20.4	5.5	25.6	6.2	17.6	20.2	21.5
1993	22.2	5.4	32.8	10.1	19.6	21.8	23.3
1994	22.8	5.9	25.9	12.2	20.7	22.6	21.4
1995	28.3	4.3	28.2	13.2	18.8	23.3	21.5
1996	35.0	4.3	29.3	15.9	...	23.8	20.8
1997	40.1	...	...	...	...	23.1	21.9

Note: [a] End of year data; definitions vary across countries.
Sources: Bank for International Settlements and Institute of International Finance (1998).

Table 11.3 Cross-border transactions in bonds and equities, 1975–97[a]: selected major industrial countries (percent of GDP)

Country	1975	1980	1985	1989	1990	1993	1995	1996	1997
USA	4	9	35	101	89	129	135	160	213
Japan	2	8	62	156	119	78	65	79	96
Germany	5	7	33	66	57	170	172	199	253
France	...	5	21	32	54	187	187	258	313
Italy	1	1	4	18	27	192	253	470	672
Canada	3	9	27	55	65	153	189	251	358

Note:
[a]Gross purchases and sales of securities between residents and non-residents.
Source: Bank for International Settlements and Institute of International Finance (1998).

In terms of economic policy, the result, it is known, has been the handicapping of monetary policy and its inability to manage interest rates for internal purposes without affecting exchange rates. For example, in case of a mild deflation of the economy, the Central Bank could boost the economy by reducing the rate of discount. But in an open and well integrated financial market in which capitals are free to come and go as easily as the pressing of a key, a reduction in interest rates would be followed by a capital outflow and consequent fall in the exchange rate. Not only would the increase in the cost of imports perhaps counteract the fall in interest rates and therefore contribute to rendering the Central Bank policy ineffective (this of course depends on the elasticity of import), but an obvious element of instability would also be introduced into the system. How much capital is withdrawn following the Central Bank policy? How much "trust" in the country is forgone, with an unpredictable impact for the future? All this is really a matter of "speculation."[12]

Speculative capital flows also play a role in controlling and disciplining government fiscal policy. In particular, as we have seen, the neoliberal dogma requires that governments put public expenditures under control, especially current expenditures, and engage in structural reforms such as the privatization of services and industries. Also, the neoliberal era has witnessed a systematic attack on a series of entitlements that were central to the rise of the Keynesian era. Welfare state pillars, such as state pensions, education, health provisions, various forms of unemployment benefits and income support, have all been undermined. Movements of speculative capital also threaten any government that, under particular pressure from some interest group in civil society, would be willing to concede even a partial return to the traditional Keynesian path. Thus, a return to systematic Keynesian policies depends on the regulation of capital movements in such a way as to give more space to national governments to pursue expansionary policies.

How, then, could capital movements be curtailed? Here I want to discuss two different proposals: the first, a mild tax on capital movements, and the second, a radical redesign of the international financial system.

One of the most debated proposals to limit the movement of speculative capital flow is the so-called "Tobin tax." This is a tax levied on foreign exchange transactions and takes its name from James Tobin, who proposed it (Tobin 1974, 1978; Eichengreen, Tobin, and Wyplosz 1995, among others). It has been pointed out that there are three main rationales for the Tobin tax (Arestis and Sawyer 1997: 753–5). In the first place, this tax would be essentially a small transaction tax that would penalize short-term round-trip movements of speculative capital, thus helping to "put grains of sand in the wheels of international finance" (Eichengreen, Tobin and Wyplosz 1995). In this way, the Tobin tax would curb the profitability of short-term speculation and allow exchange rates to better reflect long-term factors in the real economy rather than short-term speculative flows. The second rationale is based on the greater autonomy this tax would give governments in pursuing economic policies, by being shielded from financial market discipline on domestic fiscal and monetary policy. Finally, the third rationale for such a tax is its revenue-raising potential. According to a UN study, a Tobin tax of merely 0.05 percent could raise $150 billion a year (United Nations 1994: 9).

What interests us here is of course the first rationale – that is, the capability of this transaction tax to serve as a restraint on international capital flows. This is indeed the main reason for discussing a Tobin-type tax. The second rationale is nothing but a consequence of the first, and the third one is an incidental result. The Tobin tax could certainly be welcomed on the ground that it serves to find resources that could be used for more honorable and ethically sounder activities than international speculation. But for this purpose a Tobin tax would merely be one among many possible ways to tax high and capital income.

The real question is whether the Tobin tax could restrain short-term capital mobility. Perhaps the most interesting contribution to this debate was provided by Paul Davidson (1997), who focused not on the practicality of the tax but rather on its theoretical foundations. According to Davidson, the Tobin tax will not make it possible to reduce international speculation, but at most arbitrage. He convincingly argues that as the Tobin tax is a transaction cost, it is "independent of the round-trip time interval" (Davidson 1997: 675). This goes against the impression given by the proponents of the tax that a small tax rate (Tobin proposed 0.05 percent, this being the "small grain of sand" in the wheels of international finance) would convert to larger rates in direct proportion to the frequency of speculative trips. According to its proponents, the tax would discourage short-term capital movements and encourage long-term investment, as the total tax levied would increase with the number of trips within a certain time interval. However, in order for the tax to operate as a disincentive to capital movements, the speculators' expected change in assets price should be lower than the very low Tobin tax. Thus Davidson concludes that

> the imposition of a Tobin tax *per se* will not significantly stifle even very short-run speculation if there is any whiff of a weak currency in the market. In fact, any Tobin tax significantly less than 100% of the *expected capital gain* (on a round trip) is unlikely to stop the sloshing around of hot money. (Davidson 1997: 678)

Thus, taking for example the case of the fall of the Mexican peso during the crisis of 1994–5, in which the peso fell by about 60 percent, a Tobin tax of about 23 percent would have been required to stop speculative run on the peso.[12]

Paul Davidson himself (Davidson 1992, 1997) provides a more radical proposal for the regulation of international finance. Following the idea behind Keynes' original plan during the Bretton Woods negotiations, the central theme inspiring Davidson's proposal is the

> need for a permanent currency fire prevention institution rather than merely relying on either fire-fighting intervention such as the suggested Emergency Fund financed by contributions of the G7 nations and managed by the IMF, or a laissez-faire policy on international capital markets that can produce currency fires to burn the free world's real economies. (Davidson 1997: 679–80)

The proposal is built upon two pillars. First, a unit of account and ultimate reserve asset for international liquidity called the International Money Clearing Unit (IMCU). No other liquid assets would be allowed to serve as reserves for international financial transactions. Second, a mechanism that puts the burden of adjustment in international finance on countries experiencing surplus in their trade balance rather than, as it is currently the case, on countries in deficit. Individual countries' Central Banks would be the sole holders of IMCUs, and they alone would be able to sell them among themselves or the International Clearing Agency. This implies that there cannot be any draining of reserves from the system, since all major private transactions are cleared between central banks in the books of the International Clearing Agency. Thus, no country could be exposed to a liquidity crunch owing to short-term speculative movements of financial capital. A system of fixed exchange rates would be put in place and international contracts would be denominated in the national currency. Any adjustment of the nominal exchange rates would be allowed only to reflect changes in the real costs of production – that is, the relation between productivity and wages in each country. Thus, competitive advantage could not be pursued by competitive devaluation, but by real factors in the economy.

While short-term imbalances between countries could be managed through an overdraft mechanism at the International Clearing Agency, allowing unused resources to finance short-term credit, the real innovation would be the setting up of a mechanism that encourages surplus nations to spend money and generate demand for countries in deficit. Surplus countries could do this in three possible ways: (a) by increasing the import demand of goods and services from deficit countries; (b) by increasing the flow of FDI to countries in deficit; (c) by providing unilateral transfers such as aid or grants to countries in deficit. A combination of these three is of course also possible. The key point is that under this provision

> deficit countries would no longer have to deflate their real economy merely to adjust payment imbalances because others are over-saving. Instead, the system would seek to remedy the payment deficit by increasing opportunities for deficit nations to sell abroad and thereby earn their way out of the deficit. (Davidson 1997: 682)

Contrary to the dominant neoliberal efficient market theory, according to which the role of international capital markets is to ensure efficiency, Davidson's proposal stems from the thesis that the role of financial capital markets is to provide liquidity. His plan is thus aimed at ensuring that the global productive machine never runs out of oil, and that a crisis could never take the form of a liquidity crisis. There are, however, some major problems with this proposal.

In the first place, in the context of a competitive global economy geared towards production for profit, liquidity crunches may well be a necessary requirement to ensure that standards of competitiveness or movements towards further global integration are *enforced*. Liquidity crises are always accompanied by negotiations about conditions between debtors on the one side and creditors and international institutions on the other. The latter are generally willing to either reschedule debt repayment or inject new liquidity in the forms of new loans only on the condition that structural reforms affecting both the openness of the country to global capital and the basic parameters of accumulation are implemented. But the implementation of these reforms leads of course to a confrontation with civil society, as the conditions always entail some form of reduction in the social wage, abolition of entitlements, and so on. It is for this reason that the ability of national governments to present this as a necessity posed by external objective factors (such as a liquidity crisis and its consequences) is of paramount importance for the legitimization of unpopular reforms. In other words, without liquidity crises, or the threatened risk of liquidity crises, governments and national capitals would be more vulnerable to those forces in society that have do not have efficiency, competitiveness, and global integration as their priority, but the simple protection of entitlements and rights. Liquidity crises in this sense are used by global financial institutions as *disciplinary devices* coherently linked to the priorities of capitalist accumulation and its contested nature.

A second weakness in Davidson's argument can be seen in the mechanism that puts the onus of adjustment on countries in surplus. As noted, this could take the form of a purchase of imports from countries in deficit, FDI or grants and aid. This principle is linked to the previous one – that is, the need to guarantee a well oiled international economic system and avoid liquidity crises. Let us suppose the surplus countries aim at increasing imports from the deficit countries as per Davidson's proposal. A first problem can be seen by reflecting upon the reasons for the trade deficit. Within the framework of a competitive global economy, to the extent that trade deficits are caused by problems in the competitiveness of the traded goods of deficit countries, then it is contrary to any economic logic for surplus countries to increase their imports from deficit countries. Why would consumers and producers in the surplus countries have to buy goods that are relatively more expensive and/or of poorer quality than, say, commodities that are domestically produced or supplied by another more competitive country? But perhaps surplus countries could increase the imports of those commodities that are not produced domestically. Again, this would require either, first, that deficit countries were the sole international suppliers of that commodity, or, second, that they were able to supply them on competitive terms. As any lack in this second condition leads us back to the problem of economic logic mentioned before, the first condition would be a very unlikely case of absolute monopoly, which would allow the monopolist country to reap an economic rent. Alternatively, Davidson's proposal could imply the promotion of exports in commodities in which the country has a relative advantage. This case, however, is vulnerable to all the traditional criticisms stressing the socioeconomic devastation and the vicious cycle of dependency linked to export promotion for countries with a limited range of internationally tradable goods.

The mechanism of adjustment could take the form of capital movements from surplus countries to deficit countries in the form of FDI. However, for these to take the form of planned long-term investments, the deficit countries need to be able to guarantee a stable economic and political environment suitable for increases in competitiveness, and thus profitability, which is the ultimate attractor of foreign investment. In principle, then, FDI cannot be the solution to a persistent trade deficit, but itself *presupposes* that structural reforms are implemented so as to attract FDI. These structural reforms are precisely the ones that follow a liquidity crisis and are embedded within the logic of financial deregulation, unless another institutional mechanism can be used.

The last of the instruments proposed is aid and grants from surplus to deficit countries. First, we are here entering the realm of discretionary policy, constrained by the amount of resources available to use as aid and grants, and by the political and economic motivations of the economic agents (banks, multinational corporations, governments, etc.) that have surplus resources at their disposal. It is known that unilateral transfers of resources from surplus to deficit countries often come with "strings attached," which aim at subordinating the deficit countries' domestic social, political and economic priorities to those of the donor countries.[14] This is, of course, the basic condition for continuing the perpetual vicious cycle of dependency and poverty in which many countries of the South are caught. Furthermore, scholars studying the new aid agenda warns us that rather than pursuing the old developmentalist goal of "incorporation" of peripheral areas into the world system, today aid is instrumental for policies of management and containment of politically insecure territories on the edge of the global economy (Duffield 1996). The idea is that aid today is increasingly used to improve "governance" in the technocratic speak of World Bank and IMF – that is, with the aim of providing a political and social environment suitable to neoliberal economic reforms. In this sense, unlike in the past in which the recipients of aid were national governments, today aid targets a plurality of actors, NGOs, businesses, communities and their grassroots organizations. The leverage exercised through aid (and the threat of its withdrawal) therefore directly meddles with national internal affairs. The general principle encompassing old and new aid agenda therefore is the following: to the extent there is a political economic rationale for aid, the resulting dependency is a tools in the hand of vested interests. Aid could serve to address the problem of international imbalances only to the extent that a mechanism of *expropriation* of financial resources from surplus to deficit countries is set in place. However, such a case would be compatible only with a framework of international political economy that is not geared toward competitive production and trade liberalization, which is the framework assumed by Davidson's analysis.

In conclusion, paradoxically, the fundamental flaw of Davidson's proposal seems ultimately to reside in his deeper grasp of the contradictions of capitalist production *vis-à-vis* mainstream economic theory. Unlike neo-classical theory, his approach recognizes the conflictual nature of capitalist production, but stops at the phenomenal recognition of this conflict and, once economic policy proposals are made, urges solutions which imply nothing less than the wishing away of the essential nature of this conflict and these contradictions. In order to solve the resulting circularity, the analysis engages in a normative twist:

> The alternatives to a peacefully coordinated income and exchange rate policy for affecting income distribution are a Darwinian free market struggle in which the resulting stagflation is likely to impoverish most of the inhabitants or a bloody political revolution. Darwinian struggles as well as political revolutions *should be banished as uncivilized behavior in real world democratic systems*. The existence of large economic entities and/or groups with significant economic power sufficient to devastate the economic landscape if a struggle should break out, threaten the basis of any productive entrepreneurial system and the standards of living of all its inhabitants. (Davidson 1992: 248, my emphasis)

Haw can anybody ban "Darwinian free market struggles" or "political revolutions" from history, when the social relations of production themselves are a locus of conflict? For example, how is it possible to ban "Darwinian free market struggles" without infringing the interests of those who prosper from them? And how can these interests be infringed without at the same time turning the defenders of these interests into a *danger* for society, as they react to protect their interests? Davidson's proposed "ban" implicitly addresses this problem, with a call for reason and the promise of prosperity through growth:

The rich and powerful should adopt a view of *noblesse oblige* towards those lower down in the economic distribution, while the poor must not act on the basis of a "misery loves company" view which delights in reducing all to the lowest common denominator. Instead, those in the lower ranks of the distribution of income must recognize that greater net gains are most likely to be achieved within an entrepreneurial system of co-operation and growth which fosters equitable changes at a rate which is compatible with the social conscience of most. Education, not extermination, of the rich is necessary if the latter are unaware of the needs of the poor. (Davidson 1992: 249)

Thus, the bottom-line rationale for replacing neoliberal economic rationality and inducing countries in surplus to shoulder the burden of adjustment is a moral call combining *noblesse oblige* for the rich with education (aimed at the acceptance of the capitalist rules of the game) for the poor, in other words, a reconciliation among the classes based not on the transcendence of a social system reproducing classes, but on the acceptance of the optimality of this system. Thus, the recognition of conflict is not as an ontological reality of the capitalist relations of production that *needs* to be transcended by a radically different social organization, but as an unnecessary nuisance that *should* be stopped so society can grow and prosper.[15] The historical and political short-comings of this position are revealed when we consider how, unlike individuals, the social roles borne by economic agents within capitalist production cannot be subjected to normative prescriptions. The social roles themselves must be reformed. Also, the priority given to growth and its uncritical association with prosperity reflects an unfortunate acceptance of the all-pervasive economic dogma of growth for growth's sake, a dogma sadly linked not with the promotion of prosperity, but of prosperity *and* poverty, development *and* underdevelopment, as with all the other contradictions of capitalist accumulation.

Class composition

Capitalist accumulation requires that the conflict inherent in capitalist social relations be dealt with not simply through moral calls, but by bringing about an institutional social environment to regulate and manage that conflict, hence another reason why a traditional Keynesian solution cannot be a sustainable scenario for world accumulation today. It relies heavily on institutions other than the market to regulate class relations (expressed in terms of the

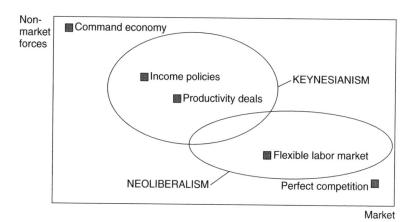

Figure 11.1   Governing the parameters of accumulation ($\pi - w$)

management of the spread between social productivity and social wage). Indeed, capitalist production can be pursued only by managing this relation, and the form of this management always lies in an intermediate position between pure non-market and pure market management. In Figure 11.1, I provide a brief illustration of this point.

On the horizontal and vertical axis of the box, I (figuratively) measure respectively the role of market and non-market forces in the regulation of the spread between productivity and wages at the social level. The two extreme positions are a purely state-regulated command economy and an economy with perfect competition. Both these cases are of course mythical, as the market or non-market forces (such as the state, a dominant political party, the unions, etc.) not only never dominate exclusively, but also are mutually reinforcing.[16] Union-managed productivity deals and, when these were not effective, income policies, were two major ways for the management of class relations at the social level during Keynesianism, and as we have seen they both presupposed a strong presence of bureaucratic unions and state intervention in one way or another. However, the process of the restructuring and globalization of production has contributed enormously not only to weaken the grassroots militancy of Fordist-type workers, but also to form a new market-driven system for managing the parameters of accumulation.

State-promoted market deregulation has provided greater competition within labor markets through the pursuit of labor market flexibility. Competition and flexibility are in turn becoming central pillars for the regulation of the parameters of accumulation at the social level, through such well known phenomena as the casualization of labor, the extensive use of part-time work, reductions in rights and entitlements, the implementation of workfare regimes, and so on. In those sectors in which a union presence is still important, flexibility can be obtained also through negotiations. In these negotiations, however, the starting point is the trade unions' compliance with market realities, rather than market adaptation to the bargaining strength of unions in different sectors, as was often the case during the Keynesian period. Within the context of the neoliberal period, the role of the state and unions is thus still important, but in a different way than during the "golden age" of Keynesianism. The state acts as an agent promoting the market, both domestically (for example, through reforms of the welfare state aimed at eliciting competition among discouraged unemployed, as in the case of workfare experiments in the United States and Britain) and in the international arena (through the shaping of global institutions such as the WTO, free trade areas such as the European Union and NAFTA, failed agreements such as MAI, and the management of international money and debt through the IMF, etc.). Whether as a result of a process of state decollectivization in employment relations or greater individualism in employment or society at large (Williams 1997), official unions, where they are present, are expected to function more as defenders of the rights of individual members, rather than as institutions for the regulation and recuperation of collective action. Also, in the context of an increasingly competitive global economy, the official unions' role is increasingly becoming that of a "partner" to management for the implementation of "lean" production strategies (Moody 1997) to better face the competition.

Going back to the viability of systematic Keynesian policies today, it must be pointed out that the fragmentation within the labor market brought about by the extreme casualization of work, the increased dispersion of production not only across a region or a nation, but throughout the world economy, makes trade unions (in their function of representing and recuperating grassroots demands) ineffective. Vertically structured trade unions can demand wage increases in exchange for productivity increases only to the extent they have a leverage on a large workforce concentrated in major industries (see, for example, the discussion of grievance procedures in Chapter 7 p. 90). When production is increasingly dispersed geographically and labor contracts are increasingly casualized, market forces have thus far served accumulation much better than large vertical hierarchical unions. Although the traditional scope for labor organization (gaining collective strength *vis-à-vis* powerful profit-driven forces in society) is currently stronger than ever (with a large casualized, part-time section utterly unorganized), the current form taken by the new unionization is far from being compatible with the top-down management of the parameters of accumulation. The new character of grassroots organizational drives is anti-hierarchical and for horizontal forms of organization, with a strong push to build alliances that are multi-issue and cross national barriers (Moody 1997; Waterman 1998).

Where does this leave Keynesianism? If we accept Kalecki's thesis, according to which full employment brings about a political problem concerning the stability of class relations and the parameters of accumulation, then from the perspective of capitalist accumulation, full employment policies cannot be systematically promoted without a strong institutional setting that provides the required stability. The Keynesian era in the West found a form of governing class relations through state and official labor unions. But today, after two decades of neoliberal restructuring, these classical mechanisms of representation, governance, and mediation of class relations are not and cannot be made operational, because of the diminished presence of official unions and their changed role. Furthermore, "the working class" itself has taken on characteristics that it did not have during the Fordist period. The working class is today more structurally fragmented and divided, with an income hierarchy that cuts along not only domestic but also international lines. Exposed to the titanic yet seemingly impersonal force of global competition and integrated within a chain of production that recognizes no borders, this new working class cannot be systematically turned into a force enhancing the growth of *domestic* capital. This is for at least three reasons (Caffentzis 1998).

First, it is becoming less and less relevant to talk about domestic capital and a domestic working class. For example, capital *owned* by US citizens is increasingly employed abroad not only for the commercialization of products in foreign markets, but even in their own domestic market. Also, workers employed by US capital (what used to be considered the US working class) increasingly include non-US citizens. It must be noted that the effect of this globalization of capital and labor power on the power relations shaping wages and productivity greatly depends on the real and perceived *threat* of capital mobility rather than simply on the absolute amount of national capital actually located abroad. This threatened mobility can in fact be used as a disciplinary device in wage settlements.

Second, and consequently, in the context of the global market, the increasing importance of export-oriented production allows employers still located within the national borders room to escape the constraints of workers' domestic purchasing power.

Third, global competition allows wages to be cheapened not only because of the wage restraint obtained by greater competition in the labor market, but also because of the cheapening of the commodities entering the wage basket and flooding the global economy. Import-consumption is thus part of a process reducing what Marx would call the value of labor power.

These three interrelated factors represent a mechanism for the regulation of the parameters of accumulation in ways that are incompatible with traditional Keynesian solutions. Domestic markets are increasingly being replaced by global markets as sites to realize sales. Productivity deals have been replaced by real or threatened capital movements to curb workers' wage aspirations and enforce productive discipline. From the perspective of neoliberal capital accumulation today, a return to systematic Keynesian policies would imply the dismantling of the composition of the global working class, the promotion of bureaucratic structures for its representation, and the establishment of a global productivity deal. Such a titanic enterprise would certainly run counter in many ways to the interests of the corporate and financial elite who rule the global economy today.

11.5   What then?

The previous discussion has emphasized that a return to the basic elements of Keynesian orthodoxy, even in a form that is compatible with the current global economy, could only with great difficulty represent a solution to the problems we face today. As the analysis of the social multiplier has shown, both the extension of aggregate demand (as emphasized by the Keynesians) and the parameters of accumulation (as emphasized by the supply-siders of various backgrounds) are strategic variables of capitalist relations. It is the existence of these capitalist relations of production that constitutes the problem. Critics of the mainstream neoliberal orthodoxy have for far too long focused on the problems raised by economic fluctuations and the business cycle, with its disruptive ups and downs, rather than on a critique of the underlying rationales of the cycle – that is, the regulation of the contradictions of a society geared to profit-making. Certainly, if the modern social movements mentioned earlier gain momentum and are able to build alliances in such a way as to force the question of radical political transformation back on the historical agenda, things could be different. In this case, it is worth asking whether the corporate and financial elite ruling the global economy may want to consider the possibility of a global Keynesianism for the twenty-first century as a way to recuperate these movements in a manner analogous to what the old Keynesianism did to the movements at the beginning of the twentieth century. Thus, at this point, we can ask the question: assuming systematic Keynesian policies of growth promotion were possible, would they be desirable? Again, it is important to say, at the risk of repetition, that here I am not talking about growth policies for this or that sector, or this or that area. I am talking about Keynesian-style growth policies as a pervasive principle of economic management in society.

Paradoxically enough, Keynes himself urges us to answer negatively to the question of the desirability of Keynesian policies today. The rationale for this answer is not based on short-run macropolicy considerations, but on a deeper reflection on the human condition and the potential for human emancipation embedded in the level reached by the productive power of labor, by society's knowledge and its potential ability to tackle its most fundamental problems. In his "Economic Possibilities for our Grandchildren," published in 1930, Keynes dared to abandon the short run with its associated sense of urgency and took an historical perspective, as he reflected on what would constitute the "economic problem" one hundred years hence – only thirty years from now! In this essay, Keynes moves from the problem of *technological unemployment*, which he describes as "a new disease of which some readers may not yet have heard the name, but of which they will hear a great deal in the years to come" (Keynes 1930b: 325). Technological unemployment is "unemployment due to our discovery of means of economizing the use of labor outrunning the pace at which we can find new uses for labor" (Keynes 1930b: 325). However, technological unemployment is for Keynes only the reflection of a "temporary phase of maladjustment" because, in the long run, the accumulation of the discoveries of means to economize the use of labor implies that *"mankind is solving its economic problem"* (Keynes 1930b: 325, original emphasis). By economic problem Keynes means the problem of satisfying what he defines as absolute needs, that is, those human needs that "we feel ... whatever the situation of our fellow human beings may be," as compared to the relative needs "in the sense that we feel them only if their satisfaction lifts us above, makes us feel superior to, our fellows" (Keynes 1930b: 326). For Keynes, it is this latter kind of needs that may well be insatiable, but not the former. Technological development enables humanity precisely to reduce the amount of work necessary to satisfy absolute needs, and thus would give people the freedom to choose whether to continue working in order to run after a moving goal-post, or rather dedicate themselves to less mundane and more humanly meaningful activities.

In this essay, Keynes was predicting a three-hour shift or a fifteen-hour week in thirty years' time from today, not because it will be necessary to work so much, but simply because "the old Adam will be so strong in us that everybody will need to do *some* work if he is to be contented" (Keynes 1930b: 328). But if we look carefully, we don't even need to wait thirty years. Keynes was looking into the future by assuming that "the standard of life in progressive countries" would increase between four and eight times. In the United States, for example, real GDP measured in 1992 dollars was almost $720 billion in 1930, and almost $7270 billion in 1997, ten times higher, while measured in terms of real GDP *per capita*, the "standard of life" has increased almost five times in the same period.

However, today, especially in the Anglo–Saxon world, mainstream public debates very seldom address what Keynes called "the economic problem." Yet, the information revolution and the developments in communication technologies have enormously extended the frontiers of our potentials as society and as individuals within that society. In principle, the resolution of the fundamental economic problem need be postponed no longer; we do not need to wait until proper growth rates are obtained, or until this or that target of economic integration is reached, or until the "proper" structural adjustment program and "proper" standards of competitiveness are met. In fact, all such goals are ways that will not only postpone the solution of the economic problems, but also exacerbate them. The United Nation (1998) estimates that the wealth of the three (!) richest people on earth equals that of the 49 poorest countries. It also estimates that the abolition of global famine would cost a mere 4 percent of the wealth of the largest economies. Isn't this a price worth paying? The answer is "yes," if human needs are at the center of our perspective. The answer is "no," if we are pervaded with the humanly "absurd" position that prioritizes money over life.

But this is only the tip of the iceberg. The real issue is not *simply* income redistribution, although this does need urgent tackling, especially after twenty years of world-wide neoliberal policies that have made the rich richer and the poor poorer. The real issue is *existential*, the issue of the "purposiveness" of our toiling (and therefore of its methods, extension, and results) in the potentially plentiful dawn of the twenty-first century. Here again, Keynes is enlightening. He predicts that the liberation from toil will enable us

> to afford to dare to assess the money-motive at its true value. The love of money as a possession – as distinguished from the love of money as a means to the enjoyments and realities of life – will be recognized for what it is, a somewhat disgusting morbidity, one of those semi-criminal, semi-pathological propensities which one hands over with a shudder to the specialists in mental disease. (Keynes 1930b: 329)

It must be noted that the object of Keynes' "disgust" here is not only the passion for money of the rentier, but also of the industrialist, the trader, in brief of whoever and whatever institution is engaged in accumulation, in the pursuit of monetary profit, the *pursuit of money for money's sake.*[17] In this, his definition of "money as a possession" is similar to Marx's definition of *money as capital* – that is, money thrown into circulation not in order to satisfy a need, but *in order to* make more money. Capitalist society is indeed organized around the accumulation of this abstract wealth, which in turn is translated into the pursuit of growth for growth's sake. However, unlike Marx, Keynes is not able to see the ontological substance of this inherently boundless drive for wealth creation. For Keynes, this true question of "microfoundation" is a question only of quantitative measure detached from the quality of what is to be measured. Thus, while for Marx the immanent measure of value (what he calls "socially necessary labor time") is the quantitative expression of an inhuman and alien reality constituting the qualitative aspect of the substance of value (what he calls "abstract labor") (De Angelis 1995), for Keynes efficiency wages and labor measure economic quantities with no link to a social "substance."

For this fundamental reason, Keynes' prediction that technical progress would automatically liberate humanity from unnecessary toil and the economic problem is naive. To the extent that the world is dominated by the humanly "absurd" profit motive, and since the substance of this profit is unpaid *labor*, more technology and higher productivity is the cause not of higher, but lower social profits, as Marx's insight about the tendency of the rate of profit to fall reminds us. And this implies that in society today there are strong forces that, instead of directing technological development to address human problems, will attempt to counterbalance the corresponding fall in profitability by exacerbating these problems. Reducing entitlements and wages, expanding global competition, shifting production to lower wage areas, increasing the intensity of labor, using child labor and other forms of bonded and modern slave labor, and the commodification of an increasing number of spheres of life at a planetary level, etc. – these are just some of the form taken by these "counter-tendencies."

The fact that the "discovery of means of economizing the use of labor" outruns "the pace at which we can find new uses for labor" (Keynes 1930b: 325) does not simply imply short-term technological unemployment and the long-run solution to the economic problem of humanity, as Keynes puts it. On the contrary, it means that at any point in the path of capitalist development, humanity is at a cross-roads, and the choice, so to speak, is between the continuation of the humanly "absurd" (poverty in the midst of plenty, overwork for some and unemployment for others, famine in the midst of plentiful resources) or tackling things by the roots. Humanity is now once again facing that crossroads.

We must, however, acknowledge that in his essay Keynes forces us to touch upon the fundamental character of the human condition in our age. This character is, as already noted, permeated with *absurdity* which, as the French philosopher Albert Camus put it (1942), describes the situation of modern humanity as strangers in an inhuman world. It is the absurdity of extreme poverty amidst plenty, of famine next to warehouses full of food, of overstressed commuters and workers worried about *their* economic problems in a society that could guarantee dignified lives for all at a fraction of the amount of work that the "privileged" employed are currently required to do. Absurdity of course does not mean irrational. The state of current contradictions, which are simply the multiplication of those existing at the time of Keynes' writing, are perfectly *rational* from the perspective of social priorities that are not *simply* the satisfaction of human needs, but the satisfaction of human needs *in forms and measures compatible with capital accumulation*. In other words, the capitalist form of satisfying human needs imposes a *limit* to how and how much of these needs can be satisfied. Demand within capitalism is always *effective* demand, demand for use-values backed by money in the hands of private individuals, rather than human demand backed by the social power of labor. Precisely because technological development is not neutral, but a site of conflict between the rationale of profit-making and the rationale of needs, it can only provide the horizon for human liberation, a set of opportunities, it can never automatically lead society to transcend its "love for money as a possession."

Today, the perspective of the humanly "absurd," of the passion for money and growth for growth's sake, still pervades the spectrum of economic policies proposed by neoliberal orthodoxy and even by many of its vehement critics. They thus fail to acknowledge that Keynes' long run is now upon us, infusing the present with a renewed sense of urgency, that of addressing the core problems of our human condition. These problems surely often need to be tackled by growth (in the sense of *more* health services and structures, *more* convivial public spaces, *more* structures addressing basic needs, *more* entitlements, *more* democracy, and so on), but at the same time many of the problems facing humanity today will also have to be addressed by decline (in the sense of *less* arms production, *less* automobile production, *less* packaging and advertisement, *less* commercialization of life, *less* financial trading, *less* working time, and so on). The fundamental political question is thus a question of vision and the criteria of selection, and it is all played out in the contrast between the humanly absurd vision that subordinates everything to accumulation, and the vision that takes humanity and its natural context as its only worthy principle of social organization.

Notes

1 Introduction: the social meaning of economics

1. However, this must be qualified in at least two ways. First, the ongoing and profound involvement of governments in the economy has made it impossible to fully exorcise the ghost of Keynes. As James K. Galbraith (1994–5) has argued, the anti-Keynesianism of the last few decades is indeed a form of repressed Keynesianism. Governments have pursued the stimulation of fiscal policies in pre-electoral years or have engaged in what Galbraith calls NIMB ("not in my budget") Keynesianism, which occurs when "U.S. authorities habitually enjoin Germany and Japan to run larger budget deficits so as to stimulate global growth and U.S. exports" (Galbraith 1994–5: 258). Second, different forms of more "self-conscious" Keynesianism are increasingly put forward, in the face of the disastrous human, social and economic consequences of neoliberal policies. Many economists have attempted to revive Keynesianism by arguing for its continued validity. They remain confident in classical fiscal stimulus policies and adduce evidence to disprove the alleged domestic and international "crowding out" effect (see, for example Fazzari 1994–5), among others.

2 The making of the Keynesianism of Keynes

1. For a discussion of different nuances taken by classic economic liberalism from Smith through Senior, Bentham, J.S. Mill and Marshall see Frankel (1979).
2. Thus, for example, ancient Greek's wisdom says through the voice of Achilles, whose soul whispers to Odysseus from the darkness of Avernus:

   > Odysseus, don't console me for my death. *I'd rather be a serve and serf another*, some poor man who has not enough to live on, than be the lord of all the dead who've perished. (Odyssey, XI. 487–491, my emphasis)

   To have a price is to be dependent upon another person's personal whim and command. This is so despicable that the second worst after being dead appears to be, in Achilles's words, "to be a serf and serve another." The tradition that regards labour as despicable (and therefore its "price" as unworthy for human beings) continues in different forms and nuances up to the Calvinist and Lutheran cultural revolution. For an historical survey see, for example, the first two chapters of De Grazia (1994).
3. According to Fetter (1977), Keynes *invented* Lenin's statement. This is another indication of how the revolutionary threat – symbolised here by the figure of Bolshevism and Lenin – played a substantial role in the construction of the economic discourse.

4. "The party of Catastrophe – Jacobins, Communists, Bolsheviks, whatever you choose to call them – ... can only flourish in an atmosphere of social oppression or as a reaction against the Rule of Die-Hard" (Keynes 1925a: 299).
5. See also (Keynes 1925b).
6. For an account of the general strike see, for example, Morris (1976).
7. See also the testimony of R.H. Harrod (1951: 375).
8. The letter was drafted by Pigou and signed also by J.M. Keynes, D.H. MacGregor, Walter Layton, Arthur Salter, and J.C. Stamp. See Keynes *et al.* (1932: 138).

3   Keynes' scientific system

1. For a detailed discussion, see Chick (1983: Chapters 7 and 8).
2. Despite all his work to sustain capitalism, Keynes really did think that it was doomed in the long run (see, for example, Keynes, 1930b). Also, it must be added that Keynes really did not like capitalism, although he thought it was the only viable option for the foreseeable future. Moggridge (1992), for example, points out how Keynes repeatedly denounced greed and money grubbing as a way of organizing human affairs.
3. Jean Baptiste Say's (1803) argument was that production creates a demand for other products. This is because the reason for producers to sell their products is to buy other goods. James Mill (1808) extended this assertion by claiming that general overproduction was impossible, because the demand for goods comes from income, and the latter increases with the increase in production. See Backhouse (1985: 50–1).
4. The similarity with Marx's analysis in Chapter 3 of Volume I of *Capital* is striking. Even if Keynes never read Marx in any depth, he was aware of the logic of the money circuit of capital M–C–M', the fragility of the M–C and C–M' transformations, the fact that they presupposed a separation between decisions to "save" and invest, etc., and therefore of Marx's discussion of the possibilities of crisis inherent in hoarding.
5. In turn, expected profits were associated with the "marginal efficiency of capital" – that is, the rate of discount that makes the present value of the future return of a capital asset equal to the supply price of that asset (Keynes 1936). The demand for capital goods today therefore depends on the excess of the discounted value of their expected earnings over their price, that is to say, the spread between expected profit and interest rate.
6. Robinson relies mostly on Keynes (1937), but evidence can also be found in Keynes (1936:Chapters 22 and 24). See Dow (1985: 125).

4   The mass worker and Ford's strategy

1. See Marx (1867, Chapters 13, 14, and 15) for the concept of the social co-operation of labor.
2. "A walking man is not productive" Ford seems to have said to philosophically motivate the introduction of moving chains (Nevins 1954).

3. Industrial espionage at Ford dates back to 1906. As general foremen of motor assembly William Klann reports, "there were certain men who weren't going to do much work the next day; they were going to lay down so you had better put a man to watch them ... So we put a man there who would work fast and then we'd see what they would say to him ... They'd talk back to him and we'd trace the story down and fire the man" (quoted in Meyer 1981: 172–3).

4. Through the IWW, the early mass workers were able to exploit both their inherent mobility and their detachment from capitalist work in order to shape new methods and contents of struggles. In December 1906 they staged their first sitdown strike in New York at a plant of the General Electric Company. Direct action methods became their basic forms of struggle. Sabotage, in the words of the Wobbly poet Ralph Chaplin, was synonym of the struggle for the separation of income from work: "The hours are long, the pay is small, So take your time and buck'em all" (Meyer 1981: 92). The well known mobility of Wobbly militants even originated a complete sign code which left traces on fences and walls and was used by activists on the road to communicate to fellow comrades and "hobos" what to expect from the hospitality of towns and local families and from the local police. For a survey of the politics and history of the IWW, see Kornbluh (1988).

5. "As the size of the labor force increased ... control of the men had to be more largely deputed. Once the worker was put on the payroll, equipped with a badge, and sent to his department, he was under the all but absolute authority of his immediate foremen. The size of his wage-check, the severity of the production standard assigned him, the time given him to learn his job, his chances of promotion or transfer, his tenure – all this lay within the range of the foreman's discretion. Above all the foreman's right of arbitrary and unchallengeable discharge was accepted as the cornerstone of efficient labor practice. This was true of most large American factories at the time; it was true of practically all big motor work. Many foremen were arbitrary, prejudiced, and brutal – and hence the chronic galling turnover of men." (Nevins 1954: 526)

6. For a discussion of the link between fear of the IWW and Ford's reforms of 1914, see Russel (1978). The relation between labor problems as discussed above and Ford's response is analyzed in Meyer (1981). According to historians Roediger and Foner (1989: 190), labor militancy, the struggles of the unemployed organized by the IWW and the movement for the reduction of working time to eight hours "deserves to be considered a serious motivation for [Ford's] reforms."

7. Ford said, "We have settled on the eight-hour day ... because it so happens that this is the length of time which we find gives the best service from men, day in and day out" (quoted in Roediger and Foner 1989: 191). Ford's introduction of the eight-hour day allowed him to anticipate workers' struggles which were at the time organizing for that goal.

8. In his essay "Americanism and Fordism" (Gramsci 1971) written in prison, Antonio Gramsci establishes the connection between the company's control on workers' lives and the policy of prohibition, and identifies Ford's goal as the creation of "a new type of worker and man." For a critical review of this essay from an autonomist perspective see Bologna (1991).

9. An incentive devised by Ford's managers for the compliance of reluctant workers was the possibility for the latter to regain part of all the "profit-sharing" they were excluded from. See Meyer (1981: 112–13).
10. These included: The policy of forbidding discharge by foremen and trying men in various departments to test their aptitudes; the sick leave allowances soon introduced; the new savings and loan association; the English School for immigrants opened in 1914 and the technical school which Henry Ford, against opposition from other officers, instituted in 1916 – all this had an effect upon the spirit of the shop. The various welfare measures, from better medical care for the injured to an extra five minutes for lunch, must be lumped together. Weighing their effects after two years, the Educational Department in 1916 declared that the whole set of innovations, including profit sharing, a brighter factory environment, and educational work, when regarded from the cold-blooded business standpoint, was "the very best investment" the Ford Company ever made. (Nevins 1954: 550)
11. Some observers

> believed that many workers resented the questionnaires. Comments of job seekers at the Labor Bureau of the Employers' Association (many of them discharged Ford employees, to be sure, and hence prejudiced witness) revealed an undercurrent of discontent. Doubtless the spectacle of an earnest inquirer writing down an array of facts on his blue form aroused conflicting emotions in many breasts. (Nevins 1954: 555)

Workers' attitude provoked the investigators to be suspicious.

> The investigators, who were recruited from the plant ... were asked to throw a "deep, personal interest" into every visit. Sometimes this was cordial and helpful. Sometimes it was tinged with suspicion; the mere word of an employee that he was married was not taken as sufficient, and the agents were instructed to use some ingenuity in getting information *positively*. The inquiry necessarily had to go beneath the surface. Branch managers were instructed, for example, to be vigilant and to make sure "beyond the shadow of a doubt that the money is paid to those deserving, and to no others." (Nevins 1954: 555)

5 War, class war and the making of the social microfoundation of Keynesianism

1. As I discuss later, wartime strikes differ from those of the 1930s, especially because the early ones were often to gain union recognition, whereas during the war the unions were already becoming part of the problem for the working class. See Glaberman (1952, 1980).
2. For an idea of the problems posed by the war as discussed by economists close to the WPB, see, for example, the war years of the *Federal Reserve Bulletin*. For a thorough account of the WPB, see Civilian Production Administration (Bureau of Demobilization) (1947).
3. In five industrial cities of Ohio alone eviction orders were issued against nearly 100 000 families in the two and a half years beginning in January, 1930. In Chicago 3611 families, including 26 515 children, were evicted during the year beginning in December, 1931. During the eight months

ending June 30, 1932, some 185 794 families in New York City were served with dispossess notices, but 77 000 of these families were moved back into their premises by the people of the Unemployed Council. (Boyer and Morais 1955: 261)

4. Boyer and Morais (1955: 261).

5. Three thousand members of the Unemployed Council marching in St. Louis forced the passage at city hall of two relief bills. In Chicago 5000 members of the Council forced the improvement of conditions involving 20 000 jobless living in municipal lodging. With most cities approaching bankruptcy, with President Hoover still staunchly against federal relief, unemployment insurance, or anything except loans to Big Business, such demonstrations were necessary to avoid starvation. Their value is attested by Mauritz H. Hallgren, who wrote in his *Seeds of Revolt*:

> 'Social workers everywhere told me that without street demonstrations and hunger marches of the Unemployed Councils no relief whatever would have been provided in some communities, while in others even less than that which had been extended, would have been forthcoming.' (quoted in Boyer and Morais 1955: 263)

6. For a survey of these struggles see Piven and Cloward (1977: 48–60).

7. See Boyer and Morais (1955: 264). Wolters (1969, 1970) provides a study of the general condition of blacks during the Great Depression. An important collection of articles on the same subject is provided by Foner and Lewis (1980). For a detailed and insightful case study of black class composition and organization in this period see Greenberg (1991). A flavor of the life in Harlem in this period is given in the novel *Harlem Glory* by Claude McKay (1990).

8. "For the first time in history there was virtually no scabbing during a depression, the unemployed instead appearing on the picket line behind the banner of the Unemployed Council helping win the strikes of those fortunate enough to be employed. Its primary function was agitation and mass demonstration to the end that people might be fed. It increased the relief allotments of literally millions, championed for public works and unemployment insurance." (Boyer and Morais 1955: 260–1)

9. "Unlike the top-down generalship which unfortunately became all too typical of the CP's trade-union 'influentials' after 1938, the Communist strike leaders of 1936–37 (Mortimer and Travis in auto, Emspak in electrical, and so on) were genuine tribunes of the rank and file, who worked with relentless energy to expand and deepen mass participation in strike organization". (Davis 1986: 60) Davis thus continues to comment:

> It is not exaggeration to claim that a fecund synthesis was temporarily achieved between the highly participationist and egalitarian tradition of struggle derived from the Wobblies, and some of the best elements of American Leninism's emphasis on organization, discipline and strategy. (Davis 1986: 60)

10. For an informative discussion of the practice of sitdown strikes, see Fine (1969).

11. "The device was simple enough, consisting of staying inside the struck plant beside the machines and the assembly line, after going on strike without notice or warning, but it had all the elements of genius. Safe and

secure inside, protected from the rain or snow, cold or heat, the strikers were also safe from the assaults of police and vigilantes against picket lines. They held their places before their machines and so long as they were there no strike-breakers could take their jobs. The factory was a fort, sometimes relatively easy to defend because of the owner's fear that his machines would be injured if the workers were attacked." (Boyer and Morais 1955: 293)

12. This is an example of CP wartime leaflet: "Advocates of strike threats or strike actions in America in 1945 are SCABS in the war against Hitlerism, they are SCABS against our Armed Forces, they are SCABS against the labor movement" (quoted in Davis 1986: 80 n. 45).
13. For a general account of women's condition and struggles in production during the war, see Milkman (1987).
14. For a discussion of the relation between CIO and black unionism, see Olson (1969).
15. Roediger and Foner (1989: 261) reports that "Turnover was great among both sexes, especially before War Manpower Commission curbs on job changes began in September 1943." *Labor* (October 28, 1941) reports labor turnover the "highest in history." See also Glaberman (1980: 54–7).
16. About the myth that women went from the home to the factory, see Green (1975: 27).
17. "Women workers, burdened with household as well as wage labor, and poorly supported by social services, proved especially likely to quit jobs and to take time off from six-day weeks. One study concluded that, in Detroit alone, as many as 100 000 worker/hours per month were lost to the necessity of women workers staying home to do laundry" (Roediger and Foner 1989: 261). See also Anderson (1981).
18. "Thus the issue in these strikes was chiefly the control of production and maintenance of discipline. A GM vice-president reported that most of the 1944 strikes in the corporation's plants were "caused by the refusal of small groups of workers to meet production standards." That year, GM reported that about 52 percent of all strikes were a result of "necessary disciplinary action," up from 15 percent in 1940, when wage and recognition issues predominated. Of man-hours lost, almost 83 percent involved disputes over discipline, compared to 4 percent in 1940. The Bureau of Labor Statistics figures for the auto industry, which capture only the larger and longer strikes (at least a shift in duration), show the same trend. Work stoppages to protest discipline, work assignments, and working conditions increased from 205 to 452 between 1943 and 1944 and rose as a percentage of all stoppages from 31 to 43 percent." This view is also expressed by Glaberman. (Lichtenstein 1982: 121–2)

> "Although money was a factor, combined with the continual irritations of commodity shortages, housing shortages, and excessive overtime, the most common concern seems to have been the numerous kinds of grievances around production and discipline that challenged management's right to run their plants. Despite the opposition of the top union leadership and, often enough, local union leaders; despite the pressure of the government through uniformed officers present in the plants; despite the pressure of the draft boards to get rid of the militants; despite the loss of militants, including stewards and committeemen, through company dismissals;

despite the fantastic pressure of the daily papers which bitterly and viciously attacked striking workers; wildcats continued to increase in number as the war went on" (Glaberman 1980: 50).

19. "It should be noted that military officers in uniform were present in all the war production plants during the war and they regularly intervened in strikes and potential strikes. In other words, the reality of the war and the role of the government were concretely present to workers who went on strike or who threatened to go on strike" (Glaberman 1980: 49).

20. In the words of a labor militant, Jess Ferrazza,

> Management would not settle grievances. They would tell us to take them to the War Labor Board. The War Labor Board, although they tried to do a job, was not properly staffed to handle the job that had to be done. The result was that grievances took a year or a year and a half to be processed. Many of the workers thought that this was the long course around. They after a while became impatient when their grievances remained unsettled. The result was that during the war we had many unauthorized work stoppages. (quoted in Glaberman 1980: 42–3)

In the post-war years, the practice of diffusion of grievances became embodied in the multi-years contract, which this time made the unions directly accountable to the management for its application.

21. Historian Lichtenstein describes most of these strikes as:

> "quickie" stoppages, involving from half a dozen to a few hundred employees who halted work for a shift or less. They typically began when management retired an operation or changed a job assignment and then insisted that the employees meet the new standard or perform the task. If they refused or proved sluggish, managers took disciplinary action by either firing or suspending those who failed to meet their new duties. At this point, the strike issue became less the original grievance than the discipline itself, and an entire department might go out in defence of those penalized. (Lichtenstein 1982)

22. In other cases, however, also of "concern" was "the substitution of unskilled workers for skilled workers ... (a cause of much of the hostility against blacks and women on the part of the veteran white workers)" (Noble 1984: 22).

23. "Wage rate inequalities within a single plant or department proved an even more vexing and persistent cause of working-class discontent. Each employee knew well the wages paid his or her coworkers, and because no general pay increase seemed in the offing to take the sting out of such differentials, those that remained were particularly irksome. In the steel industry, for example, U.S. Steel maintained more than 26 000 different rates, most of them purposely designed to fragment and divide the workforce. "A man at the blast furnace does the same work another fellow does at the open hearth, but gets a few cents an hour less," reported a United Steel Workers of America district official in 1942. "Now frankly it's not a question of starving, much as he could use the money. It's just not right. A man does not see any sense in it and gets pretty mad. Who wouldn't?" As a result, local unions came under

direct pressure from rank and file to equalize such wages, and local leaders soon flooded the NWLB with intraplant wage inequality cases, some covering but a handful of workers, other involving thousands. Although its work was slow, the NWLB could not resist accommodating to this pressure, if only because it recognized the "adverse effect upon employee morale and productive efficiency" of such internal inequalities. By the spring of 1943, the upward equalization of wages had become one of the union movement's most promising ways of circumventing the Little Steel formula." (Lichtenstein 1982: 115)

In the end, Roosevelt ordered to NWLB to correct wage inequalities.

24. "The alienation of the foreman from the ranks of factory supervision proved another key element in this process" (Lichtenstein 1982: 117).
25. Management "had pursued labor peace and adequate manpower by the maladministration of wage systems as a way of getting around strict NWLB prohibitions against direct wage increases. Widespread practices included the 'demoralization' of incentive schemes and production standards, misclassification of jobs, rapid upgrading of workers to supposedly more skilled positions, and allowing excessive overtime" (Harris 1982: 63).
26. "What is involved in struggles for improved income is not impoverishment but a combination of two factors. One factor was the awareness of discriminatory treatment of workers. Workers could see both the tremendous profits and the tremendous waste all around them and they could not see why they had to accept limits that were not applied to any other section of the population. The other factor was power. This was the first time since the beginning of the Great Depression that there was anything like a shortage of labor. That is to say, this was the first time in anyone's memory that workers had the means to exert considerable pressure for improved wages. That, in fact, is why the government rushed to freeze wages at a ridiculously low level. The result was that workers imposed many back door deals on management, circumventing the wage freeze by changing job descriptions, promotions, supply of tools, work clothes, etc. which had previously been purchased by the worker, and so on." (Glaberman 1980: 41–2)
27. "At Ford, ten percent of the 250-odd wildcats in 1943 were sympathy stoppages" (Jennings 1975: 86).
28. For the following description of the events which led to the formation of the NWLB, I draw on Harris (1982) whose work represents an exellent detailed analysis of the industrial relation policies during the war and post-war years.
29. "The NWLB had to fight against a stubborn rearguard action by managements far from reconciled to having to deal with a union, and attempting to maintain a "hands off" or "arm's length" policy, confining recognition of the union's institutional existence and legitimacy to an absolute minimum. The NWLB had to give such firms an education in the

practical and procedural necessities of labor relations, just as it had "instructed" them in the need to accept maintenance of membership." (Harris 1982: 51–2)

30. The mine workers' union abrogated the no-strike pledge and called or even engaged in official strikes. For a thorough analysis of the role of the CIO during world war two see Lichtenstein (1982).

31. "What had preceded the wartime period was a mere four years of continuing organizing activity. What happened during the war years, as we shall see, was the rapid bureaucratization of the top, while local union officers, generally speaking, retained close ties to the rank and file. When some of the early militants were railroaded into the army because they were active in the struggle against the no-strike pledge, they retained the support of their fellow union members, no matter how new or old these were." (Glaberman 1980: 34)

32. Labor organizations thus "would appear to their own members, not as leaders who had been elected to represent the interests of their members, but as politicians whose function it had become to get their members to sacrifice for the war effort" (Glaberman 1980: 14).

33. An example of the bureaucratic attitude of union leaders can be provided, for example, by the minutes of a meeting of the UAW executive board in Cleveland on March 28, 1942, where among other things it is stated that "The rank and file does not seriously realize or appreciate the grave predicament of our country and, therefore, is not prepared to forfeit its overtime provisions" (quoted from Glaberman 1980: 5). "The Board decided to combat the lack of understanding of the membership by refusing to permit them to elect the delegates to the special conference and by refusing to permit either the members or the delegates to study in advance the program that was to be presented to the conference" (Glaberman 1980: 6).

34. "In the spring of 1942 a few important CIO locals had already begun to disintegrate, while serious dues-collection difficulties were encounter in steel, textiles and aircraft" (Lichtestein 1975: 53).

35. "In this potential crisis the government sought to strengthen the institutional power of the CIO's politically cooperative leadership. In prewar years CIO leaders had unsuccessfully demanded union-shop contracts as a guarantee that hostile employers would not seek to weaken the new unions during periods of slack employment. Now the government's WLB gave CIO unions a modified union shop – maintenance of membership – in order to assure membership stability and a steady dues flow during the difficult war years. The WLB's policy solved the chronic financial problems of many CIO unions, assured their steady wartime growth, and made cooperative union leaders somewhat "independent" of rank-and-file pressure." (Lichtenstein 1975: 53)

36. Incidentally Rawick (1972b) notes that the loss of workers' control of unions brings doubts to the use of union membership figures as a proxy for working class militancy.

6 War planning and the rise of the Keynesian orthodoxy

1. Boyer and Morais (1955: 274) remind us that among the legislative measures there was

   the CCC, the Civilian Conservation Corps, to give employment to the impoverished youth of the country; there was the AAA, the Agricultural Adjustment Act, to help the hard-pressed farmers of the nation; there was the NIRA, the National Industrial Recovery Act with its section 7(A), the opening wedge for workers to organize unions of their own choosing; there was the Wagner Act or National Labor Relations Act, to guarantee wage earners for the first time the right to bargain collectively and the right to strike by prohibiting specifically coercive anti-union activities on the part of the employers; and there was the Fair Labor Standards Act, to prescribe maximum hours of work and minimum wages and regulate child labor in interstate commerce.

2. It should be recognized that before publication of the *General Theory*, and even before publication of Keynes' 1933 pamphlet, *The Means of Prosperity*, some established and outstanding economists, such as J.M. Clark, James Rogers and Jacob Viner understood that recovery required an expansion of aggregate demand and understood clearly the argument for a planned expansion of loan-financed expenditure, but in 1932 and even later they nevertheless thought such a programme unwise. (Salant 1988: 64)

3. According to (Salant 1988: 65):

   the early New Deal, at least during Roosevelt's entire first term, was not an exercise in Keynesian economics. The centre-piece of the recovery programme in the early years was the National Recovery Administration (NRA), established under the National Industrial Recovery Act, which, among other things, put floors under prices and hourly wages. That legislation did not expand demand for goods and services, and it was the deficiency of demand that was the actual problem. Most of the federal budget deficits during the first years of the New Deal were the result of the depression, and the resulting fall in tax revenues and tax expansions of relief and other depression-related expenditures.

4. Not long before he was elected president, Governor Roosevelt remarked: "Our people have to be put back on their feet ... it will have to be soon. They are getting restless. Coming back from the West last week, I talked to an old friend who runs a great Western railroad. 'Fred,' I asked him, 'what are the people talking about out here?' I can hear him answer even now. 'Frank,' he replied, 'I'm sorry to say that men out here are talking revolution'" (quoted in Boyer and Morais 1955: 272).

5. In Britain the same process was occurring as Arthur Salter recalls: "All the relevant information was at our disposal. We were able over a great range of controversial questions, to make unanimous recommendations which would, if adopted, have profoundly changed the policy of the time. In retrospect they can, I think, be seen to have anticipated much that later became orthodox in Whitehall and elsewhere" (Salter 1961).

6. "Another important result was the official backing given to the collection, refinement, and publication of national income and related statistics. From relatively humble beginnings in 1941 an important branch of economic statistics has developed, without which the application of macroeconomic theory to policy problems would be practically impossible ... The value of the national income accounts is, of course, not confined to the problems of war finance; they are of central importance in any well-designed policy for controlling the level of economic activity." (Winch 1969: 266)

7. Alvin Johnson wrote in his presidential address at the forty-ninth Annual Meeting of the American Economic Association: "With due credit to the economists who composed the original 'brain trust,' we must still admit that the policies grouped together under the term 'New Deal' have been little influenced by the professional economist. The economists were slow to realize the need for action, and were inclined to hold back and let the politicians assume all the responsibility" (Johnson 1937: 2).

8. "Perhaps one of the most important results of the Second World War for economics lay in the recruitment of economists into the machinery of government. In the United States, notably in the latter years of the New Deal, the employment of economists by various agencies within the Administration was already a well-established practice. Close relations existed between Washington officials and those universities where active research was being carried out on problems connected with immediate policy concerns. The Fiscal Policy Seminars conducted by Alvin Hansen and J.H. Williams at Harvard in the late thirties, for example, were frequently attended by economists working in government. And as early as 1934 the Department of Commerce had co-operated with Simon Kuznets and a group of statisticians at the University of Pennsylvania and at the National Bureau of Economic Research to produce national income estimates. But in Britain this kind of inter-change of personnel and ideas hardly existed before the Second World War. Economists were drafted into government service during the First World War, but they tended to merge imperceptibly with other temporary civil servants. After the war their services were used mainly on *ad hoc* committees and Royal Commissions. The chief exception to this, however, was the Economic Advisory Council created by MacDonald in 1930." (Winch 1969: 264–5)

9. "The significance of this recruitment of economists during the war was that a substantial number of leading members of the academic profession, and those who later became members of that cadre, gained access to information and valuable administrative experience. The process of education worked both ways; civil servants taught economists and vice versa. It led to a substantial injection of realism into economic studies and greater respect for expert economic knowledge on the part of officials. The conferences ... took place in Keynes's room at the Treasury" (Winch 1969: 266).

10. Indeed, these "sins" may have contributed, together with the lack of payment of dues, to the drop of professional economists affiliated with the American Economic Association during the depression. In 1933 the Report of the Secretary at the American Economic Association Annual Meetings explains that "the prolonged depression is responsible for this decline, as the correspondence has shown that many members and libraries as well

had to suspend their affiliation with the Association on account of a lack of funds." Also, there was a large number of "removals for non-payment" (Deibler 1933: 180).

11. Robbins acknowledged the impact that the war had on his opinion on the capacity of the system to have equilibrium without government intervention: "I owe much to Cambridge economists, particularly to Lord Keynes and Professor Robertson, for having awakened me from dogmatic slumbers in this very important respect" (Robbins 1947: 68).

12. For a provocative and insightful analysis of German economic planning techniques see Götz and Heim (1988).

13. See for example Samuelson (1944); Eccles (1944); Goldenweiser and Hagen (1944).

14. "An examination of the popular and learned periodicals issued during the last war shows almost no preoccupation with problems of postwar planning. As victory finally loomed ahead, a number of programs for Reconstruction did emerge, but these were almost exclusively international. A few cautious souls warned that temporary problems of glut in the labor market might arise if soldiers were demobilized too rapidly, and that consequently the speed of discharges should be regulated with reference to unemployment. But on the whole, in the radical and in the conservative press, there was little concern over the problem of achieving or maintaining full employment." (Samuelson 1944: 1449)

15. As an analysis this is very similar to that of the gap between potential and actual GNP, which will be extensively used subsequently.

16. "'[F]from a purely self-interested point of view,' Harry C. Hawkins, the director of the State Department's Office of Economic Affairs stated on April 1944, 'trade cooperation ... will help us a great deal. As you know, we've got to plan on enormously increased production in this country after the war, and the American domestic market can't absorb all that production indefinitely. There won't be any question about our needing greatly increased foreign markets'" (Kolko 1968: 253).

17. For example, in 1960, if the United States reduced imports by 1 percent of GNP, this would have represented a reduction of effective demand on the world market of 4 percent. See Moore (1985), who offers also a history of the trends and institutions of international trade since the war.

18. It must be noted that the principles of the Bretton Woods agreement were not fully met immediately after their ratification. For a large number of reasons which will not be explored here, formal full implementation of the Bretton Woods agreement could not begin before January 1959 – that is, before the full convertibility of all major European currencies (Burk 1991: 11–17). Thus contrarily, for example, to the interpretation of the social structure of accumulation school proposed by Gordon, Weisskopf and Bowles (1987) this element of international Keynesianism served the social structure only for the period between 1959 and 1971. A very small "era" if we also consider the few years of international pressures before the official suspension of convertibility of dollar into gold in 1971 (Phillips 1980). This obviously serves as further reminder of the crucial difference between regarding international and domestic Keynesianism as "strategy" embodying a particular set of principles which is always defined *vis-à-vis* the working class, and Keynesianism simply as

"golden age" based on a fixed "deal" regarded as the prime source of a (inherently static) social structure.

19. The role of the Italian Communist Party (PCI), for example (the largest Communist Party in the Western World for the entire period of the cold war), is significant. During the late years of the war, its obedience to Stalinist line allowed its acceptance of the national over the socialist question. To Togliatti, historical leader of PCI, the war of resistance was not a way toward social revolution but a war of national liberation together with the allies. When it became clear that this was not an idea shared by many men and women fighting the resistance, Togliatti assured the American authorities that the PCI he was leading had nationalistic and patriotic tendencies (Kolko 1990: 68). In a conference on economic questions in August 1945 Togliatti rejected central planning in favor of the principle of international economic cooperation (Sassoon 1990; Togliatti 1984; for a critical analysis of the implications of this party line in the post-war period, see Del Carria 1977).

20. Despite this, however, to date Italy still does not have a comprehensive social security system including unemployment subsidies.

7 The institutional features of post-war Keynesianism

1. For a discussion of the political debates and the comparison between these two pieces of legislation, see Winch (1969: 268–77).

2. See Winch (1969: 276).

3. While in the "First World" growth theories on the demand side were flourishing, in the "Third World" this was the case for supply-side theories. See Cleaver (1981).

4. For an analysis of the development of statistical methods of national accounting in relation to state policies, see Lintott (1982).

5. "A large number of distinguished academic economists descended on Washington to serve the new Administration in one capacity or another" (Winch 1969: 303). The author recalls, among others, Walter Heller, Paul Samuelson, J.K. Galbraith, James Tobin, James Duesenberry, Otto Eckstein, Arthur Okun, Gardner Ackley, Seymour Harris, Robert Solow, Kermit Gordon, Gerhard Colm, Walter Salant, Joseph Pechman, and Charles Schultze (Winch 1969: 303 n.3). Particularly in this period, there is the Council of Economic Advisers. One of its Chairmen, Gardner Ackley, stressed that "Through participating in the work of the Council of Economic Advisers or in hearings before the Joint Economic Committee – both institutions created by the Employment Act – more economists have had more to say about economic policy than in the previous 170 years of our Nation's history" (Ackley 1966: 169).

6. "Government, in its operations, has come as well to redefine more and more of its functions in a way that business understands. 'True economy,' Kermit Gordon, the Budget Director, testified recently, 'is the most efficient allocation of resources,' and he pledged his $98-billion budget to advance that end. Though such entrenched semi-socialist projects ...

continue to thrive, the new governmental managers have been happy to pass along to industry the major new areas of development, notably commercial satellite communication and atomic power. On business' side some redefining has been going on too. The rising generation of chief executive officers have come to realize their dependence on government in their international operations, and if they have any complaint it is simply that government should be better managed. On the home front, whole industries, such as space, defence, system planning, ocean mining, etc., look to government as their legitimate parent." (Benks 1965: 98)

7. See also Meek (1967: 194–5, 217–22).
8. See, for example, the famous Okun's law according to which there is a $2\frac{1}{2}$ percent gap between potential and actual GNP for every 1 percent of unemployment above the natural rate. See also Heller (1966). Heller was Kennedy's earliest appointment to the post of Chairman of Council of Economic Advisers.
9. The scarcity of labor power had come to be felt by 1943 and increased in 1944. The *Federal Reserve Bulletin*, for example, reported several articles on the issue, describing possible or already implemented strategies for facing the problem. Intensive strategies were utilized when the extensive exploitation of workers was no longer possible:

> Manpower controls became progressively tighter and more direct throughout the year [1943]. Wage and price stabilization policies designed to "hold the line" restricted the use of increased wage differentials as a method of channeling workers into the most essential jobs, and non-wage methods of manpower control were utilized to an increasing extent. Employment stabilization programs were extended throughout the country and in especially critical areas, such as the West Coast, strong measures were placed in operation to direct available workers to the most essential jobs, reduce needless turnover, eliminate hoarding of labor, and utilize more fully manpower supplies available. (Federal Reserve 1944a: 6)

For an larger review of the strategies of work control during this last period of the war see Federal Reserve (1944b: 415–23).
10. Incidentally, this wave of US labor movement coincides with the threat to US interests abroad posed by armed sections of the European working class after the experience of resistance against fascism.
11. Thus, those approaches such as the Social Structure of Accumulation school (Gordon, Weisskopf and Bowles 1987) which interpret the post-war period in terms of, among other things, a "capital–labor accord," miss the central point that this accord between labor bureaucracies and capital was unstable and crisis-prone even, in the period of the so-called "golden age of capitalism" after the Second World War.
12. Incidentally, the cultural dimension of the early post-war period reflects the ideal of a prosperous society in which the basic aspects of class conflict have been resolved. For a review, see Cartosio (1992).
13. "The system was still connective, however, due to the fact that the national union was heavily involved in monitoring local union affairs

and functioned as a channel of communication up and down the union hierarchy particularly through its involvement in the administration of the grievance procedure and by way of the patter following that standardized employment conditions within and across the companies." (Katz 1985: 37)

14. See also Sachs (1980). Among the factors that are believed to have played a role in the decreased cyclical response of wages and price inflation there is, for example, increasing concentration, higher ratios of value added per shipment, increased unionization, and the large increase in investment in human capital. For disagreement on this issue, see Gordon (1986).

15. For an analysis of the labor market segmentation in the big corporate sector, see Gordon, Edwards and Reich (1982).

16. As historians Boyer and Morais argue:

> If the cold war began on the diplomatic front in 1945 with the dropping of the atom bomb, it began on the home front late in 1945 and early in 1946 as the employer answer to the great strikes against the wage freeze. From then on a curious parallelism developed: every move in the cold war abroad was matched by a move against civil liberties and the labor movement at home. The great strikes of 1945–46 frightened monopoly, convincing its leaders that the cold war was constantly growing in size, militancy and unity. (Boyer and Morais 1955: 343)

17. Historian George Rawick (1974: 145) argues that the process of capitalist integration of society, which received a crucial impetus starting with the state intervention during the New Deal, remained incomplete until the working class lost control of the union – that is, beginning from the post-war period.

18. "The contract is a contradictory thing. To begin with, it records the gains made by the workers, the wages, the hours, the right to representation. Putting these gains in a contract makes them secure, or so it appears. But for every advance made in a contract a price must be paid. The fundamental cost was the reestablishment of the discipline of the company. The contract gave to the company what the workers had taken away – the right to organize and control production. The complete recognition of a grievance procedure meant the establishment of a structure of red tape where the worker lost his grievance. To end the constant battle over members, the union won the union shop and the dues checkoff – and paid by removing the union another step from its membership." (Glaberman 1952: 19)

19. "The more 'victories' it recorded, the bigger and more technical the contract became. The union militants of '36 and '37 began to drift away and the contract lawyers and porkchoppers and specialists took over. Workers stopped going to membership meetings because instead of activity and to chance to solve their own problems directly they were presented with debates on technicalities and the manoeuvring of rival factions. The initiative was taken away from the workers and given to the officials". (Glaberman 1952: 20)

20. "The first evidence of this came in 1955 when Walter Reuther won his precedent-setting demand of supplemental unemployment benefits (SUB) in which workers were compensated by the companies in addition to their

governmental unemployment compensation when they were laid off. Like all of Reuther's great victories it was granted by the auto corporations in exchange for labor peace, that is, union cooperation in keeping the workers quiet in the face of automation, speed-up and reorganization of production. But the workers were having none of this. An unprecedented wave of wildcat strikes broke out from coast to coast precisely when the contract was signed. All of them were directed at what was called "local grievances," that is the assertion of workers' power in the plants, in the process of production. Reports in the press at that time (as well as reports during the 1964 strikes) indicated thousands of unresolved local grievances. That implies a total collapse of the union as representative of the workers in the day-to-day life in the plants". (Glaberman 1966: 22)

21. "What are these specific local grievances? They involve production standards: the speed of a line, the rate on a machine, the number of workers assigned to a given job, the allowable variations in jobs on a given line. They involve health and safety standards: unsafe machines, cluttered or oily floors, rates of production which prevent the taking of reasonable precautions, the absence or misuse of hoists or cranes, protection from flames or furnaces, protection from sharp, unfinished metal, protection from welding or other dangerous chemicals or fumes, the right to shut an unsafe job down until the condition is changed.

They involve the quality of life in the plant: the authoritarian company rules which treat workers like a combination of prison inmate and kindergarten child, the right to move about the plant, the right to relieve yourself physically without having to get the foreman's permission or the presence of a relief man, the right to reasonable breaks in the work, the right to a reasonable level of heat in the winter or reasonable ventilation in the summer. And so on and on". (Glaberman 1975: 25)

22. Schor (1991: 83–106) provides a detailed analysis of how technology failed to reduce labor time in the domestic sphere.

23. The following interpretation of the post-war agricultural transformation is based on Cleaver (1977).

24. The recent high level of European unemployment has sparked a vast literature on the issue of the high proportion of discouraged unemployed workers. The persistence of such a high proportion threatens the economic function of unemployment – that is, its ability to depress real wages.

25. The hierarchical structure and grading system of the university was accompanied in spring 1966 by its connection with military draft eligibility, to which the student struggles responded massively. As Caffentzis notices: "Once the 'F' began to mean death in the jungle no crap about the 'community of scholars' was needed to attack the grading process. Once grading showed its immediate quality as a wage in the social factory sequence of school–army–job, the struggle against it became nation-wide" (Caffentzis 1975: 133).

8 The theoretical features of post-war Keynesianism

1. Modigliani (1963) surveyed the major developments in macroeconomics in the early 1960s by presenting an updated IS–LM model.
2. Large econometric models consisting of several hundreds of equations were disaggregated into IS–LM structures, as in the case of MPS model.
3. In a reappraisal of the IS–LM model Hicks (1983), for example, highlights a basic tension between the time periods appropriate to IS and LM, the former being a locus of alternative *flow*-equilibria while the latter the locus of alternative *stock*-equilibria. For a reply in post-Keynesian terms, see Chick (1992). For a summary of the internal logical problems of the IS–LM model, see Alex Leijonhufvud (1988).
4. For example, see the use of IS–LM model in the debate over economic policies between Friedman and his critics (Gordon 1973).
5. Modigliani (1944) clarified the role played by nominal wage rigidity in the Keynesian model. The interpretation of Keynesian unemployment as the product of the rigidity of some prices and quantities was discussed in Patinkin (See, for example, 1956: Chapter 13 n.3) and illustrated in Smith (1956). Hicks' (1957) review of Patinkin's book clarifies the difference between Patinkin's formulation and Keynes' original thought. This debate is also recollected in Hicks (1979).
6. Patinkin (1956); Smith (1956).
7. The effect that a change of prices exercises on the real value of money stock, the so-called "Pigou effect," was analyzed for the first time by A.C.Pigou (1948, 1949). For the description of the "Pigou effect" and some of the post-war criticism it has originated see Samuelson (1963). Samuelson reports here Leontief commenting around 1935–6 on the "Pigou effect" as resulting in what was known later as disguised unemployment: "If wages are low enough, this dime in my hand will employ everyone in the nation; and my only requirement on them is that they not show up at my office for work" Samuelson (1963: 333). For a simple but insightful account of the "Pigou effect" vs the "Keynesian effect" using the IS–LM model, see Peterson (1988: 401–2).
8. "Reductionism" is defined by the author as, very broadly, consisting "of analysing markets on the basis of the choices made by individual traders." This method is called "reductionism" "on the ground that the central idea is the *reduction* of market phenomenon to (stylized) individual choices" (Coddington 1983: 92).
9. It is useful to point out here that this does not imply that prices do not play any role in Keynesianism. It is instead a matter of degree and centrality of prices within the economic paradigm (Coddington 1983: 103).
10. Keynes' discussion of "animal spirits" in relation to long-run expectations is to be found in Keynes (1936: Chapter 12).
11. For a review of the debate on expectations in Keynes see Dow and Dow (1985).
12. A point of equilibrium presupposes a given set of expectations but does not discuss the intertemporal formation of expectations between equilibria. Modern economic analysis therefore must discuss how expectations change. See Begg (1982).

9 Economic modeling and social conflict: 1 – the fiscal multiplier

1. For a theoretical analysis of the general relation between class relations and economic theory, see De Angelis (1996).
2. See for example Bowles, Gordon and Weisskopf (1986); Gordon, Edwards and Reich (1982); Bowles and Boyer (1990).
3. As examples of some classic statements on this subject see Aglietta (1979) and Lipietz (1987) for the Regulation approach. See also Bowles, Gordon and Weisskopf (1983); Bowles, Gordon and Weisskopf (1986), Gordon, Edwards and Reich (1982) for the Social Structure of Accumulation approach.
4. See also Myrdal (1970).
5. Bowles and Boyer (1990: 188), respectively a writer in the Social structure of Accumulation tradition and a French Regulation School theorist, give us a perfect example of this when they write: "we integrate the two approaches Keynesian and Marxian – by means of a model in which the income distribution is at once a key determinant of aggregate demand, as in the Keynes–Kalecki tradition, and the endogenous result of the level of employment and economic activity, as in the neo-Marxian class conflict view."
6. Marx argues that from the standpoint of the worker

    [w]hat is essential is that the purpose of the exchange ... is the satisfaction of his needs ... not exchange value as such ... What he obtains from the exchange is therefore not exchange value, not wealth, but a means of subsistence, objects for the preservation of his life, the satisfaction of his needs in general, physical, social etc. (Marx 1858: 284)

    From this follows the definition of savings from the standpoint of the worker:

    The most [the worker] can achieve on the average with his self-denial is to be able better to endure the fluctuations of prices high – and low, their cycle – that is, he can only distribute his consumption better, but never attain wealth. And that is actually what the capitalists demand. The workers should save enough at the times when business is good to be able more or less to live in the bad times, to endure short time or the lowering of wages... maintain themselves as pure labouring machines and as far as possible pay their own wear and tear. (Marx 1858: 286)

7. This is of course true independently of the *actual* use of these savings by the capitalists in the financial or industrial system. This use, as often argued by Marx and acknowledged by Keynes, is contingent upon profit expectations and positions in the cycle.
8. "The capitalist process of production ... seen as a total, connected process, i.e. a process of reproduction, produces not only commodities, not only surplus-value, but it also produces and reproduces the capital-relation itself; on the one hand the capitalist, on the other the wage-labourer" (Marx 1867: 724).

9. To avoid misunderstanding, it must be pointed out again that the part of workers' income that is saved *today* is necessary to the reproduction of the working class *in the future*. For this reason, whatever workers save today must be considered a component of the social wage in the future.

10. In case public expenditures were greater than zero, the social wage thus defined would include the part of public expenditures that goes for the reproduction of labor power.

11. In 1991 for the United States, proprietors income represented a mere 8 percent of total national income, that is $368 billion over $4544.2. As total consumption for that year was $3887.7 billion, the average propensity to consume, that we calculate over personal disposable ($4209.6 billions) income was 0.92. Assuming that this figure is the same for both workers and capitalists, an assumption generous to the capitalists, capitalists would have consumed $338.56 billion which, once subtracted from total consumption and using this figure to calculate the new "working-class" average consumption over their disposable income (total disposable income *minus* proprietors income, $4209.6 − $368) = $3841.6 billion. This "working-class" average consumption would be still 0.92, which corresponds to the national average. Of course, once we take under consideration the lower capitalist propensity to consume, the working-class propensity to consume would move slightly up, although not much, as the proportion of property income over total national income is very small. Therefore, in considering πb as the social wage rate, we may be only slightly underestimating it.

12. To stress the distinction further, the social wage rate is not a representation of what workers *get* in their pay check, but a representation of what is necessary, in a given period, to *reproduce* them as labor power.

13. For different formulations regarding what has been called the "value of money" or the "monetary expression of labour", see Foley (1982) and Ramos (1995).

14. Kliman (1988, 1996), among others, has reopened an old debate by arguing that Marx's theory on the tendency of the falling rate of profit formulated in the third volume of *Capital* (Marx 1894) is valid also in presence of continuous technological change and increase in the capital–labour ratio.

15. Within conventional Marxist literature it is common to argue that labour productivity depends on technology rather than on class relations. While making my disagreement explicit on this point, I invite the interested reader to consult Panzieri (1961) and Noble (1984). Marx (1867: 563) puts it bluntly and clearly: "It would be possible to write a whole history of the inventions made since 1830 for the sole purpose of providing capital with weapons against working-class revolt."

16. In 1943, Keynes maintained that the task of keeping wages per unit of output stable (what he called "efficiency wages") is a political rather than an economic problem and in 1944 he acknowledged the problem of restraining real wages in the presence of full employment and collective bargaining (Winch 1989: 107; Glyn 1995: 37).

17. Schor (1991) argues that in the United States during the 1980s the downward trend of working time was even reversed.
18. By "income policies", I mean those governments' strategies aimed at controlling the rate of price and wage inflation. For a given level of productivity growth, this implies the control of the denominator of the social multiplier. Income policies can of course take different forms. They can be the result of a negotiated agreement between trade unions, employers' representatives and government, or simply be imposed by government as in the case of Nixon's wage–price freeze in 1971. For a survey of income policies in the United States, see Pencavel (1981: 160–5), while for the European case see Addison (1981: 219–42).
19. This is recognized in different ways and with different implications by the writers in the Regulation school and the Social Structure of Accumulation approach cited before and by others; see ZeroWork Collective (1975); Cleaver (1979); Armstrong, Glyn and Harrison (1984).

10   Economic modeling and social conflict: 2 – inflation and the Phillips curve

1. According to the "widow's cruse" theory of distribution, capitalists' increase in investment led to an increase in prices and therefore profit. Thus however much profits are spent, they will never be exhausted. This theory has strong similarities with Kalecki's (1933) one, according to which capitalists consume what they spend.
2. For a useful review of the evolution of the Phillips curve analysis and its different use by policy-makers, see Humphrey (1973).

11   Conclusion: looking ahead

1. For example, Eric Helleiner (1995) discusses three areas in which states have supported financial liberalisation, the most developed form of globalisation. first, by granting freedom to market actors through liberalisation and deregulation; second, by preventing major financial crisis and coming to the rescue of fragile financial institutions; third, by choosing not to implement controls on capital movements. Amin (1996: 231), echoing Polanyi, reminds us that "deregulation ... is itself a deliberate policy which must be consciously undertaken rather than a natural state of affairs which imposes itself". Other forms of globalisation, such as trade and investment, are of course also linked to state-promoted institutions which define rules and regulations, such as GATT and, later, WTO, or the G7 attempts to define a Multilateral Agreement on Investment.
2. As an example, take the issue of intellectual property rights. In every culture in the history of humanity, knowledge has been accumulated and passed on to further generations as a natural matter of human social interaction. Just as language and agricultural and farming methods and skills of various kinds are the cultural basis of any society, without which no society would survive, so genes are the building blocks of life itself. Yet, in the last few

years, there has been increasing pressure by large multinational corporations to introduce legislation that "encloses" knowledge and genes. These forms of enclosure go under the name of "intellectual property rights," the consequences of which are potentially devastating. Drug companies claim that patenting is necessary for guaranteeing the maintenance of investment in the sector. This is to ensure the development of further research. However, many researchers argue that patenting promotes secrecy, and therefore would channel funds into what is commercially profitable rather than the public good. Thus, instead of promoting research, this would threaten it. Also, the patenting of life legitimizes biopiracy, promotes the private appropriation of knowledge built up collectively by generations of anonymous experimenters (especially at the expense of the peoples of the South), and provides multinational corporations with new means of establishing control over areas of nature previously held in common by communities in the South.

For the many small-scale farmers of the South, the consequences are serious. The establishment of patents over some of the genes of a particular plant or animal curtails the ability and right of Third World farmers to grow that crop or raise that animal and to trade it. Farmers may have to pay for what had been for generations free and theirs. Increased debt and dependency on the cash economy, bankruptcy and dispossession is likely to be the result for large sections of the population, especially the poorest. (See CornerHouse 1997.)

3. See, for example, the project of the Kensington Welfare Rights Union, "a multi-racial organisation of, by and for poor and homeless people" in the United States. In their Call for Testimony and Documentation they write:

> WELFARE CUTS = HUMAN RIGHTS VIOLATIONS. The United Nations Universal Declaration of Human Rights, signed in 1948, guarantees every man, woman and child the right to housing, food, education, health care and living wage jobs. Recent federal and state welfare reforms in the United States violate these rights. People who have been receiving public relief are told to "get a job" while millions of unemployed and under-employed people can't find jobs. With the new welfare laws, those who cannot find a job are no longer guaranteed the right to food, housing, clothing and health care. As a result of this, more and more people are unable to feed, house and clothe their families." See the union site at <http://www.libertynet.org/~kwru>.

4. Examples of blurring this distinction are provided by the wave of anti-NAFTA struggles in the few years before 1994; the emerging coalitions against social exclusion and unemployment in Europe; the mushrooming of committees organising (and in so doing learning and practicing direct democracy) the first and second Intercontinental Meetings for Humanity and against Neoliberalism, etc. On the labor front, Brecher and Costello (1994: 160) report that the organizing of the new labor activism is based on practices such as (a) worker-to-worker exchanges; (b) cross-border organizing; (c) labor rights; (d) international strike support; (e) global labor com-

munications (Internet, etc.): "LaborNet also ties into other 'nets' dedicated to social movements like the environmental movement, peace movement, and human rights movement. Labor communication expert Peter Waterman has suggested that the increasing use of computers by labor and social movements constitutes a 'communications internationalism,' which he dubs a 'fifth International.'" Also in this case, the blurring of the distinction between the national and the international is evident in the practice of the movement itself.

5. Brecher and Costello (1994: 150) note:

> Curiously enough, the architects of American labor's foreign policy during the Cold War regarded themselves as anti-communist internationalists. They co-operated closely with the CIA to break left-led strikes (for example in France in 1949) and overthrow leftist governments (for example in Guatemala in 1954). *Business Week* described the AFL–CIO's global operations, such as its International Affairs Department in Washington and its American Institute for Free Labor Development in Latin America, as "labor's own version of the Central Intelligence Agency, a trade union network existing in all parts of the world." In 1988, most of the AFL–CIO budget in overseas activity still came from the US government. The collusion of the AFL–CIO with US foreign policy was mocked by American grassroots militants by calling the union organization AFL–CIA.

6. For a discussion of the Zapatista phenomenon and its implications in the context of contemporary social movements and the globalization of capital, see Holloway and Peláez (1998) and De Angelis (2000). To access primary sources and general debates around the Zapatistas and their international network see Chiapas95 at <gopher://mundo.eco.utexas.edu//11/mailing/ chiapas95.archive> and the EZLN web page at <http://www.ezln.org/> where it is possible to link to numerous other sites of various movements.

7. For PGA see <http://www.agp.org/agp/index.html>; for ASEED see <http://antenna.nl/aseed>.

8. See for example the Jubilee 2000 coalition at <http://www.oneworld.org/jubilee2000>.

9. See for example the Globalisation and the MAI information center, where it is possible to link to various sites: <http://www.isleandnet.com/~maisite />.

10. See, for example, <http://www.oneworld.net/campaigns/wto/index.html>.

11. Senior derived government duty and right to perform a certain function or promote a certain policy from the principle of expediency – that is, from the evaluation of a certain policy as being "appropriate" or "advantageous." As has been argued,

> Senior never proved that expediency ought to be the regnant principle, just as Bentham did not prove utility and the natural-rights theorists did not prove the validity of their first principles. He assumes that expediency is the only valid basis of government and the only feasible test of any particular proposed measure. That this argument offers much greater potential scope to governmental intervention than the principle of laissez-faire, whether grounded on natural rights (as in Smith) or on

the utility principle (as in Bentham and J.S. Mill), is obvious. The government is only limited, once the expediency of a proposed measures is established, by its power. Where the government can claim expediency for an act, it has the duty and the right to proceed, so that the only remaining question is whether it has the power to accomplish its objective. Frankel (1979: 140–1)

12. This problem could in principle be avoided if countries or Central Banks were to "coordinate" their policies – for example, by simultaneously setting an interest rate reduction. However, as different countries are exposed to different pressure groups and their economies are situated in different phases of the cycle, coordination in the presence of capital mobility would risk either being ineffective or exacerbating the domestic problems faced by each country.

13. Davidson provides a simple formula. "All that is required to set off speculative flows is an expected change in the exchange rate that is $[(1 + x)/(1 - x)]$ greater than what would set off speculation regarding the exchange rate in the absence of the Tobin tax" (Davidson 1997: 678). "x" is the size of the Tobin tax rate.

14. For a critical review of the rationale and impact of IMF and World Bank policies, see Chossudovsky (1997).

15. The unfortunate identification of "revolution" with threat, understood as the "menace of the starving poor," must also be noted. This perspective is ahistorical and reductionist, and hides the constitutive and creative power of collective movements and struggles. For Davidson, the ability to create the new is confined to the realm of "education" for both the "rich" and the "poor." The rich *ought* to understand the pleading of the poor. And the poor too *ought* to be educated not to wish to "exterminate" the rich. Revolution is thus reduced to the clash between the "insensibility" of the rich on one side and the desire to exterminate on the other. But if both "rich" and "poor" could avoid revolution through "education," Marx's famous question would once again become relevant: who educates the educators? Davidson's solution embeds an unfortunate postulate, that the educators have been educated by the profit-driven rules of the game of the capitalist system, and that these rules cannot be transcended and must be accepted as given.

16. For example, the case of perfect competition presupposes policies of deregulation and state maintenance of perfect competition *vis-à-vis* social forces aiming in the opposite direction. See, for example, Polanyi (1944). On the other hand, the rule of the state in a command economy is always complemented by some forms of alternative interaction, often but not uniquely taking a market form (such as, for example, the vast underground economy that many command economies generally have displayed).

17. In *The General Theory*, Keynes suggests that the "rentier aspect of capitalism" is a "transitional phase which will disappear when it has done its work" (Keynes 1936: 376). Keynes believed this disappearance or "euthanasia" would be a gradual process, certainly not requiring a revolution. The reason for its gradual disappearance would have been the increase in the volume of capital, thus drastically reducing its scarcity, "so that the functionless investor will no longer receive a bonus" (Keynes 1936: 376). Today,

almost seventy years later, Keynes' prediction cannot be justified. The sphere of influence of the "functionless" investor has increased enormously, as the development of financial markets demonstrates. Also, any attempt to curtail the power of finance is met with blind resistance, urging us not to "disappoint the markets," and warning of the terrible consequences if we do so. What does look quite certain is that the "euthanasia" of the rentier as a historical figure will not take place gradually, if it happens at all.

References

Ackley, Gardner (1966) The Contribution of Economists to Policy Formation, *Journal of Finance*, 21(2): 169–77.

Addison, John T. (1981) Income Policy: the Recent European Experience. In, J.L. Fallick and R.F. Elliott (ed), *Income Policies, Inflation and Relative Pay*, London: George Allen & Unwin.

Aglietta, Michel (1979) *Theory of Capitalist Regulation*, London: New Left Books.

Akerlof, George A. and Janet L. Yellen (eds) (1986) *Efficiency Wage Models of the Labor Market*, Cambridge: Cambridge University Press.

Amin, Samir (1996) The Challenge of Globalization, *Review of International Political Economy*, 3(2): 216–59.

Anderson, Karen (1981) *Wartime Women: Sex Roles, Family Relations and the Status of Women During World War II*, Westport, CT: Greenwood Press.

Ando, A. and F. Modigliani (1963) The "Life Cycle" Hypothesis of Saving: Aggregate Implications and Tests, *American Economic Review*, 53(1): 55–84.

Arestis, Philip (1992) *The Post-Keynesian Approach to Economics: An Alternative Analysis of Economic Theory and Policy*, Aldershot: Edward Elgowe

Arestis, Philip and Malcolm Sawyer (1997) How Many Cheers for the Tobin Transaction Tax?, *Cambridge Journal of Economics*, 21, 753–68.

Armstrong, Philip, Andrew Glyn, and John Harrison (1984) *Capitalism since World War II*, London: Fontana.

Arrow, Kenneth J. (1951) *Social Choice and Individual Values*, New York: Wiley.

Asimakopulos, Athanasios (1977) Profit and Investment: A Kaleckian Approach, in G.C. Harcourt (ed.), *The Microeconomic Foundations of Macroeconomics*, London: Macmillan. 328–42.

Backhouse, Roger (1985) *A History of Modern Economic Analysis*, Oxford, NY: Basil Blackwell.

Baldi, Guido (1972) Theses on Mass Worker and Social Capital, *Radical America*, 6(3): 3–21.

Barone, Enrico (1935) The Ministry of Production in the Colectivist State, in Friedrich A. von Hayek (ed.), *Collectivist Economic Planning*, London: Routledge: 245–50.

Becker, Gary S. (1964) *Human Capital: A Theoretical and Empirical Analysis*, New York: National Bureau of Economic Research.

—— (1965) A Theory of the Allocation of Time, *Economic Journal*, 75(299): 493–517.

Begg, David K.H. (1982) *The Rational Expectations Revolution in Macroeconomics. Theories and Evidence*, New York: Philip Allan.

Bell, Peter F. and Harry Cleaver (1982) Marx's Crisis Theory as a Theory of Class Struggle, *Research in Political Economy*. 5: 189–261.

Benjamin, Walter (1955) Theses on the Philosophy of History, in Hannah Arendt (ed.), *Illumination*, London: Fontana: 255–66.

Benks, Louis (1965) The Economy Under New Management, *Fortune*, 21(5): 97–9.

Bernstein, Irving (1970) *The Lean Years: A History of the American Worker, 1920–1933*, Baltimore: Penguin.

Beveridge, William (1944) *Full Employment in a Free Society: A Report*, London: George Allen and Unwin.

Beynon, Huw (1973) *Working for Ford*, London: Allen Lane.

Blaug, Mark (1980) *The Methodology of Economics*, Cambridge: Cambridge University Press.

Böhm-Bawerk, Eugen (1896) Karl Marx and the Close of His System, in Paul Marlor Sweezy (ed.), *Karl Marx and the Close of His System*, New York, Nelley, 1949.

Bologna, Sergio (1972) Class Composition and the Theory of the Party, *Telos*, 4(13): 4–27.

—— (1991) The Theory and History of the Mass Worker in Italy, *Common Sense*, 11: 16–29; 12: 52–78, Edinburgh

Bonefeld, Werner, Richard Gunn and Kosmas Psychopedis (1992) Introduction, in Werner Bonefeld, Richard Gunn and Kosmas Psychopedis (eds.) *Open Marxism. Theory and Practice*, II, London: Pluto Press: xi–xviii.

Bowles, Samuel and Robert Boyer (1990) A Wage-led Employment Regime: Income Distribution, Labour Discipline, and Aggregate Demand in Welfare Capitalism, in Stephen A. Marglin and Juliet B. Schor, *The Golden Age of Capitalism. Reinterpreting the Postwar Experience*, Oxford: Clarendon Press.

Bowles, Samuel, David M. Gordon and Thomas E. Weisskopf (1983) *Beyond the Waste Land: A Democratic Alternative to Economic Decline*, New York: Anchor Press.

Bowles, Samuel, David M. Gordon and Thomas E. Weisskopf (1986) Power and Profits: The Social Structure of Accumulation and the Profitability of the Postwar US Economy; *Review of Radical Political Economics*, 18(1&2): 132–67.

Boyer, Richard O. and Herbert M. Morais (1955) *Labor's Untold Story*, New York: United Electrical, Radio & Machine Workers of America.

Braid, Mary (1993) The Shameful Secret of Britain's Lost Children, *The Independent*, Tuesday, 13 July.

Branson, William H. (1989) *Macroeconomic Theory and Policy*, New York: Harper & Row.

Braverman, Harry (1974) *Labor and Monopoly Capital: The Degradation of Work in the Twentieth Century*, New York: Monthly Review Press.

Brecher, Jeremy (1972) *Strike!*, San Francisco: Straight Arrow Books.

Brecher, Jeremy and Tim Costello (1994) *Global Village or Global Pillage: Economic Reconstruction from the Bottom Up*, Boston: South End Press.

Brody, David (1975) The New Deal and World War II, in John Breaman, Robert H. Bremner and David Brody (eds), *The New Deal: The National Level*, Columbus: Ohio State University Press: 267–309.

Bukharin, Nikolai I. (1919) *Economic Theory of the Leisure Class*, New York: International Publishers, 1927

Burk, Kathleen (1991) The International Environment, in Andrew Graham with Authory Seldnom (eds), *Government and Economies in the Postwar World*, London: Routledge: 9–29.

Caffentzis, George (1975) Throwing Away the Ladder: The Universities in the Crisis, *ZeroWork*, 1: 128–42.

—— (1998) *From Capitalist Crisis to Proletarian Slavery. An Introduction to Class Struggle in the US 1973–1998*, Jamaica Plain, Mass.: Midnight Notes.

Cagan, Phillip (1956) The Monetary Dynamics of Hyperinflation, in Milton Friedman (ed.), *Studies in the Quantity Theory of Money*, Chicago: University of Chicago Press: 25–120.

Camus, Albert [1942 1975] The Myth of Sisyphus, London: Penguin.

Carpignano, Paolo (1973) Italy in the Sixties: The Rise of the Mass Worker, *Typescript*, March 1, New York: CUNY.

—— (1975) US Class Composition in the 1960s, *Zerowork*, 1: 7–32.

Cartosio, Bruno (1992) *Anni Inquieti. Società, Media, Ideologie negli Stati Uniti da Truman a Kennedy*, Roma: Editori Riuniti.

Carvalho, Fernando (1983–4) On the Concept of Time in Shacklean and Sraffian Economics, *Journal of Post-Keynesian Economics*, 6(2): 265–80.

Checkland Sydney (1983) *British Public Policy. 1776–1939. An Economic, Social and Political Perspective*, Cambridge: Cambridge University Press.

Chick, Victoria (1983) *Macroeconomics After Keynes: A Reconsideration of the General Theory*, Oxford: Philip Allano University of London.

—— (1992) *On Money, Method, and Keynes: Selected Essays*, in Philip Arestis and Sheila Dow (eds.), London: Macmillan: 1–193.

Chossudovsky, Michel (1997) *The Globalisation of Poverty*, London: Zed Book.

Civilian Production Administration (Bureau of Demobilization) (1947) *Industrial Mobilization for War, History of the Production Board and Predecessor Agencies 1940–1945. Volume I. Program and Administration*, Washington: United States Government Printing Office.

Clark, Peter K. (1979) Investment in the 1970s: Theory, Performance, and Prediction, *Brookings Papers on Economic Activity*, (1): 73–124.

Clarke, Simon (1988) *Keynesianism, Monetarism and the Crisis of the state*, Aldershot: Edward Elgor.

Cleaver, Harry (1977) Food, Famine and International Crisis, *Zerowork*, 2: 7–70.

—— (1979) *Reading Capital Politically*, Austin: University of Texas Press.

—— (1981) Supply-Side Economics: Splendori e Miserie, *Metropoli*, 3(7): 33–48.

Clower, Robert W. (1965) The Keynesian Counter-Revolution: A Theoretical Appraisal, in F.H. Hahn and F.P.R. Brechlin (eds), *The Theory of Interest Rates*, London: Macmillan: 103–25.

Coddington, Alan (1983) *Keynesian Economics. The Search for First Principles*, London: George Allen & Unwin.

Cohen, Gerald A. (1978) *Karl Marx's Theory of History: A Defence*, Oxford: Oxford University Press.

Command Paper 3331 (1929) *Memoranda on Certain Proposals Relating to Unemployment*, London: 43–54.

Coriat, Benjamin (1979) *La Fabbrica e il Cronometro. Saggio Sulla Produzione di Massa*, Milan: Feltrinelli.

CornerHouse (1997) From No Patents of Life!, *The CornerHouse*, Briefing, 1, September.

Crotty, James R. (1980) Post-Keynesian Economic Theory: An Overview and Evaluation *American Economic Review, Papers and Proceedings*, 70(2): 20–5.

Crozier, Michel, Samuel P. Huntington and Jdju Watanuki (1975) *The Crisis of Democracy: Report on the Governability of Democracies to the Trilateral Commission*, New York: New York University Press.

Daal, J. Van and A.H.Q.M. Merkies (1984) *Aggregation in Economic Research: From Individual to Macro Relations*, Dordrecht: Reidel.

Dalla Costa, Mariarosa (1983) *Farmglia, Welfare e State tra Progressismo e New Deal*, Mulan: Franco Angeli.

Dalla Costa, Mariarosa and Selma James (1972) *The Power of Women and the Subversion of the Community*, Bristol: Falling Wall Press; reprinted in Ellen Malos (ed.), *The Politics of Housework*, London: Allison & Busby, 1980: 160–95.

Davidson, Paul (1992) *International Money and the Real World*, London: Macmillan.

—— (1997) Are Grains of Sand in the Wheels of International Finance Sufficient to do the Job when Boulders are Often Required?, *The Economic Journal*, 107, May: 671–86.

Davis, Mike (1986) *Prisoners of the American Dream*, London: Verso.

De Angelis, Massimo (1995) A Political Reading of Abstract Labour on the Substance of Volume, *Capital and Class*, 57: 107–34.

—— (1996) Social Relations, Commodity-Fetishism and Marx's Critique of Political Economy, in *Review of Radical Political Economics*, 284.

—— (1997) Class Struggle and Economics: The Case of Keynesianism, *Research in Political Economy*, 16: 3–53.

—— (1999) Capital Movements, Tobin Tax, and Permanent Fire Prevention: a Critical Note, *Journal of Post Keynesian Economics*, Winter 1999–2000, 22(2): 189–198.

—— (2000) Globalization, New Internationalism and the Zapatistas, *Capital and Class*, 70: 9-35.

De Grazia, Sebastian (1994) *Of Time, Work and Leisure*, New York: Vintage Books.

Del Carria, Renzo (1977) *Proletari Senza Rivoluzione. Storia delle Classi Subalterne in Italia*, V. Roma: Savelli.

de Jonquières, Guy (1998) Network Guerrillas, *Financial Times*, 30 April.

de Vroey, Michel (1982) On the Obsolescence of the Marxian Theory of Value: A Critical Review, *Capital and Class* (17): 34–59.

Deibler, Frederick S. (1933) Report of the Secretary of the American Economic Association, *American Economic Review*, 23(1): 176–80.

Dillard, Dudley (1984) *The Economics of John Maynard Keynes. The Theory of a Monetary Economy*, Westporton: Greenwood Press.

Dow, A.C. and Dow, S.C. (1985) Animal Spirit and Rationality in T.H. Lawson and M.H. Pesaran (eds), *Keynes Economics: Methodological Issues*, London: Croom Helm: 46–65.

Dow, Sheila C. (1985) *Macroeconomic Thought. A Methodological Approach*, Oxford, NY: Basil Blackwell.

Drucker, P.F. (1959) *The New Society*, New York: Harper & Row.

Duffiled, M. (1996) The Symphony of the Damned: Racial Discourse, Complex Political Emergencies and Humanitarian Aid, *Occasional Paper*, Birmingham, School of Public Policy, University of Birmingham, 2 March.

Duisenberry, J.S. (1948) Income-Consumption Relations and their Implications, in L.A. Metzler (ed.), *Income Employment and Public Policy: Essays in Honor of A. H. Hansen*, New York: New York University Press: 53–65.

Duménil, Gerard (1983) Beyond the Transformation Riddle: A Labor theory of Value, *Science and Society*, 47(4): 427–50.

Duménil, Gerard, Mark Glick and J. Rangel (1987) The Rate of Profit in the United States, *Cambridge Journal of Economics*, 11(4): 331–59.

Eccles, Marriner S. (1944) The Postwar Price Problem. Inflation or Deflation?, *Federal Reserve Bulletin*, 30(5): 1156–62.

Edwards, Richard (1979) *Contested Terrain*, New York: Basic Books.

Eichengreen, B., J. Tobin and C. Wyplosz (1995) The Case for Sand in the Wheels of International Finance, *The Economic Journal*, 105: 162–72.

Eisemberger, Robert (1989) *Blue Monday. The Loss of the Work Ethic in America*, New York: Paragon House.

Fazzari, Steven M. (1994–5) Why Doubt the Effectiveness of Keynesian fiscal Policy?, *Journal of Post Keynesian Economics*, 17(2): 231–48.

Federal Reserve Board (1940–5) *Federal Reserve Bulletin*, Washington DC: Federal Reserve System.

Federal Reserve (1944a) War Production and Consumer Supplies, *Federal Reserve Bulletin*, 30(1): 1–10.

—— (1944b) Manpower for War, *Federal Reserve Bulletin*, 30(5): 415–23.

Federici, Silvia (1975) Wages Against Housework, in, Ellen Malos (ed.), *The Politics of Housework*, London: Allison & Busby, 1980: 253–61.

Fetter, F.W. (1977) Lenin, Keynes and Inflation, *Economica*, 44(173): 77–80.

Fine, Sidney (1969) *Sit-down: The General Motors Strike of 1936–7*, Ann Arbor: University of Michigan Press.

Fisher, Stanley (1981) Relative Shocks, Relative Price Variability, and Inflation, *Brookings Papers on Economic Activity*, 2: 381–441,

—— (1987) Samuelson, in John Eatwell, Murray Milgate and Peter Newman (eds) *The New Pelgrave: A Dictionary of Economics*, New York: The Stockton Press: 234–41.

Foley, Duncan K. (1982) The Value of Money, the Value of Labour-Power, and the Marxian Transformation Problem, *Review of Radical Political Economics*, 142.

Foner, Philip S. and Ronald L. Lewis (1980) *The Black Worker: A Documentary History From Colonial Times to the Present*, Philadelphia, PA: Temple University Press.

Frankel, Paul Ellen (1979) *Moral Revolution and Economic Science: The Demise of Laissez-faire in Nineteenth-century British Political Economy*, Westport, CT: Greenwood Press.

Friedman, Milton (1953) *Essays in Positive Economics*, Chicago: University of Chicago Press.

—— (1957) *The Theory of the Consumption Function*, Princeton: Princeton University Press.

—— (1968) The Role of Monetary Policy, *American Economic Review*, 58(1): 381–441.

Galbraith, James K. (1994–5) John Mayherd Nosferatu, *Journal of Post Keynesian Economics*, 17(2): 249–60.

Gartman, David (1979) Origin of the Assembly Line and Capitalist Control of Work at Ford, in A.S. Zimbalist (ed.), *Case Studies in the Labour Process*, London: Monthly Review Press: 193–205.

Georgescu-Roegen, Nicholas (1971) *The Entropy Law and the Economic Process*, Cambridge, MA: Harvard University Press.

Glaberman, Martin [1952 1973] *Punching Out*, Detroit, MI: Bewick Editions.

—— (1966) *Be His Payment High or Low: The American Working Class in the Sixties*, Detroit: Facing Reality Publishing Committee.

—— (1975) Unions vs Workers in the Seventies: The Rise of Militancy in the Auto Industry, in *The Working Class and Social Change*, Toronto: New Hogtown Press.

—— (1980) *Wartime Strikes. The Struggle Against the No-Strike Pledge in the UAW During World War II*, Detroit, MI: Bewick Goitons.

Glyn, Andrew (1995) Social Democracy and Full Employment, *New Left Review*, No, 211, May/June.

Gobbini, Mauro (1972) Lo Sciopero Generale Inglese del '26, *Operai e Stato*, Milan: Feltrinelli, 1980.

Goldenweiser, E.A. (1944) Research and Policy, *Federal Reserve Bulletin*, 30(4): 312–30.

Goldenweiser, E.A. and Everett E. Hagen (1944) Jobs after the War, *Federal Reserve Bulletin*, 30(5): 424–31.

Gordon, David M., Richard Edwards and Michael Reich (1982) *Segmented Work, Divided Workers. The Historical Transformation of Labor in the United States*, Cambridge: Cambridge University Press.

Gordon, David M., Thomas E. Weisskopf and Samuel Bowles (1987) Power Accumulation and Crisis: The Rise and Demise of the Postwar Social Structure of Accumulation, in, Robert Cherry *et al.* (eds), *The Imperiled Economy*, 1, New York: Union for Radical Political Economics.

Gordon Robert J. (ed.) (1973) *Milton Friedman's Monetary Framework: A Debate with His Critics*, Chicago: University of Chicago Press.

—— (1986) *The American Business Cycle. Continuity and Change*, Chicago: University of Chicago Press.

Götz, Aly and Susanne Heim. (1988) The Economics of the Final Solution: A Case Study From the General Government, in *Five Articles on War and Class Composition*, London: Red Notes; a shorter version is in *Common Sense*, 11: 42–60, Edinburgh, 1991.

Gramsci, Antonio (1971) Americanism and Fordism, in Antonio Gramsci, *Selection From the Prison Notebooks*, New York: International Publishers.

Graziani, Augusto (1981) *Teoria Economica. Macroeconomia*, Naples: Edizioni Scientifiche Italiane.

Green, James (1975) Fighting on Two Fronts: Working Class Militancy in the 1940's, *Radical America*, 9(4): 7–48.

Greenberg, Cheryl Lynn (1991) *or Does it Explode?: Black Harlem in the Depression*, New York: Oxford University Press.

Haberler, Gottfried (1962) Sixteen Years Later, in Robert Lakachman (ed.), *Keynes' General Theory. Reports of Three Decades*, New York: St Martin's Press London: Macmillan: 289–96.

Hannington, Wal (1977) *Unemployed Struggles 1919–1936: My Life and Struggles Amongst the Unemployed*, London: Lawrence & Wishart.

Hansen, Alvin H. (1953) *A Guide to Keynes*, New York: McGraw Hill.

Hansen, Bent (1951) *A Study in the Theory of Inflation*, London: Macmillan.

Harris, John H. (1982) *The Right to Manage. Industrial Relations Policies of American Business in the 1940s*, London: The University of Wisconsin Press.

Harrod, Roy H. (1951) *The Life of John Maynard Keynes*, London: Macmillan.

Harvey, David (1989) *The Condition of Postmodernity*, Oxford, MA: Basil Blackwell.

Hayek, Friedrich A. von. (1935) The Present State of the Debate, in Friedrich A. von Hayek (ed.), *Collectivist Economic Planning*, London: Routledge: 201–43.

Helleiner, Eric (1995) Explaining the Globalization of Financial Markets: Bringing States Back In, *Review of International Political Economy*, (2)2: 315–41.

Heller, Walter W. (1966) *New Dimensions of Political Economy*, Cambridge, MA: Harvard University Press.

Hicks, John (1937) Mr. Keynes and the "Classics": A Suggested Interpretation, *Econometrica*, 40(1): 129–43.

—— (1957) A Rehabilitation of Classical Economics?, *Economic Journal*, 67(266): 278-89.

—— (1974) *The Crisis in Keynesian Economics.*, Oxford, NY: Basil Blackwell.

—— (1979) On Coddington's Interpretation: A Reply, *Journal of Economic Literature*, 17(3): 989–95.

—— (1983) IS-LM: An Explanation, in Jean-Paul Fitoussi (ed.), *Modern Macroeconomics*, Oxford: Blackwell: 49–63.

Hines, Albert G. (1964) Trade Unions and Wage Inflation in the U.K. 1863–1961, *Review of Economic Studies*, 38(88): 221–52.

Hirshman, Albert O. (1989) How the Keynesian Revolution Was Exported From the United States, and Other Comments, in Peter A. Hall (ed.), *The Political Power of Economic Ideas: Keynesianism across Nations*, Princeton: Princeton University Press: 347–59.

Holloway, John (1987) A Note on Fordism and Neo-Fordism, *Common Sense*, 1, Edinburgh.

—— (1992) Crisis, Fetishism, Class Composition, in Werner Bonefeld, Richard Gunn and Kosmas Psychopedis (eds.), *Open Marxism. Theory and Practice*, II, Boulder, CO: Pluto Press: 145–69.

Holloway, John and Eloína Peláez (1998) *Zapatista! Reinventing Revolution in Mexico*, London: Pluto Press.

Hoover, Calvin B. (1940) Economic Planning and the Problem of Full Employment, *American Economic Review*, 30(1): 263–71.

Humphrey, Thomas M. (1973) Changing Views of the Phillips Curve, *Monthly Review*, Federal Reserve Bank of Richmond, 7: 2–13.

James, Selma (1975) *Sex Race and Class*, Bristol: Falling Wall Press.

Jennings, Ed. (1975) Wildcats: The Wartime Strike Wave in Auto, *Radical America*, 9(4): 77–105.

Johnson, Alvin (1937) The Economist in a World of Transition, *American Economic Review*, 27(1): 1–3.

Kahn, Richard F. (1931) The Relation of Home Investment to Employment, *Economic Journal*, 41(162): 173–98.

Kaldor, Nicholas (1956) Alternative Theories of Distribution, *Review of Economic Studies*, 30(23): 83–100.

Kalecki, Michal (ed.) (1933) An Outline of a Theory of the Business Cycle, in Michal Kalecki, *Studies in the Theory of Business Cycles. 1933–1939*, Oxford: Basil Blackwell, 1969.

—— (1943) Political Aspects of Full Employment, in Osiatynski (ed.), *Collected Works of Michael Kalecki*, 1, Oxford: Oxford University Press, 1990.

Kanth, Rajani (1986) *Political Economy and Laissez-Faire. Economics and Ideology in the Ricardian Era*, Totowa, NJ: Rowman & Littlefield.

Kapp, Karl W. (1939) Economic Regulation and Economic Planning. A Theoretical Classification of Different Types of Economic Control, *American Economic Review*, 29(4): 760–73.

Katz, Harry C. (1985) *Shutting Gears: Changing Labor Relations In the US Automobile Industry*, Cambridge, Mass: Mit Press.

Katz, Harry C. Thomas A. Kochan and Robert B. McKersie. (1986) *The Transformation of American Industrial Relations*. New York: Basic Books.

Keynes, John Maynard (1919) The Economic Consequences of the Peace, in *The Collected Writings of John Maynard Keynes*, II. London: Macmillan, 1971.

—— (1922a) A Revision of the Treaty, in *The Collected Writings of John Maynard Keynes*, III, London: Macmillan, 1971.

—— (1922b) Lecture to the Institute of Bankers, in *The Collected Writings of John Maynard Keynes*, XIX, London: Macmillan, 1971.

—— (1923a) Bank Rate at Four Percent, in *The Collected Writings of John Maynard Keynes*, XIX, London: Macmillan, 1971.

—— (1923b) Currency Policy and Unemployment, in *The Collected Writings of John Maynard Keynes*, XIX, London: Macmillan, 1971.

—— (1923c) Letter to *The Times*, 14 February 1923, in *The Collected Writings of John Maynard Keynes*, XIX, London: Macmillan, 1981.

—— (1923d) Population and Unemployment, in *The Collected Writings of John Maynard Keynes*, XIX, London: Macmillan, 1981.

—— (1923e) A Reply to Sir William Beveridge, in *The Collected Writings of John Maynard Keynes*, XIX, London: Macmillan, 1981.

—— (1923f) *A Tract on Monetary Reform*, in *The Collected Writings of John Maynard Keynes*, IV, London: Macmillan, 1971.

—— (1924a) Does Unemployment Need a Drastic Remedy?, in *The Collected Writings of John Maynard Keynes*, XIX. London: Macmillan, 1981.

—— (1924b) To the Editor of *The Times*, 28 May 1924, in *The Collected Writings of John Maynard Keynes*, XIX, London: Macmillan, 1981.

—— (1925a) Am I a Liberal?, in *Essays in Persuasion, The Collected Works of John Maynard Keynes*, IX, London: Macmillan, 1972.

—— (1925b) The Economic Consequences of Mr. Churchill, in *The Collected Works of John Maynard Keynes*, IX, London: Macmillan, 1972.

—— (1926a) Industrial Reorganization: Cotton, in *The Collected Works of John Maynard Keynes*, XIX, London: Macmillan, 1981.

—— (1926b) The End of Laissez-Faire, in *Essays in Persuasion, The Collected Works of John Maynard Keynes*, IX, London: Macmillan, 1972.

—— (1929) Mr. Churchill on the Peace, in *The Collected Writings of John Maynard Keynes*, X. London: Macmillan, 1972.

—— (1930a) A Treatise on Money, in *The Collected Works of John Maynard Keynes*, V, London: Macmillan, 1971.

—— (1930b) Economic Possibilities for our Grandchildren, in *The Collected Works of John Maynard Keynes*, IX, London: Macmillan, 1971.

—— (1936) *The General Theory of Employment, Interest, and Money*, New York: Harvest/HBJ Books.

—— (1937a) Letter to R.F. Kahn. 20 October 1937, in *The Collected Writings of John Maynard Keynes*, XIV, London: Macmillan, 1973.

—— (1937b) The General Theory of Unemployment, *Journal of Economics*, 51, February: 20g–23.

—— (1940) How to Pay for the War, in *Essays in Persuasion, The Collected Works of John Maynard Keynes*, IX, London: Macmillan, 1972.

—— (1941) Letter to Walter A. Salant. 27 July 1941, in *Essays in Persuasion, The Collected Works of John Maynard Keynes*, IX, London: Macmillan, 1972.

Keynes, John Maynard *et al.* (1932) To the Editor of the Times. 17 October 1932, in *The Collected Writings of John Maynard Keynes*, XXI, London: Macmillan, 1982.

Keynon, Peter (1980) Discussion of Tarshis, *American Economic Review, Papers and Proceedings*, 70(2): 26–7.

Klein, Lawrence (1947) *The Keynesian Revolution*, New York: Macmillan.

Kliman, Andrew (1988) The Profit Rate Under Continuous Technological Change, *Review of Radical Political Economics*, 20(2&3).

—— (1996) A Value-Theoretic Critique of the Okishio Theorem, in Alan Freeman and Guglielmo Carchedi (eds), *Marx and Non-Equilibrium Economics*, Cheltenham: Edward Elgar.

Kolko, Gabriel (1968) *The Politics of War. The World and United States Foreign Policy*, New York: Pantheon Books.

Kornbluh, Joyce L. (ed.) (1988) *Rebel Voices. An IWW Anthology*, Chicago: Charles H. Kerr.

Kregel, Jan A. (1976) Economic Methodology in the Face of Uncertainty, *Economic Journal*, 86(342): 209–25.

Kuhn, Thomas S. (1970) *The Structure of Scientific Revolutions*, Chicago: The University of Chicago Press.

Le Pan, Don (1988) *The Birth of Expectation: A Cognitive Revolution in West Culture*, London: Macmillan.

Leijonhufvud, Alex (1988) IS–LM analysis, in John Eatwell, Murray Milgate and Peter Newman (eds) *The New Pelgrave: A Dictionary of Economics*, New York: The Stockton Press: 1002–4.

Lichtenstein, Nelson (1975) Defending the No-Strike Pledge, *Radical America*, 9(4): 49–76.

—— (1982) *Labor's War at Home. The CIO in World War II*, Cambridge, NY: Cambridge University Press.

Lintott, John (1982) *Political Arithmetic: National Accounting, Ideology and the State*, Ph D thesis, London: Birkbeck College, University of London.

Lipietz Alain (1987) *Mirages and Miracles. The Crisis of Global Fordism*, London: Verso.

Lipsey, Richard G. (1960) The Relation Between Unemployment and the Rate of Change of Money Wage Rates in the United Kingdom 1861–1857: A Further Analysis, *Economica*, 27(105): 1–31.

Lucas, Robert E. and Thomas J. Sargent (1979) After Keynesian Macroeconomics, *Federal Reserve Bank of Minneapolis Quarterly Review*, 3(2): 1–16.

Maier, Charles S. (1978) The Politics of Productivity: Foundations of American International Economic Policy after World War II, in Peter J. Katzenstein (ed.) *Between Power and Plenty: Foreign Economic Policies of Advanced Industrial States*, Madison: The University of Wisconsin Press: 23–49.

Marazzi, Christian (1977) Money in the World Crisis: The New Basis of Capitalist Power, *Zerowork* 2: 91–111.

Marshall, Alfred (1890) *Principles of Economics*, London: Macmillan, 1960

Marx, Karl (1844) Economic and Philosophical Manuscripts, in Karl Marx, *Early Writings*, New York: Vintage Books, 1975.

—— (1845) The Holy Family. Or Critique of Critical Criticism, in Karl Marx and Frederich Engels, *Collected Works*, 4. London: Lawrence & Wishart, 1975.

—— (1858) *Grundrisse*, New York: Penguin, 1974.

—— (1867) *Capital*, 1, New York: Penguin, 1976.

—— (1894) *Capital*, 3, New York: Penguin, 1981.

Mattick, Paul (1969) *Marx and Keynes: The Limits of the Mixed Economy*, Boston: Pozter Sergent.

—— (1972) Samuelson's "Transformation" of Marxism into Bourgeoise Economics, *Science and Society* 36(3): 258–73.

—— (1980) *Economics, Politics and the Age of Inflation*, London: Merlin Press.

—— (1981) *Economic Crisis and Crises Theory*, New York: M.E. Sharpe.

McKay, Claude (1990) *Harlem Glory*, Edinburgh: Ak Press.

Meek, Ronald L. (1956) *Studies in the Labour Theory of Value*, London: Lawrence & Wishart.

—— (1967) *Economics and Ideology and Other Essays: Studies in the Development of Economic Thought*, London: Chapman & Hall.

Merrington, John (1968) Introduction, in Toni Negri, *Revolution Retrieved: Selected Writings on Marx, Keynes, Capitalist Crisis and New Social Subjects 1967–83*, London: Red Notes, 1988: 5–7.

Meyer, Stephen (1981) *The Five-Dollar Day: Labor Management and Social Control in the Ford Motor Company. 1908–1921*, New York: Albany.

Milgate, Murray (1982) *Capital and Employment. A Study of Keynes' Economics*, London: Academic Press.

Milkman, Ruth (1987) *Gender at Work. The Dynamic of Job Segregation by Sex During World War II*, Urbana: University of Illinois Press.

Mill, James (1808) *Commerce Defended*, in Donald Winch (ed.), *James Mill: Selected Economic Writings*, Chicago: University of Chicago Press, 1966: 85–159.

Milward, Alan (1984) *The Recovery of Western Europe 1945–51*, London: Methuen.

Minsky, Hyman Philip (1975) *John Maynard Keynes*, New York: Columbia University Press.

Mises, Ludwig von (1922) *Socialism*, London: Jonathan Cape, 1936.

Modigliani, Franco (1944) Liquidity Preference and the Theory of Interest and Money, *Econometrica*, 12(1): 45–88.

—— (1963) The Monetary Mechanism and its Interaction with Real Phenomena, *Review of Economics and Statistics*, 45(1): 79–107.

Moggridge, Donald E. (1992) *Maynard Keynes. An Economist's Biography*, London: Routledge.

Monthly Labor Review, (1976) May: 36–7.

Moody, Kim (1997) *Workers in a Lean World. Unions in the International Economy*, London: Verso.

Moore, Lynden (1985) *The Growth and Structure of International Trade since the Second World War*, Brighton: Wheatsheaf Books.

Morris, Margaret (1976) *The General Strike*, Baltimore: Penguin.

Moulier, Yann (1982) Les Théories Américaines de la "Segmentation du Marche du Travail" et Italiennes de la "Composition de Classe" à Travers le Prisme des Lectures Françaises, *Babylone*, O: 175–217.

Mowat, Charles L. (1955) *Britain Between the Wars*, Whitstable: Methuen.

Myrdal, Gunnar (1953) *The Political Element in the Development of Economic Theory*, London: Routledge & Kegan Paul.

—— (1970) *Objectivity in Social Research*, London: Duckworth.

Nader, Ralph and Lori Wallach (1996) GATT, NAFTA, and the Subversion of the Democratic Process, in Jerry Mander and Edward Goldsmith (eds), *The Case Against the Global Economy and For a Turn Towards the Local*, San Francisco: Sierra Club Books.

Negri, Antonio (1968) Keynes and the Capitalist Theory of the State Post-1929, in Antonio Negri, *Revolution Retrieved: Selected Writings on Marx, Keynes, Capitalist Crisis and New Social Subjects 1967–83*, London: Red Notes, 1988: 5–42.

—— (1971) Crisis of the Planner-State: Communism and Revolutionary Organisation, in Antonio Negri, *Revolution Retrieved:Selected Writings on Marx,*

Keynes, Capitalist Crisis and New Social Subjects 1967–83, London: Red Notes, 1988: 91–148.

—— (1982) Archeology and Project: The Mass Worker and the Social Worker, in Antonio Negri, *Revolution Retrieved. Selected Writings on Marx, Keynes, Capitalist Crisis and New Social Subjects*, London: Red Notes, 1988.

—— (1992) Interpretation of the Class Situation Today. Methodological Aspects, in Werner Bonefeld Werner, Richard Gunn Richard and Kosmas Psychopedis (eds), *Open Marxism. Theory and Practice*, II, London: Pluto Press: 69–105.

Nevins, Allan (1954) *Ford. The Times, The Man, the Company*, New York: Charles Scribner's Sons.

Noble, David (1984) *Forces of Production: A Social History of Industrial Automation*, New York: Knopf.

Nussbaum, Bruce (1998) Time to Act, *Business Week*, September 14.

O'Connor, James (1973) *The Fiscal Crisis of the State*, New York: St Martin's Press.

Olson, James S. (1969) Race, Class, and Progress: Black Leadership and Industrial Unionism, 1936–1945, in Milton Cantor (ed.), *Black Labor in America*, Westport, CT: Negro University Press: 153–64.

Osiatynski, J. (ed.) (1990) *Collected Works of Michael Kalecki*, 1, Oxford: Cluzenolon.

Panzieri, Raniero (1961) The Capitalist Use of Machinery: Marx Versus the "Objectivists," in Phil Slater (ed.), *Outlines of a Critique of Technology*, Atlantic Highlands: Humanities Press, 1980: 44–68.

—— (1964) Surplus Value and Planning: Notes on the Reading of Capital, in Raniero Panzieri, *The Labour Process and Class Strategies*, CSE Pamphlet, 1: 4–25, 1976.

Pasinetti, Luigi (1962) Rate of Profit and Income Distribution in Relation to the Rate of Economic Growth, in *Review of Economic Studies*, 91(1).

Pareto, Vilfredo (1867) *Cours d'economie Politique*, 1, Laousanne.

Patinkin, Don (1948) Price Flexibility and Full Employment, *American Economic Review*, 38(4): 543–64.

—— (1956) *Money Interest and Prices*, New York: Harper & Row.

Pencavel, John H. (1981) The American Experience with Income Policies, in J.L. Fallick and R.F. Elliott (eds), *Income Policies, Inflation and Relative Pay*, London: George Allen & Unwin.

Peterson, Wallace (1988) *Income, Employment, and Economic Growth*, London: W.W. Norton.

Phelps, Edmund S. (1967) Phillips Curves, Expectations of Inflation and Optimal Unemployment Over Time, *Economica*, 34(135): 254–81.

Phillips, A.W. (1958) The Relation Between Unemployment and the Rate of Change of Money Wage Rates in the United Kingdom 1861–1857, *Economica*, 25(100): 283–99.

Phillips, Ronnie J. (1980) *Global Austerity: The Evolution of the International Monetary System and World Capitalist Development, 1945–1978*, Ph D Dissertation, Austin: University of Texas at Austin.

—— (1985) The Failure of Keynesianism and the Collapse of Bretton Woods, *Research in Political Economy*, 8: 1–25.

Pigou, Arthur C. (1941) *Employment and Equilibrium*, London: Macmillan.

—— (1948) The Classical Stationary State, in Friedrich A. Lutz and Leoud W. Mints (eds), *Readings in Monetary Theory*, Pennsylvania: Blakiston, 1951.

—— (1949) Economic Progress in a Stable Environment, in Friedrich A. Lutz and Leoud W. Mints, *Readings in Monetary Theory*, Pennsylvania: Blakiston, 1951.

Piore, Michael J. and Charles F. Sabel (1984) *The Second Industrial Divide: Possibilities of Prosperity*, New York: Basic Books.

Piven, Frances Fox and Richard Cloward (1972) *Regulating the Poor: The Functions of Public Welfare*, New York: Vintage.

—— (1977) *Poor People's Movements. Why They Succeed, How they Fail*, New York: Vintage Books.

Polanyi, Karl (1944) *The Great Transformation. The Political and Economic Origins of our Time*, Boston: Beacon Press.

Ramonet, Ignacio (1998) Japan in Danger in *Le Monde Diplomatique*, English edn, *The Guardian Weekly*, 159(17), 25 October: 1.

Ramos, Alejandro M. (1995) The Monetary Expression of Labor: An Interpretation of the Relation Between Value-Substance and Value-Form, paper presented in the third miniconference of the International Working Group in Value Theory at EEA, Boston, 15–17 March, 1996.

Rawick, George P. (1972a) Anni Venti: Lotte Operaie USA, *Operai e stato*, Milan: Feltrinelli.

—— (1972b) Anni Trenta: Lotte Operaie USA, *Operai e stato*, Milan: Feltrinelli.

—— (1974) *The American Slave: a Composite Autobiography*, Westport, CT: Greenwood Press.

Reich, Robert (1991) *The Work of Nations*, London: Simon & Schuster.

Robbins Lionel (1935) *An Essay on the Nature and Significance of Economic Science*, London: Macmillan.

—— (1947) *The Economic Problem in Peace and War. Some Reflections on Objectives and Mechanisms*, London/New York: Macmillan.

—— (1956) *The Economist in the Twentieth Century*, London/New York: Macmillan.

Robertson, D.H. (1920) Review of "The Economic Consequences of the Peace," *Economic Journal*, 30(117): 77–84.

—— (1949) *Banking Policy and the Price Level: An Essay in the Theory of the Trade Cycle*, New York: Kelley.

Robinson, E.A.G. (1946) John Maynard Keynes, in Robert Lekachman (ed.), *Keynes' General Theory. Reports of Three Decades*, London/New York: Macmillan and St Martin's Press, 1964: 12–86.

Robinson, Joan (1956) *The Accumulation of Capital*, London: Macmillan.

—— (1958) Full Employment and Inflation, in Joan Robinson, *Collected Economic Papers*, 2, Oxford: Basil Blackwell, 1960.

—— (1962) Review of Harry Johnson's *Money, Trade, and Economic Growth*, in Joan Robinson, *Collected Economic Papers*, 3, Oxford: Basil Blackwell, 1979.

—— (1974) Inflation West and East, in Joan Robinson, *Collected Economic Papers*, 4, Oxford: Basil Blackwell, 1979.

—— (1978) History versus Equilibrium, in Joan Robinson, *Contribution to Modern Economics*, Oxford: Basic Blackwell.

—— (1962) *Economic Philosophy*, New York: Anchor Books.

—— (1973) *After Keynes*, Oxford: Basil Blackwell.

—— (1977) What are the Questions?, in Joan Robinson, *Collected Economic Papers*, 5, Oxford: Basil Blackwell, 1979.

Roediger, David R. and Philip S. Foner (1989) *Our Own Time. A History of American Labor and the Working Day*, London: Verso.

Russel, Jack (1978) The Coming of the Line: The Ford Highland Park Plant, 1910–1914, *Radical America*, 12(3): 28–46.

Sachs, Jeffrey (1980) The Changing Cyclical Behavior of Wages and Prices 1890–1976, *American Economic Review*, 70(1): 78–90.

Salant, Walter S. (1988) The Spread of Keynesian Doctrines and Practices in the United States, in Omar F. Hamouda and John N. Smith (eds), *Keynes and Public Policy After Fifty Years, Vol. I: Economics and Policy*, Aldershot: Edward Elgar: 61–76.

Salter, Arthur (1961) *Memories of a Public Servant*, London: Faber & Faber.

Samuelson, Paul A. (1944) Full Employment After the War, in Paul A. Samuelson, *Collected Scientific Papers*, II, Cambridge, MA: MIT Press.

—— (1948) *Economics. An Introductory Analysis*, New York: McGraw-Hill.

—— (1955) *Economics. An Introductory Analysis*, 3rd edn, New York: McGraw-Hill.

—— (1957) Wages and Interest: A Modern Discussion of Marxian Economic Models, *American Economic Review*, 47(6): 884–912.

—— (1959) What Economists Know, in E. Stiglitz (ed.), *Collected Scientific Papers*, II, Cambridge, MA: MIT Press, 1966.

—— (1960) American Economics, in Paul A. Samuelson, *Collected Scientific Papers*, II, Cambridge, MA: MIT Press, 1966.

—— (1963) A Brief Survey of Post-Keynesian Development, in Robert Lekachman (ed.), *Keynes' General Theory. Reports of Three Decades*, London/New York: Macmillan/St Martin's Press.

Samuelson, Paul A. and Robert M. Solow (1960) Analytical Aspects of Anti-Inflation Policy, *American Economic Review*, 50(2): 177–94.

Santomero, Anthony M. and John J. Seater (1978 The Inflation–Unemployment Trade-Off: A Critique of the Literature, *Journal of Economic Literature*, 16(3): 499–544.

Sassoon, Donald (1990) Italy, in Andrew Graham and Anthony Seldon (eds.), *Government and Economies in the Postwar World*, London: Routledge: 104–24.

Say, Jean Baptiste (1803) *A Treatise on Political Economy*, trans C.R. Prinsep, London, 1821.

Schor, Juliet B. (1987) Class Struggle and the Macroeconomy: The Cost of Job Loss, in Juhet B. Schor, *The Imperiled Economy*, 1, New York: Union for Radical Political Economics.

—— (1991) *The Overworked American*, New York: Basic Books.

Schumpeter, Joseph (1954) *History of Economic Analysis*, London: Allen & Unwin.

Shackle, George L.S. (1951) Twenty Years On: A Survey of the Theory of the Multiplier, *Economic Journal*, 61(242): 241–60.

—— (1968) *A Scheme of Economic Theory*, Cambridge: Cambridge University Press.

Shaikh, Anward (1987) The Falling Rate of Profit and the Economic Crisis in the US, in Robert Cherry *er al.* (eds.), *The Imperiled Economy*, 1, New York: Union for Radical Political Economics.

Skidelsky, Robert (1922) *John Maynard Keynes. The Economist as Saviour 1920–1937*, London: Macmillon.

Slater, Phil (ed.) (1980) *Outlines of a Critique of Technology*, London: Ink Links.

Smith, Warren L. (1956) A Graphical Exposition of the Complete Keynesian System, *The Southern Economic Journal*, 23(2): 115–25.

Spiegel, Henry W. (1983) *The Growth of Economic Thought*, Durham, NC: Duke University Press.

Tarshis, L. (1980) Post-Keynesian Economics: A Promise that Bounced?, *American Economic Review, Papers and Proceedings*, 70(2): 10–14.

Taylor, Fred M. (1929) The Guidance of Production in a Socialist State, *American Economic Review*, 19(1): 1–8.

Taylor, Frederick W. (1903) Shop Management, in Frederick W. Taylor, *Scientific Management*, Westport, CT: Greenwood Press, 1972.

—— (1911) The Principles of Scientific Management, in Frederick W. Taylor, *Scientific Management*, Westport, CT: Greenwood Press, 1972.

—— (1912) Testimony Before the Special House Committee, in Frederick W. Taylor, *Scientific Management*, Westport, CT: Greenwood Press, 1972.

Termini, V. (1981) Logical, Mechanical, and Historical Time in Economics, *Economics Notes by Monte dei Paschi di Siena*, 10(3): 58–104.

Thompson, Edward P. (1963) *The Making of the English Working Class*, New York: Vintage Books.

—— (1974) *The New Economics One Decade Older*. The Eliot Janeway Lectures on Historical Economics in Honour of Joseph Schumpeter, 1972, Princeton; Princeton University Press.

—— (1978) A Proposal for International Monetary Reform, *Eastern Economic Journal*, 4, (3–4): 1153–9; Reprinted in *James Tobin, Essays in Economics: Theory and Policy*, Cambridge Mass: MIT Press.

Togliatti, Palmiro (1984) *Opere*, 5, 1944–1955, Rome: Editori Riuniti.

Tronti, Mario (1966) *Operai e capitale*, Torino: Einaudi.

—— (1973) Social Capital, *Telos*, 5(17): 98–121.

United Nations (1994) *Human Development Report*, New York and Oxford: Oxford University Press.

—— (1998) *Human Development Report*, New York and Oxford: Oxford University Press.

Vaneigem, Raoul (1983) *The Revolution of Everyday Life*, London: Left Bank Books and Rebel Press.

"Wages for Students'" Students (1976) *Wages for Students*, Amherst, Pamphet.

Wallace, Peterson (1988) *Income, Employment, and Economic Growth*, London: W.W. Norton.

Walton, John and David Seddon (1994) *Free Markets and Food Riots. The Politics of Global Adjustment*, Oxford: Blackwell.

Waterman, Peter (1998) *Globalization, Social Movements, and the New Internationalism*, Washington, DC: Mansell.

Weisskopf, Thomas E., Samuel Bowls and David M. Gordon (1983) Hearts and Minds: A Social Model of US Productivity Growth, *Brookings Papers on Economic Activity*, 2: 381–441.

Williams, S. (1997) The Nature of Some Recent Trade Union Modernization Policies in the UK, *British Journal of Industrial Relations*, December: 495–514.

Winch, Donald (1969) *Economics and Policy. A Historical Study*, London: Hodder & Stoughton.

—— (1989) Keynes, Keynesianism and State Intervention, in P. Hall (ed.), *The Political Power of Economic Ideas*, Princeton: Princeton University Press.

Winner, Langton (1986) *The Whale and the Reactor: A Search for Limits in an Age of High Technology*, Chicago: University of Chicago Press.

Wolters, Raymond (1969) Closed Shop and White Shop: The Negro Response to Collective Bargaining, 1933–1935, in Milton Cantor (ed.), *Black Labor in America*, Westport, CT: Negro University Press: 137–52.

—— (1970) *Negroes and the Great Depression: The Problem of Economic Recovery*, Westport, CT: Greenwood Press.

ZeroWork Collective (1975) *ZeroWork*, 1, New York.

Index